HOW TO BE ENOUGH

Also by Ellen Hendriksen

How to Be Yourself

HOW TO BE ENOUGH

SELF-ACCEPTANCE FOR SELF-CRITICS AND PERFECTIONISTS

ELLEN HENDRIKSEN, Ph.D.

ST. MARTIN'S
ESSENTIALS
NEW YORK

First published in the United States by St. Martin's Essentials, an imprint of St. Martin's Publishing Group

www.stmartins.com

Designed by Steven Seighman

The Library of Congress Cataloging-in-Publication Data is available upon request.

ISBN 978-1-250-29187-5 (hardback)
ISBN 978-1-250-29188-2 (ebook)

Our books may be purchased in bulk for promotional, educational, or business use. Please contact your local bookseller or the Macmillan Corporate and Premium Sales Department at 1-800-221-7945, extension 5442, or by email at MacmillanSpecialMarkets@macmillan.com.

First Edition: 2025

10 9 8 7 6 5 4 3 2 1

For Adrien and Davin, with all my love

Contents

Author's Note

All HIPAA identifiers and other potentially identifying details have been changed to honor therapy's confidentiality pledge and to render clients unrecognizable, even to themselves, while retaining the essence of their stories. In many cases, to further disguise identity, I have created composite characters from several clients. In the case of the Tice, Bratslavsky, and Baumeister study, the story comes directly from their methods section, but I invented the details of journals from 1975, *Tetris*, *People*, as well as the color of the aromatherapy candle.

Prologue

A Tale of Two Titans

IT WAS HARD to tell what shone most brightly that December evening in 1937. Powerful beams of light from the hand-operated spotlights searched the sky above the Carthay Circle Theatre in Los Angeles. Pure star power emanated from the red carpet. Flashbulbs popped as tuxedoed and bejeweled celebrities like Clark Gable, Marlene Dietrich, Cary Grant, and Shirley Temple made their way into the theater, past the thousands of fans who spilled into the street, craning their necks for a glimpse. But brightest of all, perhaps, were the hopes of thirty-six-year-old Walt Disney, the creator of the first full-length animated feature to be unveiled that night, *Snow White and the Seven Dwarfs*.

Entering the theater, Walt was both elated and profoundly anxious. Charlie Chaplin had wired him a telegram that morning: AM CONVINCED ALL OUR FONDEST HOPES WILL BE REALIZED TONIGHT. And over the course of the next eighty-eight minutes, they were. The audience even applauded the backgrounds, without a single animated character on the screen. When Snow White was poisoned by the apple and laid out on her funeral bier, audible sniffling and nose-blowing could be heard throughout the theater. Walt had been fretting for months over whether viewers would be emotionally moved by animated characters, but at the end of the film, when the audience leaped to its feet in a standing ovation, he felt a knot release within him. It was all right. People liked it. He hadn't failed.

Snow White might have been a historic success, but the road to that success was excruciating. Walt hired a small army of six hundred artists and drove them into the ground—three eight-hour shifts every day, around the clock—drawing, inking, and painting over a quarter million stills. The work hours totaled two hundred years' worth of labor. Furthermore, the film, first budgeted at $250,000, had exceeded its budget more than sixfold. His studio owed the bank a million dollars, a mind-bending sum during the heart of the Great Depression.

But to Walt, the time didn't matter. Money was no object. The only thing that mattered was that he had pushed and scraped and, through sheer force of will, achieved that elusive "just right" feeling. If the movie didn't feel right in his bones, not only would it fall short, so would he. He *was* his movies.

Chasing that feeling was intense and agonizing, not only for Walt but also for everyone around him. Since Walt couldn't draw each cel himself, he had to let go of absolute control, but he couldn't bring himself to trust the world-class staff he had so carefully handpicked. Even after animation began, Walt screen-tested more than 150 young women for the role of Snow White, a marathon time suck of exhausting comparison. When it came time to paint, Walt had the studio grind its own pigments, then painstakingly measured each with a spectrometer—one of only twenty in the world at the time—creating an expansive library of 1,200 different colors that pointlessly exceeded Technicolor's existing technology. Undaunted, Walt had the staff create a seven-foot-tall chart displaying exactly how each pigment would translate to the screen.

Even in the final, combustible days leading up to the movie's release, Walt couldn't stop micromanaging. "Have the hummingbird make four pick-ups instead of six," he corrected. Regarding one of the dwarfs: his "fanny in the last half of the scene is too high." The Queen's eyebrows were too extreme. One of Grumpy's fingers was too big. In an irony visible only to his exasperated staff, Walt worried aloud that the constant revisions would suck the spontaneity from the film. Far from Walt's office, on the studio floor, the supervising director threw drawing boards across the room, screaming, "We gotta get the picture out!"

When the film was finalized, Walt could only see the flaws. To a reporter, he admitted, "I've seen so much of Snow White that I am conscious only of the places where it could be improved. You see, we've learned such a lot since we started this thing! I wish I could yank it back and do it all over again."

Ultimately, the colossal success of *Snow White* publicly cemented Walt's place in cinematic history. For a time, it was the highest-grossing American film ever, making nearly $92 million in today's dollars during its initial release. Away from the spotlight, however, it solidified Walt's perpetual dissatisfaction. His triumph only set the bar higher for Disney magic. Despite Walt's carefully crafted public image of the sheepish, aw-shucks "Uncle Walt," a journalist visiting the studios noted that Walt "appeared to be under the lash of some private demon."

After the war, faced with the realities of budgets and bank loans, the studio went through a round of layoffs and budget cuts. Walt, demoralized, began to lose his drive. His future films, he fretted, would never be the jewel box masterpieces—painstaking, gorgeous, almost spiritual experiences—that the earlier ones had been. Rather than making the most of what he had or looking at the new constraints as a challenge to be mastered, he grew despondent: If the films couldn't be perfect, what was the point in making them?

Walt tried immersing himself in an old interest: model trains. "Just a hobby to get my mind off my problems," he said, but he felt trapped and rule bound even in leisure. Tellingly, Walt wrote to a fellow railroad buff who had constructed a model railroad big enough to straddle and ride in his yard, "I envy you for having the courage to do what you want."

Caught between the false choice of perfection or failure, paralyzed by both his self-imposed standards and bank-imposed budget, Walt withdrew into himself. The Disney brand might have centered on happiness and community, but Walt increasingly found himself lonely and isolated, mostly through his own making. When presented with a formal dinner invitation, he would RSVP "NO!" in red crayon, underlined for emphasis. Amid the frenetic activity at the studio, Walt would slouch in his chair and complain, "It gets lonely around here. I just want to talk to somebody." When lent a listening ear, however, he would ruminate aloud about his childhood hardships, and when it was his conversation partner's turn to talk, he would leave them hanging: "Gotta get goin'!"

The world Walt Disney had created—one of fantasy, innocence, and wish-upon-a-star fulfillment of dreams—stood in stark contrast to the world he lived in, where it was too precarious to loosen his grip, enjoy a genuine interest, or be a friend instead of a taskmaster. A *New York Times* reporter who visited the studios noted, "I came away feeling sad" to find that the brilliant man who had delighted the world's imagination was now deflated, intransigent, craving approval but desperately lonely, and avoiding his problems by procrastinating with toy trains.

The popcorn machine was filled with too many kernels. As the cameras rolled on the television show *The Children's Corner*, the lid bounced open and the newly popped popcorn exploded over the sides. After filming wrapped, the show's cocreator, thirty-three-year-old Fred Rogers, said, "Now we have to do that again."

The show's star, a bubbly young woman named Josie Carey, was mystified. "Why? That was fun! The kids will love it." But Rogers was concerned that for younger children, the runaway popping and the ensuing mess could be disturbing. Carey threw up her hands. He was so particular, so exacting. To Carey, the popcorn spilling everywhere was exciting—it was exactly what made TV entertaining.

But Fred Rogers hadn't gotten into TV to be entertaining. According to biographer Maxwell King, Rogers's mission on TV was "to make it better, to make it more appropriate and educational for young children. The slapstick, pie-in-the-face quality of early television was just what he wanted to change." Rogers had high standards, deep commitment, yet also a clear-eyed vision. He paid attention to the details—he saw things and thought of nuances nobody else did.

In 1961, the head of children's television at the Canadian Broadcasting Corporation thought these traits made Fred Rogers the right person to lead a quiet revolution in children's education. "I've seen you talk with kids," said the executive. "I want you to look into the lens, and just pretend that's a child."

And so began the show that would come to be called *Mister Rogers' Neighborhood.* Over thirty-one seasons and 895 episodes, the world would witness Rogers trade a blazer and dress shoes for his cardigan and sneakers at the start of every show, a comforting, reliable signature.

Each episode underwent intense care and deliberation. Excellence was the only acceptable standard. Every script went through multiple levels of review—Rogers himself, the show's producers, and Rogers's mentor and consultant, Dr. Margaret McFarland, a child psychologist at the University of Pittsburgh.

Once, in the middle of shooting an episode, Rogers felt the script was not quite right, even after all the usual layers of input. So he did the unthinkable. He stopped production, left a highly paid, mostly unionized crew twiddling their thumbs on set, and walked down to the university campus to consult with Dr. McFarland. After about an hour, he came back, and the show rolled. But the incident was pure Rogers. If it was for the kids, it had to be right.

With such exacting standards, one might think that Rogers would be difficult, an unreasonable autocrat, or at least deadly boring. But Fred Rogers wasn't any of those things. Instead, he magically merged high standards with flexibility, responsibility with creativity. An ordained Presbyterian minister, he devoted himself to service, seamlessly combining rectitude with approachability and humility.

Rogers's mentor at the Pittsburgh Theological Seminary, the chain-smoking Dr. William Orr, taught Rogers the principle of "guided drift": staying the course of one's principles while embracing the flow of life. Uphold your integrity but take chances. Be open to change and serendipity rather than being confined by a rigid set of rules.

This philosophy showed up in the show and in life. During one taping, for instance, Rogers began as usual by swapping his blazer for a cardigan and buttoning it up, only to realize that he was one button off—the Monday button was in the Tuesday hole. Familiar with Rogers's standards, the crew expected him to call, "Cut!" and start over, but instead he ad-libbed a line and re-buttoned the sweater, noting that mistakes happen and, moreover, they can be corrected.

Another time, the script called for a shot of the fish in the set's tank eating their food. A production assistant fed the fish during rehearsal in order to calibrate the camera and avoid glare on the tank, so when actual taping came around, the fish were full. They just stared at the food as it sank unceremoniously to the bottom of the tank. Everyone settled in for a long day, assuming they'd have to wait for the fish to get hungry again so the scene could be shot as scripted. But, recalled longtime producer Elizabeth Seamans, "Fred just looked at it. And he looked at the camera and said, 'I guess the fish aren't hungry right now; you know sometimes we're not hungry.'" It was a perfectly reasonable explanation, and he trusted his young viewers to be accepting of the circumstances. The moment became a mantra for the crew: "Do the fish really need to eat?" It reminded them that rolling with the punches made for a better TV show than shoehorning fish—and by extension, life—into a preconceived script.

Despite his flexibility with others, Rogers could be hard on himself. In 1979, after more than a decade on the air, Rogers rolled a piece of paper into his typewriter and tapped out his thoughts in a clickety-clack stream of consciousness: "Am I kidding myself that I'm able to write a script again? . . . Why don't I trust myself? . . . AFTER ALL THESE YEARS, IT'S JUST AS BAD AS EVER. I wonder if every creative artist goes through the tortures of the damned trying to create? GET TO IT, FRED!"

But what truly pushed Fred Rogers was something much deeper than self-castigation. The reporter Tom Junod profiled Rogers for a 1998 cover story in *Esquire*. In the process, he watched Rogers in action on set and commented, "Fred, of course, was an amazing perfectionist who didn't—I wouldn't say he drove those people, that's the wrong word—but absolutely knew what he wanted when he wanted [it] and would not leave that day until he saw it." His staff could sense the intensity, too. "There wasn't a spontaneous bone in that man's body," observed Seamans. "He hated to go into anything unprepared."

But both Junod and the *Neighborhood* staff also understood innately that Rogers's intensity was in service of something greater than a good show. He was driven by his high but flexible standards, commitment to guided drift, his unshakable service to children, but most of all, his energy was funneled into one thing: human connection.

He forged connections quickly and deeply, with everyone. Ten-year-old Jeff Erlanger came on the show to explain how his electric wheelchair worked and why he used it. Nearly twenty years later, Jeff rolled onstage in a tuxedo at the Television Hall of Fame induction ceremony to introduce Rogers. Rogers, who had kept in touch but not seen his old friend since the original taping, leaped to his feet and clambered straight onstage, a huge smile on his face.

Rogers connected with François Clemmons, the Black, gay actor who for twenty-five years played Officer Clemmons on the show; together, they quietly broke the color barrier by cooling their feet in a shared plastic wading pool—a revolutionary act in 1969. In his memoir, Clemmons remembers, "There was something serious yet comforting and disarming about him. His eyes hugged me without touching me."

Rogers once connected with an empty-eyed boy fiercely wielding a toy sword in Penn Station, who was forced into saying hello by his starstruck mother. Rogers leaned in and whispered, "Do you know you're strong on the inside, too?" The boy, caught off guard at being given something he did not know he needed, nodded nearly imperceptibly.

Rogers even connected with Koko, the gorilla who had been taught American Sign Language. It turned out she was a fan of the show. Upon meeting, she hugged him and wouldn't let go. Then, in tribute to the opening sequence of the show she adored, she lovingly removed his shoes.

In *Esquire*, Tom Junod wrote about Rogers, "There was an energy to him . . . a fearlessness, an unashamed insistence on intimacy," and, tellingly:

> Once upon a time, a man named Fred Rogers decided that he wanted to live in heaven. Heaven is the place where good people go when they die, but this man, Fred Rogers, didn't want to go to heaven; he wanted to live in heaven, here, now, in this world, and so one day, when he was talking about all the people he had loved in this life, he looked at me and said, "The connections we make in the course of a life—maybe that's what heaven is, Tom. We make so many connections here on earth. Look at us—I've just met you, but I'm investing in who you are and who you will be, and I can't help it."

* * *

Disney and Rogers are both titans of childhood; their creations are both beloved and immortal. As personalities, they are both studies in high standards, intensity, work ethic, and focusing on the details, from the size of Grumpy's finger to the velocity of popcorn.

But despite being cut from the same cloth, they each created very different garments over the course of their lives. One man was rigid; the other was flexible. One had something to prove; the other had something to share. One avoided any possibility of error; the other made room for inevitable mistakes and hardship through a belief in service and a mission greater than himself. One disengaged from those around him; one engaged fully and with authenticity. One craved approval yet was desperately isolated; the other craved intimacy and created a life based not on control but connection.

Despite such different lives, Disney and Rogers shared a core world-view, *perfectionism*, or the tendency to demand from ourselves a level of performance higher than what is required for the situation. Perfectionism can be healthy, with high yet reasonable and flexible standards, but it quickly becomes unhealthy when standards become unrealistic and rigid. Most importantly, unhealthy perfectionism demands we perform superbly simply to be sufficient as a person. It's not a diagnosis, though it can range from mildly inconvenient to downright paralyzing. Perfectionism comes both from within as a personality style and from all around us as a reaction to a demanding environment.

If you've been nodding in quiet recognition, this book is for you, whether or not the term *perfectionism* snaps into place like that final, satisfying puzzle piece. In fact, most of us with unhelpful, Disneyesque perfectionism don't see it as the overlapping center of the Venn diagram of our struggles. I, for one, didn't resonate with the concept until I started researching it for my last book, *How to Be Yourself: Quiet Your Inner Critic and Rise Above Social Anxiety*, and I'm a clinical psychologist who supposedly has a certain degree of self-awareness about things like this.

But it turns out you and I are in a very big boat. And the boat is getting bigger. Perfectionism is on the rise. In a bold 2019 study, Dr. Thomas Curran, author of *The Perfection Trap: Embracing the Power of Good Enough*, and Dr. Andrew Hill examined perfectionism in over forty thousand college students over a generation, from 1989 to 2016, and discovered that perfectionism was on a steady upward march. Over the twenty-seven years of data, young people became more demanding of themselves, more demanding of others, and perceived that others were more demanding of them.

Demanding a lot of yourself has probably gotten you a long way. I know it's bought me a lot. Since you're reading this book, I'll bet it's the same for you. But demanding a lot can also cost us. Perfectionism can take us down the road of Walt Disney—isolation, burnout, chronic dissatisfaction. Luckily, it can also go the way of Fred Rogers—excellence, flexibility, magnanimity. And guess what? We can forge the path we take. We can learn to be good to ourselves even when we're wired to be hard on ourselves. Ready? Let's take a look.

PART I

Introducing Perfectionism

1

How We See Ourselves

SINCE YOU PICKED up this book, I'll bet you a jelly donut you identify with some part of Walt Disney's or Fred Rogers's high standards, intensity, work ethic, and commitment to doing things well. To outside observers, our lives make a lovely, framed photo of functionality, productivity, or having stuff figured out. The descriptions are flattering: overachiever, on top of everything, accomplished, successful.

But I'll bet you probably also identify with the hidden clutter just outside the frame of that lovely photo. I'm right there with you. We are our own toughest critics. Meeting our expectations for ourselves feels good temporarily but, like a burp, dissipates quickly. We have an internal cattle prod that drives us forward relentlessly, but we also get stuck in our own versions of reworking the size of Grumpy's finger or typing anxious stream-of-consciousness notes when we're supposed to be writing an episode script. Privately, we may feel like we're falling behind, inadequate, left out, or not like everyone else. Despite our eagle-eyed inner quality control inspector ensuring we do things correctly, we worry about letting others down, being judged, or getting criticized. We get called some dubious labels: type A, intense, task-oriented, driven, workaholic, neat freak. Too often, we feel like Walt Disney—lonelier and more isolated than we'd like, a feeling of disconnection that goals and tasks never seem to fill. We yearn for the heaven of Fred Rogers—compassion, purpose, community, belonging.

Don't get me wrong. Perfectionism confers some magical super-powers like high standards, strong work ethic, reliability, and deep care of others. But gone awry, it can subject us to a powerful riptide of *I should do more, do better, be more, be better.* We might look like we're hitting it out of the park, but we feel like we're striking out. For those of us who struggle with it, *perfectionism* is a misnomer: it's not about striving to be perfect. Instead, it's about never feeling good enough.

Interestingly, at the heart of perfectionism is something downright magical: conscientiousness. Conscientiousness is the least sexy super-power. Detail-oriented super vision! Single-handedly crush the marsh-mallow test! Clear the highest standards in a single bound! But it is the most potent trait for a good life. Dr. Angela Duckworth, author of the book *Grit: The Power of Passion and Perseverance*, and three col-leagues examined almost ten thousand American adults and identified conscientiousness as the most consistent predictor of both objective and subjective success—it plays a role in everything from income to happiness to life satisfaction.

Conscientiousness is deeply rooted; the word dates from the 1600s and distills down to *conscience*, our inner sense of right and wrong. It means caring deeply—caring about doing things right, caring about doing a good job, caring about being a good person. We care deeply about, and for, those around us. But at some point, conscientiousness can tip over into unhelpful perfectionism.

Trailblazing Oxford University colleagues Drs. Roz Shafran, Zafra Cooper, and Christopher Fairburn* posit that clinical levels of un-helpful perfectionism emerge when we keep pushing despite adverse consequences; we keep hammering away at the nail long after we've

---

* We'll meet many esteemed researchers in this book, representing several schools of thought. Somewhat ironically, there are differing views on perfectionism—can it ever be helpful, how many core factors are there—and the literature is full of spirited debate and polite yet searing rebuttals. Rather than staking my flag in one research camp, as a clinician and a pragmatist, I'll highlight several views and emphasize what has resonated with clients and fellow clinicians to reduce suffering and improve lives.

smashed our thumb. Two core elements lie at the heart of clinical perfectionism, both of which made my eyebrows shoot up in recognition.

First is *a hypercritical relationship with oneself.* We are our own worst critics. We focus on flaws rather than what's going well, what is lacking rather than what's good. When we don't fulfill those high expectations for ourselves, we are hard on ourselves, but when we do, we decide the expectations were insufficiently demanding in the first place.

Second is *an overidentification with meeting personally demanding standards*, which Shafran and colleagues call *overevaluation.* Our evaluation of ourselves as a person is contingent upon our performance. In other words, we conflate meeting all our expectations for ourselves (or failing to do so) with our sense of self. If we define "failure" as not reaching our standards, a mistake or shortcoming means *we've* failed, even if our standards were unrealistic. Classic examples include striver students defining themselves by their grades, people struggling with body image measuring their self-worth by their weight or body shape, social media users who confuse their worth with their number of followers, athletes who only feel as good as their last game, or anyone struggling with social anxiety who feels like every interaction is a referendum on their character. We can overevaluate almost anything: how healthy we ate today, how adeptly we handled that weird thing Jim said at work, the tidiness of our house, or how much we managed to get done today.

We're not perfectionistic about everything all the time; we're only perfectionistic about what matters to us, because meeting those demanding standards (or not) says something about us personally. I may be perfectionistic about my work and my social behavior, but I'm definitely not when it comes to the state of my home office (piles are a method of organization, right?).

Remember how I said those of us familiar with perfectionism are in a very big boat? There are actually three boats. *Self-oriented perfectionism* is when we're hard on ourselves. This is the classic version of perfectionism—what we think of when we say *perfectionism.* Since the only person we can change is ourselves, we'll hang out on this boat for most of this book.

But according to OG perfectionism researchers Drs. Gordon Flett and Paul Hewitt, there are two other boats, both of which we'll cover in chapter 5. *Other-oriented perfectionism* is when we're hard on the people around us—we have higher-than-necessary expectations for our partner, kids, or employees and get judgy and critical when they don't meet them.

The third boat is *socially prescribed perfectionism*, which is the sense that others have the highest of expectations for us and will come down harshly if we fail to live up to them. If the self-oriented kind comes from within, this type comes from all around us, from the minestrone soup of culture we all float in: capitalism, oppression in all its forms, consumerism. This is the most toxic breed of perfectionism. It's also the one that's increasing—no exaggeration here—exponentially. All three types of perfectionism are on an upward march, but in Drs. Thomas Curran and Andrew Hill's study, the trajectory of socially prescribed perfectionism looked less like a gentle slope and more like a rocket launch.

Our crystal ball shows the trend is likely to continue: in a meta-analysis of ten different studies, Flett and Hewitt found that one in three children and teens today deal with some "clearly maladaptive" form of perfectionism, where they grind themselves into the ground like a cigarette butt under a stiletto trying to meet their own standards.

And then? These kids grow up. Dr. Martin Smith of the University of British Columbia and distinguished colleagues published a meta-analytic review of twenty-five years of research on perfectionistic personalities. The biggest takeaway? While a lot of people mellow as they age, easing up on themselves and caring less about what others think, something different happens as type As get older: the wheels start to come off. As we fall short of our impossible expectations for ourselves again and again, we feel like failures. Life goes down the path of Walt Disney rather than Fred Rogers.

Or we flame out. In the words of Smith and his colleagues, "In a challenging, messy and imperfect world, perfectionists may burn out as they age, leaving them more unstable and less diligent." Life does not get easier for people with perfectionism.

One way that perfectionism does not make life easy is its contribution to actual disorders. Perfectionism itself isn't a diagnosis, but a meta-analysis of 284 different studies reiterated the link between perfectionism and depression, eating disorders, social anxiety, OCD, and non-suicidal self-injury. It even reaches its tendrils into problems that, on the surface, seem unrelated, like sexual dysfunction, mood swings in bipolar disorder, panic attacks, and migraines.

A sobering meta-analysis of forty-five different studies went even further, linking perfectionism to suicide. The Alaska Suicide Follow-Back Study tracked suicides in the state of Alaska from 2003 to 2006. With great care, the researchers interviewed grieving parents who had lost teens and young adults. Without any prompting at all, 62 percent of the bereaved parents described their deceased children as perfectionistic. The most alarming takeaway? Suicide among people with perfectionism comes out of nowhere. Many said they had no idea their children were even suffering. These promising young people hid their distress from everyone. But internally, they agonized to the point of believing the world would be better off without them. Perfectionism isn't technically a disease, but it can be fatal.

Throughout twenty years of working with clients and research participants, I've witnessed the effects of this rising tide of perfectionism. I see them in my client Gus, who came to me looking to optimize his performance at work. A tall, mustachioed product designer at a cookware company, Gus either went all out or got stuck. "I have two gears," he liked to say, "overdrive and park." His approach was all or nothing, but because it took so much time and energy to reach his "all" standards, he frequently felt stuck at "nothing." He worked long hours but was embarrassed to tell me that many of them were spent in procrastination. When he did manage to be productive, he found himself focusing on inconsequential tasks he had already mastered rather than novel, high-profile projects where he had to make decisions or figure things out on the fly. Despite receiving two promotions, he said, "I always have this scene in my head of my boss calling me, telling me she found a mistake I missed, and then firing me, saying she always suspected I couldn't cut it."

Gus's all-or-nothing mentality carried over to other parts of his life. An avid distance runner, my eyes widened when he described his last run: "I wore a heart monitor, tracked my metrics on my phone, and uploaded everything to two apps when I got home, one of which is for my coach." He loved running, but lately, he admitted, slogging through his training regimen felt like a chore. We'll get to know Gus better in chapter 7, when we talk about what to focus on besides performance.

I also see the effects of perfectionism on Francesca, a fortysomething stay-at-home-parent who came to me thinking she was depressed, lazy, and unmotivated. She was depressed for sure, but it was from setting such unrealistic standards for herself. She expected her house to look like a magazine design spread even though twin kindergarteners lived there, expected herself to get into the best shape of her life, expected herself to make everyone around her happy, and make it all look easy. No wonder she would end up eating M&M's on the couch while watching daytime talk shows. What she saw as laziness was actually feeling completely overwhelmed.

"But other people do it, so why can't I?" she would ask when I questioned her expectations. She compared herself: "I have friends who work full-time and get dinner on the table and coach their kids' soccer team and have beautiful houses. I should be able to do that, too."

Sometimes when she uttered her expectations out loud, she realized they sounded wildly unreasonable. "I have this idea that I need to have the body I had at twenty," she said. "I know that sounds insane, but internally, I feel like if I did it before, I should be able to do it again."

Last fall, Francesca and another mom teamed up to organize the annual holiday bazaar at their kids' school. The other mom was a crackerjack at designing signs and banners, planning activity booths, decorating—all the artsy-craftsy things Francesca loved and took pride in doing well. "Every time I saw something that needed to be done, she had done it already and done it beautifully," said Francesca afterward, wiping away tears. "I've never felt so useless." We'll get better acquainted with Francesca in chapter 8, when we talk about rewriting the Inner Rulebook.

I also see the effects on Carter, a hardworking college student who initially came in for mild depression but quickly uncovered the underlying issue of "I always feel like I'm letting everyone down." Carter was from a small town in central Massachusetts where, over the decades, textile mills had slowly given way to big-box stores and opioid busts. He was the smart kid, the golden boy, the big fish, bringing home straight As from his underfunded public high school. He was celebrated by the whole town when he got into his dream university, which, after he moved into his dorm, he realized was the biggest of ponds, filled with flashy and accomplished valedictorians.

Carter tried mightily not to disappoint anyone—his parents, his friends, his girlfriend, his professors, his entire hometown. But the expectation that he become a big man on campus made him feel like shrinking into a shell. Carter felt like he should be able to do it all, despite the limitations set by a twenty-four-hour day and the fact that he isn't a machine. He thought everyone expected him to be a brilliant, charismatic success story who could own the dance floor, but he felt chronically overwhelmed, self-conscious, and like he was faking everything. The discrepancy made him distant and unreliable, which put him in the very position he was trying to avoid: on the verge of making everyone upset. We'll hear more from Carter in chapter 14, when we talk about feeling our authentic emotions.

Finally, I see it in Jamila. A straight-shooting college senior, Jamila came to see me because she felt directionless, with no idea what she wanted to do after graduation. "I'm good at going to classes and taking exams," she said, "but beyond that, I have no idea." Jamila had ground her way through "should" her whole life, doing everything right to get to the next level, but now that she could pursue any path she wanted, she realized she didn't know what she liked. "It's as if I've been trying to do someone else's generic idea of the Right Thing," she said.

One session, she welled up as she described the scene in the 2019 film *Someone Great* where Gina Rodriguez's character, in a T-shirt and underwear, drunkenly unloads groceries with her best friend while they belt Lizzo lyrics and dance dorkily around the kitchen. "I don't have any friends like that," she reflected. "And you know what? Even if I did, it wouldn't occur to me that I could let loose like that with them." She sighed. She had a circle of friends, she said, but she felt peripheral, like the *Dear Evan Hansen* song: "On the outside, always looking in." She yearned to be closer—to go deeper—but wasn't sure how to make it happen. We'll dive into Jamila's story in chapter 15, where we cover building closer relationships.

And, dear reader, let me tell you, I see perfectionism in myself. There's a saying for authors: "Write the book you need." If *How to Be Yourself* was the book I needed twenty years ago, the book you're holding is the book I need *now*.

Mostly my striver traits have served me well. I have high standards for myself, which in school led to good grades and high achievement. More than one person has said to me, "Wow, Ellen, when you set a goal, you just go out and do it." I am detail-oriented—I am the one in my family who knows where the scissors are and notices when we are almost out of toilet paper, two neurons of knowledge that may seem small but make a big difference when someone is in immediate need of either. I am prudent; I've convinced my boys that I can see the future. When they're tossing water balloons in the living room or playing a game they invented called Make Me Say "Ow,"* I foresee the result and take appropriate action to prevent it.

But I've definitely tipped into problematic perfectionism in other areas. My approach to work, for years, was to overload myself, inevitably fail to keep up, and continually stress about it, wondering what was wrong with me and beating myself up when I procrastinated because I felt so overwhelmed. I felt like I wasn't doing anything well, so I kept putting more on my plate. One miraculous day, I actually crossed off

---

* Which may or may not be an improvement over the previous game, Trip.

every item on my list, but it required sixteen hours, I fell into bed with a headache and a stomachache, and it took me three days to get back on track.

For years, I missed out on the unscheduled time that often leads to random conversation—the spontaneous face time that is so vital in building relationships. I remember I was eating lunch at my computer when a visiting scholar from Belgium knocked at my door. She was shocked. "Don't you take a break?" she asked. I would take time for lunch if I had an agenda—to catch up with a friend or give career advice to a student—but it never occurred to me to take a lunch break simply to relax. There was always so much to do.

The stuff I'm least proud of is textbook problematic perfectionism. I've had a hard time enjoying professional accomplishments because I always think things could have gone better. I don't like hearing criticism and can get defensive and grumpy. Until a few years ago, delegating was an impossible task—no one could read my mind (duh) or do the work the way I pictured it, so I soldiered on solo. I have a holiday card list of friends from all stages of my life, but for too many years, I looked at the list and realized I hadn't talked to a lot of them all year.

Rumbling in my consciousness was the sense there must be a better way, but I had no idea how to start. So instead, I doubled down: work harder, plan further ahead, be more efficient. Plus, part of me resisted change, anyway. After all, what's so bad about a well-ordered schedule, knowing I can be counted on, and never running out of toilet paper? It made me feel competent and in control, which is a very appealing feeling, even when that feeling comes at a cost.

But deep down, I knew this wasn't sustainable. The costs were getting higher and more tangible. I got diagnosed with a GI problem. I woke up one morning unable to turn my head to the right, my neck muscles were so tight. I developed an overuse injury from too much typing. I felt disconnected from friends. Everything felt like a chore. I was burned out.

What do Gus, Francesca, Carter, Jamila, and I (and you) have in common? We are human, social animals—we're designed to be part of a group, a community, a tribe. Over almost twenty years of working with clients and research participants, here is one thing I know for sure: each person has a different reason that brings them in, but they all boil down to these very human needs—to feel safe, accepted, and connected.

Our needs may be ancient and universal, but they can be tough to fulfill in our modern social context. For instance, the headlines warn that we're in a loneliness epidemic—more than half of Americans consider themselves lonely. Participation is falling in the institutions of yesteryear that reflected a tighter social fabric—community organizations, neighborhoods, religious life. Social media crushes the souls of those who dare to compare their ordinary lives to otherworldly influencers armed with filters and soft box lighting. And then came the pandemic, which isolated us from one another to the point of seismically quieting the planet. It's no wonder that when it comes to finding connection, it feels like we're swimming upstream.

Interestingly, perfectionism can buy us an ersatz copy of connection. It lights a fire under us to act, think, feel, and behave as superbly as we can and therefore gets us approval, accomplishment, and admiration (or at least seems like it's keeping us buffered from rejection and criticism). This feels pretty darn close to safety, acceptance, and connection. But over time, approval, accomplishment, and admiration feel like the emotional equivalent of fast food—highly appealing but lacking in true nourishment and satisfaction.

Even worse, perfectionism does us dirty. We feel disconnected *precisely because* we're working so hard to gain acceptance. But we're barking up the wrong tree. We want to feel like we belong, but perfectionism steers us toward #goals. We want to be accepted, but perfectionism tells us we have to earn our way into the tribe by being good at things. Part of feeling safe means avoiding the criticism of others, but perfectionism instead subjects us to a steady stream of criticism by our own hand. Overall, perfectionism is a siren song that tells us we'll find social connection if we prioritize agency over communion, if we put goals before people. At first glance, perfectionism seems like an individual problem, but really, it's a social problem.

All my clients who struggle under the weight of perfectionism are beautiful humans who work hard, care deeply, and do right by others. But they can't see how capable and delightful they are. Perfectionism—the measuring stick they use for themselves—pokes holes in their sense of self like a porcupine's raincoat.

Accordingly, this book aims to lay bare the false promises of perfectionism and offer what we can do instead. It picks up where *How to Be Yourself* left off, because the heart of social anxiety is perfectionism. Drill down on social anxiety, and you'll find it's based on the same flawed perception—the felt inadequacy of never being good enough that separates us from others.

Sometimes deconstructing perfectionism can feel like putting socks on a rooster—frustrating, needless, uncontrollable. Our usual perfectionistic strategies of pushing, following the Inner Rulebook, and checking the boxes suddenly break down. Paradoxically, it's the problem we seem least able to solve. But a telling study out of Trinity Western University in British Columbia tracked several hundred participants aged sixty-five and older for several years. It found that those high in perfectionism were *more* likely to die over the study period, while those high in conscientiousness were *less* likely to die. Strangely, that's a finding filled with hope. It means we're closer than we think. All our architecture of conscientiousness is already fully built and highly functional. When we peel away perfectionism to reveal the heart of conscientiousness underneath, our lives not only get better, happier, and more satisfying, they may even get longer.

Therefore, in the pages ahead, we'll keep what works and rethink what doesn't. Luckily, there's a lot that works; we don't have to Ctrl + Alt + Delete anything about ourselves. We'll harness our dream team of traits: conscientiousness, grit, commitment to excellence. We'll keep our strong work ethic and attention to detail. In addition to using our existing powers, we'll also gain some new powers: rest without guilt, enjoyment without a goal, flexibility without anxiety, success (and failure) without overevaluation, forgiveness for mistakes (both others' and our own), and a kinder, gentler regard for ourselves. We'll grant ourselves some kindness instead of the inner nun with a ruler, some grace instead of the internal cattle prod. We're going to take this whole enterprise called life, and ourselves, both very seriously and a lot less seriously. We'll definitely mess up along the way, but paradoxically, taking that in stride will move us forward.

Most people read psychology books because they want to get their act together. But you are not most people. Your act, in fact, might be a little *too* together. Those of us with perfectionism have self-control that's gotten a little out of control. Believe me, I'm right there with you. I'm on the same journey as you. This is not a finger-wagging self-improvement book that says you're doing things wrong—you do that to yourself already. Instead, consider it permission. Permission to discover what your life might look like when you let yourself breathe. When you stop pushing so hard. When you focus on what makes life meaningful rather than your performance. *You'll still be perfectionistic, but it will work for you, not against you.* Officially, this is called *adaptive perfectionism*, but really it just means perfectionism that buys you more than it costs you.

For me, turning down the volume on my intensity is like nothing I'd ever encountered before. When I started writing this book, I dug in with typical perfectionism: I read a stack of books and papers so high it could be measured in feet. I vowed to work diligently to put what I learned into practice. In other words, I approached my type A tendencies as a problem to be vanquished like all other challenges (and yes, I fully see the irony of doubling down on letting go). Previously, if I wanted to change something in my life—start a podcast, get in shape, jump from a research career to writing—I could do it systematically: set a goal, get to work, and check it off.

But this time, there were no boxes to check. Checking boxes was actually the problem. Rather than pushing, I had to let things be. Instead of working toward a goal, I had to focus on things that defied goal-setting—like values, enjoyment, and community. Instead of trying to do everything myself, I had to be vulnerable with others. Instead of following my rules, I had to be more flexible. I had to show my process to the world, rife with setbacks and snags, not just the highlighted correct answer at the end.

My conscientious inner striver has come in handy for some of the changes. I prioritize sleep and exercise so I'm no longer running on fumes and caffeine. I remember to tell friends about both my screwups and my successes. And yes, I still have a to-do list, but it's not in unrelenting chronological order anymore, and I look at what I accomplished rather than unhappily laser focusing on what was left undone.

I've also let go a lot of the push-push-pushing that wasn't working. I've tried to let go of my worst-case-scenario predictions. When my kids overdo it on screen time or sugar, I've stopped fretting they'll be stunted and started remembering they are kids. I still get overwhelmed sometimes, but I'm much more magnanimous to myself when I find myself listening to *My Favorite Murder* when I'm supposed to be working. I trust colleagues with delegated and collaborative tasks and wonder why I didn't do this years ago. I am learning to tolerate criticism and listen for what I can agree with rather than just defending my raised hackles. I sought out a "therapist's therapist" and finally let myself be taken care of rather than doing all the caretaking.

In short, I am learning to rest. To reach out. To be real rather than impressive. To do things for enjoyment rather than improvement. To let myself off the hook. To laugh at myself. To show more of the mess. Rather than pulling harder in my personal tug-of-war, I'm learning to drop the rope.

As someone who values privacy, I find it unbelievable that I now make a living writing about my insecurities. Sometimes, when I think about it, my stomach sinks to the floor. I have a baked-in sense that my problems are unseemly and will drive people away. But then, when

I look around and see what's actually happened, I realize sharing my weaknesses with friends and readers alike has made me feel more connected to and accepted by the many, *many* people who feel the exact same way—connections I would have missed out on entirely had I gone on hiding what I thought was wrong.

A few notes about using this book: Those of us with perfectionism tend to default to gut renovations and total overhauls, but you do not need a self-improvement program. You already have lots of great traits—heck, as far as a personality style goes, conscientious is the one to choose—you already work hard and care deeply. In terms of changes, we're talking little tweaks. Being 5 percent less hard on yourself or 10 percent kinder to yourself will likely be just right. Indeed, when you're done with this book, you may not *do* anything overtly different at all; you may simply approach things with an updated mindset of willingness and flexibility.

Next, you may feel ambivalent about letting go. I've met many clients who credit perfectionism with getting them where they are today. I feel you. Society rewards us for digging deep and pushing hard. Those got me a long way, too. Even when I was sleep-deprived, disconnected, and felt like I was half-assing everything, I sure got a lot done. Rest assured, it's okay to be ambivalent. But go ahead and try some of the mindset shifts and experiments in this book. I pinkie promise you won't end up a stoner in pajama pants covered in Cool Ranch Dorito dust. If you take a test drive and don't like it, you can go back to business as usual—no hard feelings.

Finally, notice if you find yourself approaching this book at 110 percent. You might tell yourself you need to create a program out of the book ("I'll read a chapter a day," "I'll try everything in each chapter before I move on to the next one"). If that helps you, knock yourself out. But notice what pressures and contingencies it creates and whether or not that makes you *less* likely to finish it. Indeed, the myth of "the more effort you put in the better results you get" gets in the way here. So instead, prioritize what speaks to you rather than reading cover to cover. See the chapters as a menu and read what you like. You can even keep it on the toilet tank and read it when you're sitting there—I promise I won't be offended.

Today, I'd be remiss if I said I had it all figured out. I'm not a perfect imperfectionist (a concept that makes my head hurt, anyway). The word *perfection* is from the Greek *teleiōsis*. The root, *telos*, can be translated as "end" or "goal." But modern translations have begun to interpret it as "purpose" or "maturity." Rather than implying a final, flawless masterpiece, the word connotes wisdom and intention—process rather than outcome. I'm definitely still getting my sea legs, but after trying to live the changes I write about in this book, I'd like to think I'm on my way.

Ultimately, perfectionism's deepest wish is to be safe, accepted, and connected unconditionally, without having to perform at all. You've been working so hard for so long. We're not going to abandon the hard work and high standards that make you *you*, but we will make more room for rest, joy, community, and connection. It's time to welcome yourself home to your life and yourself. It's time to take a breath, take a look around, and know, deep in your bones: *I am worthy just as I am. I am enough.*

2

The Many Salads of Perfectionism

JUST LIKE A salad can be anything from panzanella to Caesar to Jell-O, perfectionism, too, has endlessly different manifestations. Line up one hundred people who struggle with perfectionism, and I'll show you one hundred different ways of being perfectionistic. For example, while some of us will orient to detail—we'll see the typos, etiquette gaffes, and crooked paintings everyone else misses—that's not the case for everyone. Others will try to do things all by ourselves—we suck at asking for help, accepting favors, or delegating. Still others of us will work hard to put on a good face; everything's fine, no matter how we really feel. The combinations are endless, and the resulting pheno-types can be as different as Niçoise and tabbouleh.

Big flashing lights here: there is no moral judgment on any of the traits and habits of perfectionism. Nearly all the tendencies we'll discuss in this book are useful and rewarding ways to operate in the world. It's only when our habits become rigid and our expectations unrealistic that they start to work against us. Let's say it again: none of our tendencies are inherently bad. In fact, most of them are quite good. It's all in what we *do* with them.

But I digress—back to salads. Again, there are endless varieties of both salad and people with perfectionism. But just like a salad retains some basic characteristics—an assortment of ingredients bound by a common dressing—perfectionism is bound by common tendencies. A flowchart is worth a thousand words. It's based on the research of Drs. Roz Shafran, Zafra Cooper, and Christopher Fairburn when they were colleagues at Oxford University. It's a psychological tur- ducken of the two core tendencies of overevaluation and self-criticism wrapped in layers of personally demanding standards, all-or-nothing self-judgment, and avoidance. When I show this to clients, almost all of them have said, "Hey, that's exactly what I do."*

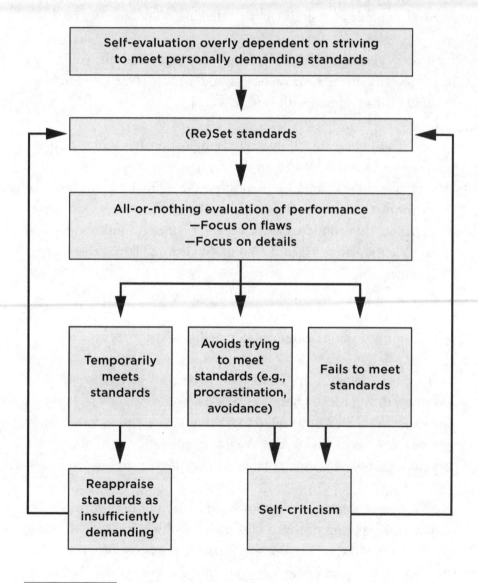

---

* Usually followed by, "Can you email this to me?"

But wait, there's more. In the literature, in my office, and in this book, we can spot seven common tendencies that go along with this cycle. While not everyone struggling with perfectionism sees themselves in all seven domains below, I'll bet you a cockatoo you resonate with many of the following statements, some of which are paraphrased from validated self-report questionnaires. Indeed, the more times your eyes widen in recognition at the examples, the more perfectionism likely plays a role in your life, both individually and interpersonally.

First up is that **hypercritical relationship with oneself**, which can bleed over into being hard on others, too. Maybe some of the following statements resonate with you:

- » I tend to beat myself up, feel disproportionately guilty, or panic when I make a mistake or do something wrong.
- » I take things harder than most people—problems, mistakes, or conflicts stick with me for a long time.
- » I often think my ideas, work, or performance are not good enough.
- » When I get criticized, I tend to shut down, blame others, or get defensive.
- » I have been told I am controlling, a micromanager, too picky, or too critical.
- » I admit I can be judgmental, whether silently or out loud.

Therefore, in Shift 1, "From (Self-)Criticism to Kindness," we'll learn how to go easier on ourselves. We'll lay off constantly trying to fix ourselves. We'll also stop trying to fix those closest to us (stage whisper: not that any of us do *that*). We'll challenge the myths of criticism and learn that we've gotten as far as we have *despite* our self-judgment.

Next is **overevaluation**. We overidentify with our performance. Our goodness as a person rises and falls with fulfilling, or failing to fulfill, all the demanding expectations we have for ourselves. We overevaluate because we're searching for acceptance and connection, but counterintuitively, all the grinding and striving gets in the way of feeling close to people, plus it's plain old stressful. Maybe these statements make you nod in agreement:

» My performance (work, grades, fitness, appearance, home, stuff I do for fun, etc.) reflects on my character, morals, or me as a person.
» There is not really a difference between doing my best and doing things right.
» I usually think of myself as a worthy person, but when I do badly at something, I sometimes feel worthless or like something is wrong with me.
» If I don't understand or can't do something well right away, I tend to blame myself.
» I set impossible expectations or deadlines for myself and then get stressed when I can't reach them.
» Even when I do something carefully, I often feel it is not quite right.
» I have to be working toward a goal or accomplishment to feel right about myself.
» I am always working to improve something (my health, my sleep, my wardrobe, my social life, my income, etc.)

Therefore, in Shift 2, appropriately named "Coming Home to Your Life," we'll shift from "I am what I do" to living a meaningful life. We'll refocus on our relationships and maybe even have a good time along the way.

Third, we **orient to rules**. The shoulds of life call out to us. We are quick to zero in on perceived duties and responsibilities and either approach them with box-checking gusto or get paralyzed with avoidance. For example, you and your friend might hold the same personal rule about maintaining a perfectly clean house, but you might manifest the rule as sparkling counters and organized Tupperware while she throws up her hands, says, "If I can't do it all, why try?" and lives in a mess. To that end, maybe some of these statements sound familiar:

» I like to know what the rules and expectations are so I can follow them.
» I've been called *stubborn*, *rigid*, or *set in my ways*.
» I think it's important to do things properly or the right way.
» I expect higher performance in my daily tasks than most people.
» When I feel pressure to do something, I sometimes resist or rebel by doing it reluctantly or not at all.

Therefore, in Shift 3, "From Rules to Flexibility," we'll rewrite the Inner Rulebook, stop twisting our wants into shoulds, roll back over-responsibility to responsibility, and learn why we balk and how to get unstuck.

Fourth, we **focus on mistakes**; we work hard to prevent them in the future and intensely regret those we made in the past. Consider these statements:

» I often worry about something I said or did.
» When I make a mistake, I tend to shut down, blame others, or get defensive.
» I ask other people how well they think I'm doing or if I'm doing things right (reassurance seeking).
» Mistakes feel like personal failures; they indicate something negative about my character.
» I tend to either over-apologize or never apologize.
» I take things harder than most people; mistakes, problems, or conflicts stick with me for a long time.
» I can get stuck or bogged down when I have to make a decision (e.g., small, like what gift to buy, or big, like which job offer to accept).

As such, in Shift 4, "Mistakes: From Holding On to Letting Go," we'll learn to forgive our past errors and regrets, as well as learn that mistakes and struggles aren't personal.

Fifth is that we **procrastinate**. This one is pretty straightforward:

> » I put off tasks that make me feel anxious, incapable, or overwhelmed.
> » If I don't know how to do something, where to start, or if I'll succeed, I get stuck.
> » I often work on inconsequential things when I should be focusing on bigger goals or tasks.
> » I regularly struggle with procrastination.

In Shift 5, "From Procrastination to Productivity," we'll learn that procrastination isn't about time management, it's about emotion management and connecting to our future selves.

Sixth, we tend to **compare ourselves to others**. This one is also straightforward.

> » I often come away from interactions or social media feeling not good enough.
> » I use other people's accomplishments and failures to determine if I'm doing well enough.
> » Comparing myself to people I know makes me feel separate or alone.

Comparison is inevitable, but in Shift 6, "From Comparison to Contentment," we'll stop coming away from comparison feeling hopelessly inadequate or problematically superior.

Finally, **our drive to do things right extends to our emotions**:

> » When I am struggling, I tell myself I'm not allowed to feel bad because other people have it worse than I do.
> » I expect myself to do things well and easily—I shouldn't get anxious, be unsure, lack confidence, or care what people think.

» When I am upset or dysregulated, I tend to think I'm doing something wrong or something is wrong with me.
» I approach leisure, socializing, or hobbies as tasks to be done right or experienced in a certain way ("I should be relaxed," "I should be happy and carefree," "I should be in the moment").

And in **how we show our emotions to others**:

» I tell others I'm fine when I'm not.
» It's mortifying to lose control of myself (e.g., cry in front of others, lose my temper, appear anxious).
» I try to look confident or nonchalant on the surface even if I'm freaking out or working frantically underneath it all.
» I laugh, look concerned, or otherwise react appropriately because it's the correct way to react for the situation, not because I actually feel that way.

Therefore, in Shift 7, "From Control to Authenticity," we'll question the idea that there is a correct feeling to have in every situation, also called *emotional perfectionism*, and an invulnerable way to behave, called *perfectionistic self-presentation*. We'll examine how to evoke social safety and be authentic, both alone and with others.

But before we get into all that, let's look backward at the origins of our personal constellation of perfectionism. We come by it honestly, so let's follow the trail back and see how it all started.

3

The Beginnings of Things

THE BRUTALIST CINDER block building that housed the Centre for Emotional Health stood in sharp contrast to the lush green campus of Sydney's Macquarie University. Outside, cockatoos perched in the gum trees; rabbits hopped about, nibbling the grass.

Inside, the center looked like a secret underground Soviet laboratory: closed-circuit video cameras kept watch from ceiling corners, illuminated signs flashed "Experiment in Progress" above the hallway doors. Despite the lack of ambiance and the jaunty brown carpet, the center was actually a safe and happy place for kids with anxiety.

Nine-year-old Charlotte was one of those kids; she and many children like her attended weekly therapy at the center, learning to be curious about their worries, test out being brave, and otherwise unwind their tightly coiled psyches.

But today was a little different. It was Saturday, the building was weekend-quiet, and most importantly, Charlotte was taking part in a first-of-its-kind study. She sat at a child-size table dutifully copying shapes from a booklet. Charlotte, always careful and deliberate, glanced back and forth between her paper and the booklet, checking the accuracy of her drawings—a square bisected diagonally, a square with a triangle perched on top like a kindergarten rendition of a house, a petite diamond. She picked up a ruler and then an eraser, considering whether or not to use either.

Jenny Mitchell, the graduate student running the study for her dissertation, sat quietly to the side of Charlotte, stopwatch in hand. "Okay, great," she said, smiling and clicking the button with her thumb. "That's one minute. Now wait here and I'll get your mum."

Next door in the observation room, Charlotte's mom, Kylie, was watching her daughter through the one-way mirror. She had been intrigued by the study when Jenny explained it to her: First, for one minute, Charlotte would copy shapes on her own. For the second minute, Kylie would join her and give her some coaching—instructions designed either to elicit perfectionism or to evoke a more easygoing vibe. And for a final, third minute, Charlotte would be left to her own devices again, her mum's instructions fresh in her mind.

Jenny appeared in the observation room doorway. "Okay, Mum, you're up," she said. As Kylie stood to go join her daughter, Jenny reviewed the instructions with her. "For minute two, I'd like you to do and say things so Charlotte knows you're not concerned about the accuracy of her picture or about her making mistakes." For instance, Jenny continued, "I'd like you to sit with a relaxed and calm posture." To demonstrate, Jenny pulled out a chair, took a seat, and struck a pose that read: unbothered. "Then, make comments so Charlotte knows you're not worried about her making mistakes. You could say, 'Close enough is good enough,' or 'I don't mind if you don't copy them exactly.' You can also remind her that nothing bad will happen if she makes a mistake, like, 'What does it matter if you don't do it perfectly?' Finally, don't draw for her, even if she asks you for help. Instead, just be encouraging. You could say, 'I'm sure you can do it fine by yourself.'"

"No problem," said Kylie, rolling her shoulders as if to warm up for a workout. "I can definitely do those things."

Let's back up. From their work at the center, Jenny, her professors Drs. Suzanne Broeren and Carol Newall, and lead researcher Dr. Jennifer Hudson, knew that lots of well-meaning parents coached their children to try their hardest, do things right, and avoid mistakes. But did it work? Or did it just stress kids out? What would a more laid-back approach do? Would kids slack off? Get lazy? To find out, they set up the most valuable yet labor-intensive type of study: a randomized experiment with actual kids and parents.

To see how the two different styles of parenting—perfectionistic or non-perfectionistic—affected the widest variety of kids, the team not only recruited kids like Charlotte, who were in treatment for anxiety, but also non-anxious kids from local schools, sports teams, and community centers. This created a perfect two-by-two grid—kids with and without clinical anxiety, perfectionistic and non-perfectionistic parent coaching—from which to investigate.

Charlotte was randomly assigned to the non-perfectionistic group, with its easy manner, low pressure, and I'm-confident-in-your-capabilities encouragement. Kylie and the other moms in their group were nonchalant about mistakes and projected confidence in their children's independence.

But for the other half of the moms, Jenny had a very different set of instructions for minute two. The pressure got cranked up. Moms were asked to show concern about the accuracy of the picture; they were told to point out that lines should be shorter, longer, or straighter. They were also asked to remind their child that bad things could happen if they made a mistake, like, "If you don't copy them properly, you won't get your best score." Finally, they were told to jump in and take over, drawing or redrawing their children's shapes themselves, or to say, "Check it again to make sure you got it right."

After their respective low- or high-pressure minute two sessions where the mom set the tone, each kid was left alone again to copy a new set of shapes during minute three.

For kids like Charlotte, who got the take-it-easy instructions, minute three was generally productive, resulting in a steady stream of nicely reproduced parallelograms and patterns. But for kids in the perfectionistic group, Jenny saw kids erase their drawings multiple times, crumple their papers to try again, and work so slowly they might still be on their first shape by the time her stopwatch hit the end of the experiment.

After all the numbers were crunched, what did the results show? One finding was intuitive: perfectionistic coaching skyrocketed perfectionistic behaviors in *all* kids—with or without clinical anxiety. They checked, erased, reworked, took forever on each drawing. Even after the experiment was over and their mothers came back in to take them home, the kids asked for reassurance: "Have I got it right?" By contrast, in the non-perfectionistic condition, these behaviors were relatively rare—kids drew their pictures and moved on to the next one.

But the second finding was a surprise. The coaching style that led to objectively better results, improving the quality and accuracy of the drawings, was the non-perfectionistic coaching. Giving kids permission to make mistakes reduced the number of actual mistakes. By contrast, all the fretting, erasing, and reworking after the perfectionistic coaching did nothing to improve kids' performance. Instead, the quality of their drawings flatlined, not improving at all over the course of the three minutes.

Four Types of Families

And that's just three minutes. Mitchell and colleagues demonstrated what a profound impact perfectionistic expectations can have on kids in the short term. But what about the long term? During our time growing up under our parents' roofs, we soak in their rules, standards, and expectations like a plugged watermelon. So what happens when three minutes gets stretched over eighteen years? In their 2002 analysis of the childhood development of perfectionism, pioneering researchers Drs. Gordon Flett and Paul Hewitt found four distinct family environments that lay fertile ground for a lifetime of being tough on ourselves.

I'm Just Trying to Help

The first family environment is the one Mitchell and colleagues tested in the Macquarie University study. It's officially called the *anxious rearing model*, but tracks firmly with overprotective, helicopter, or snowplow parents who insist, "I'm just trying to help." Anxious rearing families are cautious, exacting, instructive, or "helpful" to a degree that is disproportionate to what is needed.

Take Isabel. She was convinced her anxious overmanagement was screwing up her young daughter, but she didn't know how to stop. "We cleaned up her play kitchen the other day, and Mia put the wooden fruit away and then looked at me and asked, 'Did I do it right?' And she actually looked scared. And that just broke my heart," she said. "I know I shouldn't fix her work after she finishes it, but I can't help it. I even control her artwork," she said, rolling her eyes at herself. "The other day, she made this beautiful drawing, and then she ruined it by putting all this brown at the top. I knew better than to say out loud that she ruined it, but I'm sure she could tell I didn't like it anymore."

In anxious rearing model families, perfectionism emerges as a preoccupation with correctness—doing things the "right" or "appropriate" way. Mistakes are to be avoided, usually with a deeper goal to avoid being judged or criticized. But parents who try to protect their kids from criticism, ironically, often end up dishing out criticism themselves. Anxious rearing families promote a climate of evaluation, pronouncing outcomes good, bad, or ugly. *Why on earth did he grow that mustache? That sweater is cheap-looking—you should only buy merino sweaters. Well, she certainly gained a lot of weight.* Everything and everyone is evaluated—family members, decisions, bodies, behavior, purchases, objects, destinations, aspirations.

If this sounds familiar to you, your parents may have tried to warn you against all possible dangers, been overly worried when you did something on your own, or forbidden you from doing as many things as other kids. Anxious parents may have missed the lessons of Dory, the foil to anxious-rearing parent Marlin in *Finding Nemo*: "Well, you can't never let anything happen to him. Then nothing would ever happen to him."

I Am My Achievement

The second family environment is Flett and Hewitt's *social expectations model*. The heart of this family dynamic is contingent approval: we earn adults' time, attention, compliments, or pride because of the performances we deliver—good grades, good behavior, being "easy"—or particular attributes, like being smart, pretty, or charismatic. It starts early. When Auntie Jeanette asks you what you want to be when you grow up, even a four-year-old notices that saying, "A doctor," gets a very different reaction than saying, "A stegosaurus." Approval buys a feeling of significance.

At six years old, I found myself in an after-school Girl Scout meeting. We were making bookmarks out of felt—cutting and assembling bits into the shape of an owl nestled in a brown tree trunk. I remember cutting out a red bow tie and pasting it on. When the troop leader saw it, she said, "You are so creative." Turning to the assistant leader, she pointed at me and remarked again, "This one is so creative." The key of her praise fit perfectly into the lock of my conscientious six-year-old temperament; it clicked. I remember feeling a swell of pride, but I also remember feeling alarmed at the injured look on the face of the girl next to me. I was creative, according to the leader. But the fact that she hadn't said the same to my troop-mate meant that she wasn't. I didn't have the vocabulary to articulate it then, but now I can understand the compliment simultaneously lifted me up and differentiated me from her. I was anointed, but I was also separate.

Worse, even as I felt special, I now felt the weight of expectation. The title of "creative" was, in my young mind, now an obligation. From there on out, I intuited, if she didn't deem future craft projects "creative," I would lose my title. Or worse, her label would turn out to be untrue and I'd make a liar out of her. I liked the positive feedback—who wouldn't? But I was also afraid of letting her down and intimidated at the prospect of meeting her expectation, in my six-year-old mind, forever.

It's not just me: If we're good at math, we feel like a disappointment if we get an answer wrong. If we're the community league hockey goalie, we swear to ourselves that last goal was really, truly the last puck we're letting by us. If we generally get compliments on our appearance, gaining a few pants sizes makes us feel like we've failed.

Sometimes it's barely perceptible. Milo grew up in a family most of my clients would envy. His parents were supportive and kind; even though they were busy, he could tell they both loved and liked him. Milo remembers only one overt contingency growing up. His parents would reward him for good grades: twenty dollars per A, ten dollars per B. He remembers some covert contingencies, like sticking it out on the high school swim team long after he lost interest in it, because his mother was so enthusiastic about him being a varsity athlete.

Milo's dad would say, "I don't care what you do—be a garbageman if you want—but whatever you do, be the best at it." It came from a well-intentioned place, but it backfired into a message of, "If you're not the best at what you do, you're unworthy." It happened with teachers, too. Milo remembers one algebra test he bombed. The teacher handed it back with a look of surprised amusement and the remark, "This was unlike you." Despite the relatively mild comment, Milo felt gutted. The tone belied that he had disappointed his teacher.

None of these scenarios are unusual. In fact, they're downright gentle. But Milo's personality was particularly attuned to pleasing others and avoiding letting them down, and his sensitive antennae picked up on approval or disapproval with exacting precision. Most of the adults in his life were warm and supportive, which actually made the pressure to people-please more difficult for him to resist.

Today, Milo still struggles with giving himself permission to do what he wants rather than what will please others or avoid criticism. He chooses activities with a finish line or a final product—earning successive karate belts, running half marathons, things he can measurably excel at—rather than for fun or because he's interested in them.

In other cases, the contingencies are extreme. Some families believe it takes intense pressure to create a diamond. Take my client Ivan, a stern-looking man in his sixties with a predilection toward eye-popping neon neckties and a case of crippling anxiety.

Shortly after Ivan was born in Communist Bulgaria, his father died, leaving him, his sister, and his mother scrambling for financial stability. His mother saw Ivan's achievement as the way out, and Ivan quickly learned that his mother's love was contingent upon his performance.

He recalls his mother sitting beside him as he learned to add and subtract, monitoring his progress. Whenever he got a problem wrong, she smacked his hand. "Do it again," she growled. As life went on, the contingencies evolved from math fundamentals to elementary school grades to university admissions. All that mattered was achievement. Once, when Ivan's mother decided he should be studying rather than hanging out with his girlfriend, she slapped him with the closest item at hand—the sausage she was preparing for dinner. It was humiliating and shaming, but in a way, it worked. Of course it did: if a child thinks love is contingent upon performance, they will perform and likely do it well. Ivan became a respected engineer and, after the fall of Communism, built a comfortable life in the United States, eventually bringing his mother and sister with him. But Ivan also brought with him vast insecurities.

Today, Ivan believes if he were unable to work, the loss of prestige and income would cause his wife and kids to drop him like that same sausage, hot from the pan. Ivan can articulate that his family loves him not just for the income he provides but for his love and kindness and simply for being Ivan. Somehow, though, this belief remains in the topsoil of his brain, never quite penetrating the bedrock.

Even if you didn't suffer with a cold and harsh parent like Ivan, perhaps your parents were still demanding. When they said, "Do your best," was it clear you needed to do *the* best? Maybe they got excited when you delivered, but didn't seem to notice when you had fun, were curious, or felt deeply. Perhaps there were always lots of activities, or maybe one or two very intense activities, like gymnastics or cello, but the undercurrent made clear their purpose was for achievement, not enjoyment.*

What happened when your performance was disappointing? Sometimes the disapproval is overt. "I'm disappointed in you." "You're better

---

* In the you-are-your-performance classic *Battle Hymn of the Tiger Mother*, Amy Chua describes the decision to have her younger daughter study violin "without consulting Lulu, ignoring the advice of everyone around me." Chua chooses the violin not in response to her daughter's interests but because "I fetishize difficulty and accomplishment." The book, while a premier example of social expectations model parenting, is also unexpectedly self-deprecating and astute, even as Chua's behavior makes me shake my head.

than this." But more often, it's covert—a sigh, changing the subject, your name announced in a certain tone. Milo remembers when his parents perceived him to be behaving inappropriately, they would say his name—the ultimate in personal disapproval—in a particular tone: *Milo*.

The lock-and-key analogy of family culture and child personality is particularly salient for kids to whom accomplishment comes easily. When we are bright or talented or precocious, we impress adults and are rewarded with their time, attention, or goodwill. And then? We see how this works. So we double down. When adult approval is valued and disapproval is kryptonite, behaving superbly—being helpful, selfless, high-achieving, or attractive—becomes a life skill.

It's confusing, though. Pride does a good impression of love. But love is a freely given emotion not based on achievement or performance. Unlike pride, love isn't conditional.

It's even more confusing if we grew up in a house where parents were busy, preoccupied, task-focused, or wildly uncomfortable with warmth or affection—we might have known intellectually we were loved, but what we felt viscerally was their pride—attention, rewards, kind words, the pleased looks on their faces when we did something they deemed good and worthy. We learn the cause and effect: do something notable, get positive attention. It feels good. And it sends a message of contingency.

We might sail through for years, but inevitably, at some point, things get hard: calculus, the state music competition, varsity tryouts, college admissions. When we're used to achieving easily and suddenly find ourselves over our heads, we take it personally. Struggle, we decide, means inadequacy. The implied answer to our mumbled frustrations of "Why can't I do this?" is that we're not actually good at this, after all. Perhaps that's why Flett and Hewitt, along with their colleague Dr. Deborah Stornelli, found that in fourth and seventh graders, self- and family-driven pressures to achieve went along with elevated levels of fear and sadness.

A 2018 *Harvard Business Review* article refers to a recruiting tactic used by top firms: targeting "insecure overachievers" as they are called in the boardroom but never in public. Insecure overachievers are motivated and disciplined. They deliver long hours and exceptional outcomes. The article states, "The firm in effect tells the insecure overachiever, 'We are the best in the business, and because we want you to work for us, that makes you the best, too.'" But the targeting results in near exploitation, not exactly what well-meaning parents had in mind.

The parents of insecure overachievers—Milo's parents, Ivan's mother—all have one thing in common: good intentions. But, like another destination, the road to insecurity and anxiety is paved with good intentions. Ultimately, the message is you're not enough the way you are; you need achievements and signifiers to be enough. And therefore, what you do is more important than who you are.

If I'm Perfect, I'll Be Safe

In the third family environment, children of abusive, dramatic, erratic, or chaotic families become fiercely independent and self-reliant to cope with parental addiction, mental illness, debilitating health problems, custody battles, or the constant riptide of poverty. Flett and Hewitt call it the *social reaction model*.

Meet Katie. When she was eight, her parents got divorced. Shortly afterward, her new stepmom entreated her, an only child, to move in with her and Katie's dad. "She said, 'We're going to start a family,'" Katie remembers. "'Don't you want to have brothers and sisters and be part of a family?'" Totally sold, Katie begged her mom to let her move in with her dad and stepmom, not realizing until years later that her stepmom's invitation had less to do with welcoming Katie and more with twisting a knife in her mom's heart. But her mom let her move. The first day in the new house, her stepmom slapped her. Katie distinctly recalls thinking in that moment, *I think this is how it's going to be.* And it was, every day, for the next eight years.

A few months in, her stepmom forbade Katie from eating anything she wasn't specifically served, a new, arbitrary, and abusive rule. One day, Katie, hungry, snuck some leftover macaroni and cheese, thinking it wouldn't be noticed. Her stepmom confronted her. "You know how I know?" she asked. She showed Katie how she had drawn lines on all the containers to show where the levels of food should be. If Katie disobeyed her, even to meet her bodily needs, she would be met with wrath.

Over the years, Katie learned that if she did everything her stepmom said and made herself as obedient and deferential as possible, the abuse would happen less. It didn't stop until Katie realized, at age sixteen, that she could hit her stepmom back.

Your family may not have been abusive like Katie's; instead, your parents might have been wrapped up in their own battles. Maybe a sibling had special needs and you had to keep it all together so as not to be an additional burden. Maybe you were the elder of many and had to be the parent to your younger siblings, or even to your parent.

Children naturally believe the world revolves around them; it's a developmentally appropriate belief. But it also means that when something bad happens, kids think it's their fault. Therefore, it follows that if they can change and control their own behavior, they can change and control an out-of-control situation. Like Katie, you might have thought that if you were so good, so responsible, so helpful, your stepmom would stop abusing you. Or Mom might stop being depressed, Dad might not drink and yell so often, or your chronically ill sister would get better and your family could finally be "normal."

Regardless of your particular situation, adults like Katie who remember a childhood infused with chaos, instability, or endangerment find solace and survival through control. In Katie's case, it was obedience and deference. In other situations, it might manifest as, *If I can't control the divorce, at least I can control how thin I am. If I can't control Dad's anger, at least I can control my grades. If I can't control my stepmom hitting me, at least I can be bubbly and outgoing and the most popular girl in school.*

This technique "works," at least in the short term. In families that are chaotic, inconsistent, self-absorbed, or numbed by alcohol or drugs, a child's efforts at control help that child cope both internally and externally. Internally, attempts at control help a child hold on to a sense of mastery and self-worth; it offsets shame. Externally, they can minimize the damage and garner attentiveness and positive regard from others in their lives. Again, these techniques work, at least until we grow up and our situation changes. Once we are safe and no longer dependent on our families of origin, the overcontrolled behaviors that helped us survive cease to serve us and start to work against us.

I Learned It by Watching You

In the fourth type of family, perfectionism is infused in the air we breathe. Like spilled glitter, it sticks to everything. Flett and Hewitt call it the *social learning model*.

In social learning model families, perfectionism is like the weather: always present, always driving our choices. Hyper-disciplined, high-achieving, or hard-driving parents model hyper-disciplined, high-achieving, or hard-driving behavior to their kids. Every family immerses kids in its own microculture where kids learn standards of achievement, social niceties, health and wellness, organization, fastidiousness, and more and then internalize them as their own. Whether a parent is a retail clerk or Supreme Court clerk, a secretary or secretary of state, if they hold narrow standards of acceptable behavior or performance for themselves, or their primary source of self-worth is denying their impulses, staying on track, and keeping their eyes on the prize, they seamlessly transmit the message that these standards are normal and expected to their children.

Deon's mom, like many Black parents, drilled into him the mantra that he'd have to be twice as good to get half as far. She was strict, heavy on the shoulds and shouldn'ts. When she told Deon to do something, she meant *right now*, not after a snack or after his TV show was over. He knew to say, "Yes, ma'am," rather than explain why he could do it later—she called his reasons "excuses."

She modeled hard work for him, putting in long hours as a nursing assistant and going to school at night to advance her degree. She never complained, but she also never talked about any feelings at all, a trait Deon chalked up to being strong. "She was a rock," he remembered.

Deon learned through osmosis that the way to measure how well you were doing was how thoroughly you were denying your wants and feelings. "If you don't sacrifice for what you want, what you want will be the sacrifice" was one of her sayings. "If you don't discipline yourself, the world will do it for you" was another. Her favorite? "If it's worth doing, it's worth doing well."

This fully tracks with the social learning model, but in families like Deon's, there's an additional layer. Let's remember that our families exist in the context of the larger world. All humans react to the situations we're put in, so when our family members are put in a society infused with racism, homophobia, ableism, or other prejudice, the resulting pull to prove themselves is no longer a personality trait but the result of socially prescribed perfectionism—an understandable reaction to an environment that sends the message: you don't deserve to be here. Clients from families like Deon's often speak of never feeling good enough. They believe the problem lies within them, not the fact that our society disguises systemic inequality as individual pathology.

Forty years later, Deon is an executive at a finance firm, with a beautiful house and vacations on Martha's Vineyard. But along the way, something went awry. He had watched his mother repress her own emotions to get through the world, but when Deon tried to do the same thing, it went off the rails. He landed in my office after his wife threatened to leave him. "It's me or your work," she said. His kids said he didn't care about them. "I did the exact same thing my mom did, and this is the thanks I get?" he grumbled.

No matter which of the four types of families—or combination thereof—you were raised in, the way you turned out probably makes sense. Parents are the first and primary influencers of our beliefs and standards. But families aren't the only influence on our lives and temperaments. The flavors of our finished dish come from the ingredients we're made of. Which brings us to . . .

Born This Way

Standing at attention, my Okinawan American mother measures barely five feet tall. When paired with my father, who is six foot three and of Norwegian stock, they are a sight gag. Evolution probably didn't intend for a tiny Asian woman to carry giant Viking babies. She reports that during labor I did my best impression of a battering ram, retreating, rotating to a new angle, and trying again. This went on for hours until the attending OB took pity on us both and called for a C-section, but it was already clear: overpersistence was part of my personality.

By contrast, consider my younger brother's chill vibe. Rather than repeat my dogged ramming, four years later, when the doctor extracted and held him aloft, Simba-like, he was asleep. I have never seen him stressed. We joke his heart rate never breaks forty. As an adult, he became an emergency physician partly because he needed more stimulation in his life.

Perfectionism is baked into our bun while we're in the oven. It's in our very genes: an ever-growing mountain of research shows that the specific disorders that coil around perfectionism like a pea tendril—anxiety, depression, eating disorders—are definitely genetic, and a growing handful of studies hint that perfectionism itself may be, too. The comprehensive answer is likely as complicated as making croissants from scratch, but there are clues: a 2015 study in the journal *Psychiatry Research* examined 258 pairs of genetically identical adolescent twins and found that the heritability of self-oriented perfectionism—being hard on oneself—was 23 percent in boys and 30 percent in girls, and the genetic influence of socially prescribed perfectionism—assuming others will be hard on us—is 39 percent in boys and 42 percent in girls. In studies of perfectionism and anxiety, heritability estimates ranged as high as 66 percent, pointing to a role of common genes.

The Forces of Culture

Our genes and family environment are just two slices of the perfectionism pizza. The forces of culture play a big role as well. Culture is like an invisible, odorless gas. Despite constantly breathing it in, it's hard to remember it's all around us.

Drs. Thomas Curran and Andrew Hill, authors of the study from the prologue that showed perfectionism has been on a steady upward march over the last thirty years, hypothesize that Western cultures have "become more individualistic, materialistic, and socially antagonistic over this period, with young people now facing more competitive environments, more unrealistic expectations, and more anxious and controlling parents than generations before." Yikes. In other words, today's kids are running a rat race in a pressure cooker as helicopter parents hover overhead. We teach our kids that they can do anything, but what they hear is that they have to do everything.

What is this miasma made of? There are at least five elements of our culture that have made us harder on ourselves.

First is a culture of evaluation. When we measure, we can compare. And quantitative measurement is everywhere: social media likes and follows, one- to five-star online reviews, the leaderboard at the gym, the "How would you rate your experience?" email that came after my annual physical. My electric bill compares my energy use with my neighbors'. Even the airport restroom asked me to rate my experience by smiley or frowny face. But comparison doesn't stop at electric bills and restrooms; it extends to people, which then allows ranking or classification.

As Dr. Hill of the perfectionism-is-on-the-rise study says, "Young people are sifted and sorted more than they've ever been sifted and sorted before. . . . They're the most assessed generation of young people." The result is a culture that, as coauthor Dr. Curran notes, "prizes achievement, image, and merit above everything else."

The second element is social media. It includes the exacting standards set by the highlight reel of social media, as well as the comparison that follows. In his book *The Perfection Trap*, Curran notes that levels of socially prescribed perfectionism were "more or less flat until around 2005. Then something happened and they began to skyrocket." Correlation doesn't mean causation, but my Spidey sense reminds me that 2005 was the year a little dorm room website originally called Facemash went mainstream under a new name: Facebook. It was the year YouTube was founded. The juggernauts of Twitter, Instagram, and TikTok followed like a succession of darts hitting the bull's-eye of global culture, increasing both the pressure to present perfectly and behind-the-scenes feelings of inadequacy. We spend one-third of our time online on social media—more than news, streaming, music, and even the mysteriously large category "other," which I'm guessing is code for porn.*

That's a lot of time with our eyeballs on the parade of highlights from Maldivian over-the-water bungalows to gym selfies of abs that could grate cheese. Just like an actual parade, social media is a public performance, in that it allows us the ability to present ourselves exactly as we'd like to be seen, whether it's the Insta-perfect avocado toast and fiddle-leaf figs of the 2010s or the purposefully casual "authenticity" of hot-take-while-eating-Chipotle-in-my-parked-car of 2020s TikTok. The core remains: even with "real life" increasingly on display on social media, everything we see is still carefully staged and curated. We're still left to compare our lives to the version of real life others choose to share.

The third element feeding a culture of perfectionism is the expectation to "Live Your Best Life." Back in 2005, *O, the Oprah Magazine* published a "best of" compendium of the magazine titled exactly that: "Live Your Best Life." From there, the phrase took off (and then devolved again into a sarcastic label for weekday hangovers and multi-hour spirals of Netflix and Flamin' Hot Cheetos). But the larger result was a directive to "make over your life" or that a new year requires a "new you."

---

* Speaking of which, porn contributes to perfectionism in its own insidious way, setting a very specific and unrealistic standard for body shapes and sizes, plus a performance standard for young adults who don't realize that sex is often goofy, affectionate, and might involve someone leaving their socks on.

The need to be our best selves implies that simply being ourselves isn't sufficient.

The "live your best life" mindset highlights the gap between how we are and how we expect ourselves to be. But it goes beyond taking up meditation or trying a keto diet. Take an expectation like graduating from college. In the 1970s, around half of American high school seniors expected themselves to graduate from college. By the 2010s, the percent who expected themselves to accomplish that feat had risen to 85 percent. But the percent of Americans who actually graduate from college by their late twenties has hovered around 25 percent the whole time. In short, expectations have soared while reality has flatlined, creating an ever-more-crowded boat of people who have watched themselves fall short of their expectations.

A fourth cultural element is the one negative side effect of the happiness movement, which I'll call "Don't Worry, Be Happy." In 1998, the esteemed psychologist Dr. Martin Seligman decided to use his position as president of the American Psychological Association to turn away from the profession's emphasis on pathology and toward the rich trove of positive psychology he believed was missing from the field. The result was a still-growing mountain of research on the good life: hope, wisdom, creativity, courage, grit, resilience, and, of course, happiness. Seligman's move was necessary, overdue, and game-changing. But the tidal wave of happiness how-to books and articles that followed have set the expectation that we should be grinning from ear to ear, mindful, anxiety-free, and confident all our waking hours. Over the years, I've found that an increasing number of my clients, especially young adults, take feeling bored, sad, awkward, or uncertain as a sign that something is Very Wrong.

Not only is intolerance of unhappiness problematic in the short term, but it also shoots us in the foot in the long term. In her book, *iGen: Why Today's Super-Connected Kids Are Growing Up Less Rebellious, More Tolerant, Less Happy—and Completely Unprepared for Adulthood*, Dr. Jean Twenge shows that when we ask each successive crop of twelfth graders to predict their happiness at age thirty, we find that twelfth grade cohorts with high expectations for their adult happiness are more likely to be *unhappy* when they toss the confetti at their big 3–0. The take-away? The higher the expectations, the harder reality hits.

Finally, an environment that continually tells us we don't meet the standards because of our race, sexual orientation, gender, or other characteristics pulls for perfectionism. We may acutely feel the pressure to get everything right to prove we deserve to be there, to disprove stereotypes, or because we're functioning as a spokesperson for our group.

This all takes a toll. Indeed, a study by Drs. Sharon F. Lambert, W. LaVome Robinson, and Nicholas S. Ialongo tracked almost five hundred African American adolescents through the Baltimore public school system for several years and found that experiences with racial discrimination in seventh grade were associated with socially prescribed perfectionism in eighth grade, which in turn was linked with symptoms of depression in ninth grade.

Yowza. There are more layers to perfectionism than a deep-dish lasagna. Internally, we find lots to be proud of. We have a lot going for us. We're aware, forward-thinking, and principled. The world turns more smoothly because of us.

At the same time, we humans respond to the situations we're put in. It makes total sense that our genetics, the way we were raised, and the larger context of the world around us has shaped us like the tides shape a sandy coastline. In the chapters ahead, we'll shore up the coastline to withstand the storms that roll through, but mostly, we'll appreciate the natural beauty of that coastline—maybe in ways we'd never quite noticed before. In other words, we don't need to adjust our unrealistic expectations, "work on" our self-worth, or stop criticizing ourselves before we can see changes in our lives. We can simply approach the coastline from a new perspective. Ready? Let's dive in.

PART II

The Seven Shifts

Shift 1

FROM (SELF-)CRITICISM
TO KINDNESS

4

Beyond the Inner Critic

There are three ways to ultimate success.
The first way is to be kind.
The second way is to be kind.
The third way is to be kind.

—Fred Rogers, as paraphrased in
The Chapel Hill News, 2013

ADAM CAME TO his senses in the Junior Dresses section of Macy's and realized he probably looked creepy. He had been so stuck in his head while stomping through Housewares, Home Furnishings, Casual Sportswear, and Women's Active that he didn't register where he had ended up. Adam was in the midst of another "frustration walk," working off his anger at his "stupid stupidity." Usually, he huffed around the Dunkin'-scented sidewalks of Boston's Downtown Crossing, but today, it was raining, forcing his walk to conclude next to a rack of knee-length chiffon.

Adam was at the tail end of a twelve-week learn-to-code boot camp that he saw as his last chance. After a stint at a newspaper, another selling baseball caps, and another at a restaurant management group, he had yet to find a job he hadn't quit in frustration. By now, it was enough of a pattern that he could see the signs: get stuck on the learning curve, get mad at himself, eventually quit in a self-inflicted firestorm of anger. Repeat. Now it was all playing out yet again next to a display of floral-print minidresses.

"I just couldn't get it," Adam said when, later, he logged on for our session and told me about the impetus of that day's frustration walk. "I sat there staring at my code, and I got *so* irritated. Logically, I know I just learned this twenty minutes ago, and I know that coding is hard, but I can't help feeling that something is wrong with me. Why can't I figure this out? Other people in the class are getting this. What's my problem?"

Inner Critics come in all different flavors. We're harder on ourselves than forty-grit sandpaper. We call ourselves names, whispering, "Idiot!" under our breaths. We invalidate ourselves: "Stop complaining. I have no real problems. Other people have it so much worse." We pose harsh rhetorical questions: "What is wrong with me?" or "Why can't I do this?" We compare ourselves: "He got promoted in under a year, so I should, too," or "Why can't I be more like my sister?" We put ourselves down when we don't meet our unrealistic expectations: "I should really own my own house by this age," or simply, "I need to do better than this."

Sitting in the computer lab that morning, Adam had stewed in his own self-critical juices until he was silently seething with rage and had to get up and walk it off. He told me later, "I just shut down. I was like, 'Nobody talk to me. I'm not getting this, and it's never going to change.'"

Adam uses all three primary colors of perfectionistic self-criticism.* First is the degree of *harshness*: "Stupid stupidity." "What's my problem?" In healthy self-criticism, we might acknowledge something didn't turn out the way we wanted, be bummed, and vow to try something different next time, but in perfectionistic self-criticism, we beat ourselves up or unwittingly try to shame ourselves into better performance.

Second is the *all-or-nothing* approach: "I'm not getting this, and

---

* *Self-criticism* is the term generally favored by researchers and academics, but, as I do, you might resonate more with the term *self-judgment* or *self-blame*. I'll use all three terms interchangeably in this chapter.

it's never going to change." Perfectionistic self-judgment has a zero-tolerance policy toward our performance. Eating one cookie ruins our diet. A moment of awkward silence spoils the first date. If we can't get the whole paper written this afternoon, why even start?

Third is *personal implication*: It's me. Hi. I'm the problem; it's me. In perfectionistic self-criticism, it's our fault, such as Adam's "something is wrong with me." It's not that the thing we're trying to do is hard or didn't work out—it means we are inadequate.

It's safe to say none of this is particularly pleasant. So why do we keep doing it? Why does Adam lambaste himself to the point of quitting job after job? Why did Walt Disney keep chiding himself when his staff was so clearly frustrated and demoralized? Why did I think my inability to focus like a laser beam 100 percent of the time was the problem when clearly it was my unrealistic to-do list?

Why do we do this to ourselves? Self-judgment gets us something, even as it costs us. What are these benefits that are so hard to give up? According to Dr. Raymond M. Bergner, psychology professor at Illinois State University and author of the not-exactly-a-beach-read but incredibly insightful tome *Pathological Self-Criticism*, there are lots of reasons. Consider these six:

First, we might be tough on ourselves *to facilitate self-improvement*. We might describe it as tough love, but it's heavy on the tough and short on the love. We reason if we go hard on ourselves for making a mistake, we won't make it again. But that's like a pianist setting out to learn a new piece by remembering all the wrong notes she's ever played.

Second, we may be hard on ourselves *to keep our egos in check*. Those of us raised to be humble or unpretentious are mortified at the thought of ending up a toxic, entitled narcissist. Putting ourselves down, negating our accomplishments, and downplaying healthy pride feels virtuous. But we've confused modesty with mistreating ourselves.

Third, we might be trying *to avoid others' criticism*. We criticize ourselves before others can. That way we'll never be shot down, put in our place, or otherwise judged or rejected. Why? Because we got there first. Paradoxically, we criticize ourselves to be beyond reproach.

Fourth, we might do it *so others expect less of us*. Our self-judgment self-handicaps. If our self-judgment paints us as deficient, no one will expect or demand too much from us. No one will actually put us to the test and reveal a spectacular failure.

Fifth, we might do it *to gain a feeling of control*. So many of life's challenges are arbitrary and random, jangling our nerves like an alarm clock set to go off at the wrong time. It's disorienting and stressful. Blaming yourself means you're responsible and therefore have control over the situation. In other words, if your plane is going down, it's preferable to be the one in the cockpit rather than a blameless but helpless passenger in the last row.

Last, we might do it *to gain reassurance*. It's a stealth form of fishing for compliments. If we take ourselves down, others will naturally build us back up: "No, no—you did great. You're awesome." We hate on ourselves to receive the love of others.

In short, self-criticism buys us a lot. I mean, if there were something I thought would help me improve, be appropriate, stay free of others' judgment, relieve myself of pressure, feel in control, and be told I slay all day, you can bet a box of Frosted Mini-Wheats I would do it all the time.

And yet. A grandfather in China who goes by "Uncle Chen" went viral a few years ago for chain-smoking his way through three different marathons. He says running with a cigarette combats fatigue and having something in his mouth helps him breathe. He does pretty well, too, placing in the top third of all runners. Now, we *could* run a sub-3:30 marathon while chain-smoking, but it would probably be easier and more effective to do it differently. The cigarettes, if I may hazard a guess, are stealing the credit for his training and hard work.

The same goes for self-criticism; it steals the credit. If we go easier on ourselves, we reason, we'll be left open to dangers that self-criticism protects us from: we might perform poorly, get a big ego, miss something that others will criticize, lose all motivation, or other stomach-dropping what-ifs. Rolling back our self-criticism might take away our secret ingredient. We'd be left with . . . laziness? Mediocrity? The motivation of a sleep-deprived sloth? Not quite.

Interestingly, just like Uncle Chen, who, if he subtracted cigarettes from his road race would probably be left with greater stamina, when we subtract the self-criticism from expecting a lot of ourselves, we're left with, drumroll . . . excellence. In the research, *excellence* is the realistic, sustainable, healthy version of accomplishment. The critical (ha ha—see what I did there?) difference between excellence and perfectionism is criticism. For example, a research team at Loughborough University found that the difference between healthy exercise and perfectionistic exercise was self-criticism. Rolling it back is the key not only to feeling better but, ironically, doing better.

All that said, at its heart, the Inner Critic is trying to help us. While it's unkind, invalidating, and exhausting, self-criticism wants the same thing we want: to feel safe, accepted, and connected. Self-criticism is the core of humans' ability to self-regulate. A healthy dose of self-judgment helps us evaluate our behavior, modify it to improve ourselves, and ultimately get along more harmoniously with our fellow humans. Evolutionarily, we critique ourselves to better ourselves, which in turn betters the group and everyone's chances for survival.

Therefore, the challenge is not "How do I stop criticizing myself?" You will still expect a lot of yourself—it's what type A brains do. But we can add on some questioning: How do I talk to myself more effectively? Is self-criticism getting me what I need? Does self-blame cost me more than it buys me?

Let's introduce four very different ways to change our self-criticism from exaggerated to healthy. Like a soft-serve ice cream machine, we'll dispense two flavors—change and acceptance—plus sweet swirls of both. Importantly, these are not new rules to follow. Just like there is no "correct" favorite ice cream flavor, you get to sample different forms of self-kindness and choose what you like best.

From Evaluation to Information

It's 1965. Eighteen-year-old Kareem Abdul-Jabbar, then still Lewis Alcindor, sat on a bench awaiting the start of his first practice of his first year at UCLA alongside his impressive roster of teammates. Everyone was buzzing with excitement. The greatest freshman squad in the history of basketball—Abdul-Jabbar, the most heavily recruited high school player in the nation, plus five high school all-Americans from across the country—was combining forces with the best collegiate basketball program in the world, headed by esteemed coach John Wooden. If they had a crystal ball, they would foresee ten national championships in twelve years, including seven in a row, an untouched record to this day. Individually, Abdul-Jabbar would hold the NBA's all-time scoring record for thirty-nine years, be inducted into the Basketball Hall of Fame, and, as an activist and humanitarian, receive the Presidential Medal of Freedom.

But that afternoon in 1965, that future was yet to be written. Coach Wooden entered the gym and stood in front of the squad. "Good afternoon, gentlemen."

"Good afternoon, Coach," they intoned in unison.

Anticipation filled the air. What would come next? A rousing pep talk? Pearls of wisdom? The team leaned forward, straining with excitement. Coach Wooden cleared his throat.

"Today, we are going to learn how to put on our sneakers and socks correctly."

Abdul-Jabbar blinked. Wait, what? Everyone exchanged glances.

"We are going to talk about tug and snug," he said. He repeated himself slowly, driving the point home: "Tug. And. Snug." Coach Wooden stripped his own feet of his shoes and socks. Abdul-Jabbar later remembered, "His pale pink feet looked like they'd never been exposed to light before."

Each member of the team had come to UCLA as if on a pilgrimage, from all corners of the country. Some, including Abdul-Jabbar, had turned down full scholarships to be there. They had all come to learn at the feet of the great Coach Wooden, though they didn't realize the experience would be quite so literal.

"If you do not pull your socks on tightly, you're likely to get wrinkles in them. Wrinkles cause blisters. Blisters force players to sit on the sideline. And players sitting on the sideline lose games. So we are not just going to tug. We are going to also make it snug."

He demonstrated, pulling on his own socks. The team copied his demonstration, tugging until their socks were snug.

Unbeknownst to them, the team had been introduced to Coach Wooden's signature style. But what was the secret sauce?

A few years later, education researchers Drs. Ronald Gallimore and Roland Tharp cracked the code by studying UCLA's afternoon practices during the 1974/75 season, which culminated in their tenth NCAA title.

In the mid-1970s, teacher praise and reproof were hot topics in education research, so Gallimore and Tharp were surprised to discover Wooden seldom complimented or rebuked his players. Instead, as a former high school English teacher, Wooden did just that: He taught. He instructed. He informed. He told you what to do and how to do it: "Pass the ball to someone short!" "Don't walk." "Take lots of shots in areas where you might get them in games." "Pass from the chest!" His comments, wrote Gallimore and Tharp, were "short, punctuated, and numerous."

Wooden's players agreed. Swen Nater, who went on to play professionally, noted, "It was the information that promoted change. Had the majority of Coach Wooden's corrective strategies been positive ('Good job') or negative ('No, that's not the way'), I would have been left with an evaluation, not a solution."

Gallimore and Tharp noted that a highly successful contemporaneous football coach used instructional comments 36 percent of the time. Another revered basketball coach reached 55 percent. Wooden bested them all at 75 percent. A full three-quarters of his statements were focused on the task, not the player.

This shift from evaluation to information applies to all of us, not just college basketball stars. Pop psychology tells us to hype ourselves up with affirmations ("Today, I will be the best version of myself") or switch our critical self-talk to positive self-talk ("I can do it!"). But merely flipping from negative to positive self-talk doesn't work—there's still a sense of evaluation. The focus is still on us as a person.

From the basketball court to our work cubicle to parenting to running a household, evaluation makes it personal: "I suck." "I'm not doing enough." "Why am I not getting this?" "I screwed up."

What to do instead? Take it from UCLA basketball: turn your attention spotlight from the global self to the specific behavior. Take the stance of a sculptor eyeing a block of marble; look at the task as an entity separate from you: What to do to make *this thing* better? What would be effective for *the work*?

This shift from self-evaluation to task-focused information is subtle but profound. Evaluative self-talk is personal, general, and permanent ("I suck"). But task-focused self-talk is external, specific, and fixable ("Pass the ball to someone short"). It takes away both the harshness and personal implication of self-blame, leaving overevaluation behind like a newly shed snake skin.

Bonus? It's more effective. If the function of self-criticism is to goad ourselves into doing better, instructional self-talk accomplishes that more productively, plus it hurts a lot less.

Ava, a student majoring in viola performance who mercilessly criticized herself in the practice room while working on a particularly difficult movement, shifted from "Why can't I make this happen?" to giving herself instruction: "This movement can be slower. Adding a metronome might be helpful."

Antonio, a college first-year who scrolled TikTok instead of writing his term papers as soon as "I can't do this" entered his head, shifted to "Start with an outline."

Adam, whom we met on his frustration walk at the beginning of the chapter, channeled his best John Wooden and experimented with coaching himself through coding problems. "Try making a flowchart," he'd say to himself. "Writing some pseudocode worked last time; try that again." "Break the problem down into tiny steps." And importantly: "Take a break on your project before you get mad." It was a far cry from muttering, "What's wrong with me?" next to a rack of juniors' bodycon dresses.

> **TRY IT OUT:** Talk yourself through a task from the point of view of a supportive, no-nonsense coach. Focus on the thing you're doing, not you. If you have privacy and can talk out loud, even better. Reflect on how it feels to focus on the task versus yourself.

Why We Suck at Self-Compassion and What to Do Instead

Eunice's day started out healthy: three scrambled eggs, toast, half an avocado, some grapes. It was a good start. She even packed herself a big green salad with chicken for lunch. Today would be different, she vowed.

Eunice is a wardrobe manager at a local theater. But that day, the lead actress hated her costume and threw a hissy fit, one of the main rolling racks mysteriously disappeared, and Eunice's supervisor sent her a cryptic email asking for a meeting, stat. After Eunice got home, she figured she deserved a couple of candies from the Halloween leftovers. But two peanut butter cups turned into ten, plus three bowls of cereal and four pieces of leftover pizza. And then the self-loathing started; she spiraled with shame, guilt, and anger. She tapped out scathing texts to her boyfriend, Felix: *Why are you with me? You could do so much better. I'm holding you back. What's wrong with you that you chose me?*

He texted her back: *did u nosh just now?*

Nosh. That was the code word for a binge. Over ten years prior, when Eunice first arrived at college, she reveled in the freedom to eat whatever she wanted, a welcome relief after her immigrant mom's strict policy against American junk food. "I could even buy pints of Ben and Jerry's and bulk sour gummy candy with my meal plan," she remembered.

At first, she nibbled junk food as stress relief during midterms, but then it became a habit, a day-to-day coping mechanism. "This is what my brain learned was the go-to," she said. Most importantly, she learned that whenever she felt stressed, bad, or overwhelmed, a nosh would provide a sense of soothing, hypnotic numbness for the duration of the binge. "If I have a nosh, I forget whatever started it. Everything else fades away for the time I'm noshing," she said.

For years, Eunice tried to compensate for bingeing by running. "I know, I know—you can't outrun a binge," she said, "but I figured running was mildly healthier than, like, making myself throw up." But eventually, Eunice seriously injured her foot. She went from running sixty miles a week to not being able to walk a mile. Eunice's mood plummeted, which triggered more bingeing, a merciless cycle that eventually landed her in my office.

As I got to know her, it became clear that being hard on herself was baked into her personality, history, and family experiences. Her mom's parenting style could be boiled down to "strong and harsh feedback gets a better performance out of you than kind and constructive feedback." In a flash of understanding, Eunice remembered when her mom, a night-shift nurse, came home from an employee development training at the hospital. The instructor had said, "Every time you criticize a direct report, you should give them three compliments." Once home, her mom scoffed. "If they're doing it right, you don't need to say anything. It's when they're doing it wrong that you need to say something."

Eunice also learned to read between the lines. "She would say, 'I just want you to do your best,'" but the unsaid subtext came across loud and clear: "And I know your best is an A." Her mom pushed her to be a doctor, but Eunice fell in love with drama and costuming, throwing herself into the theater scene from high school onward. Her rebellion nagged at her. "Since I'm not going to be a doctor, I have to justify whatever I do by being the best. It can feed a not-very-healthy obsession with external accolades."

Nobody is kind to themselves all the time. We look at our muffin top, the clutter taking over our house, the metaphorical tumbleweeds drifting through our empty weekend, our remaining to-do list, and think, *I should do better than that.* But when self-criticism becomes a default setting, like Eunice's, it diminishes us in a number of ways. Self-criticism:

» *makes us feel inadequate.* When we use perfection as the standard for adequacy, we end up with mostly not-good-enough. Unless we unequivocally hit it out of the park, our Inner Critics brand our efforts as failures.

» *grinds motivation to a halt.* Why bother if it's not going to be good enough, anyway?

» *leaves us sensitive to others' criticism.* Even though we criticize ourselves, when anyone else does it, it feels like a painful jolt of electricity.

» *is stressful.* Whether our self-criticism takes the form of expletive-heavy name-calling or a low rumble of never-good-enough discontent, we're attacking ourselves, which is taxing.

» *takes the fun out of the process.* Getting there is not half the fun. In fact, it might be distinctly un-fun. It's hard—as airline pilots instruct us before takeoff—to sit back, relax, and enjoy the metaphorical flight.

» *lowers the quality of our results.* Paradoxically, when our Inner Critics are looking over our shoulders, scrutinizing and correcting, we become inefficient, procrastinate, can't think clearly, or take a long time to recover between efforts, all of which lowers our performance.

» *hinders connection.* When we self-criticize in front of others, they assume we'll be just as critical of them.

That last one is counterintuitive, especially for those of us raised to be humble or unassuming. For example, a friend recounted hosting a dinner party with his self-critical wife: "When guests would compliment her cooking, she'd try to be modest, but it would come off as rejecting: 'Thanks, but the brownies were mushy in the middle.' 'Oh, you liked the chicken? I thought it was dry.'" Self-criticism shows everyone how high our standards are, which in turn keeps everyone on eggshells and reluctant to share the self-deprecating stories that lead to "Me, too!" bonding. My friend concluded, "I think it made everybody scared to have us over in return."

In the quote at the beginning of this chapter, when Fred Rogers pinpointed kindness as the first, second, and third way to success—whatever success means to you—he might have meant being kind to others. But he also might have meant being kind to yourself: enter self-compassion.

Self-compassion, according to psychologist and researcher Dr. Kristin Neff of the University of Texas, is having compassion—warmth, caring, understanding—for ourselves when we suffer, fail, or feel inadequate. It includes being kind to ourselves, being mindful of our pain, and recognizing that personal inadequacy is part of the human condition and therefore connects us to every other person on the planet.

An avalanche of research tells us self-compassion is pretty great. Heck, a giant analysis of seventy-nine different studies involving over sixteen thousand individuals found that self-compassion corresponded with nothing short of a happier life and greater well-being.

But those of us with perfectionism, including Eunice, suck at it. I'm right there with you; I may lay a hand kindly upon my heart and tell myself, *This is hard*, but self-criticism will rise up behind me in a hockey mask and yell in my ear, *No, it's fucking not!*

Even so, I tried my best to apply it with clients. I used to try to guide clients through the classic "How would you talk a good friend in your same situation?" but we'd end up sitting in awkward silence. Both of us would feel stuck.

This is how self-criticism works. I've been a self-critic and have worked with self-critics for long enough to know that when we start to push back on our self-judgment, it rebounds faster than a Pete Davidson relationship. Remember, self-blame is trying to keep us safe and in control. Therefore, it works hard to find loopholes, exceptions, and counterpoints. Even when we find the good in our performance, our self-blame steps in to discount even the most positive experiences with that un-magic word *but*. "Yeah, I got the promotion, but I don't think it was unanimous." Or: "Meeting the Dalai Lama was amazing, but I got starstruck and babbled like an idiot."

Why is self-compassion so hard for us? Well, self-compassion is a Vitamixed smoothie of three things: self-kindness, nonjudgmental mindfulness, and connection to the larger human experience. But the perfectionistic brain is reverse threaded for all three of those things: we're wired to be hard on ourselves rather than kind, be fault-finding rather than nonjudgmental, and see our struggles as shortcomings that render us inadequate rather than common traits that connect us with others. In short, self-compassion is the opposite of self-criticism in not one but three ways. No wonder we face-plant when we try it. Luckily, there are lots of ways our brains can get on board with self-compassion.

First up: self-compassion can be *validation*, which is the recognition of thoughts, feelings, and behaviors as understandable. It's at the heart of statements that convey "that's normal" or "that makes sense." Given our unique history, personality, triggers, and vulnerabilities, it is logical that we're feeling what we're feeling and doing what we're doing.

When Eunice self-validates, she acknowledges that her self-criticism, her urges to binge, and the bingeing itself are understandable. This is different from letting herself off the hook. It's not justification or a green light. Instead, Eunice simply recognizes that her behavior and feelings make sense. And because they make sense, *she* makes sense, rather than being wrong, bad, undisciplined, lazy, or anything else the Inner Critic can throw at her as a judgy justification. Even "irrational" feelings and behaviors make sense once we understand what's under them. And when she understands herself, it's much easier to be kind to herself.

Next, self-compassion can be words. With our own-worst-critic brains and all-or-nothing approach, we often think we need to feed ourselves a steady stream of articulate, effective, self-compassionate hype. But that's unrealistic. Luckily, we can make it easier.

Rather than expecting full self-compassionate paragraphs to spring fully formed from your brain, stick to one phrase: *Easy on yourself. I must have needed that. This makes sense. I get what I'm doing. Be gentle.* Even just a word or two: *Kind. Easy. You're okay.* Repeat your kind word or phrase as often as you'd like. Or make a literal gesture of support. Touch speaks louder than words. Place a kind hand over your heart, on your stomach, on your shoulder. A reader emailed me with her method: "I put my hand on my heart and gently tap as I quietly tell myself, *I'm doing my best; I got you, kiddo.*" Want even more options? Breathe into your kind hand. Imagine sending understanding, care, or even bodacious glittery vibes through your hand.

Self-compassion can be actions. Dr. Clarissa Ong of the University of Louisville and coauthor of *The Anxious Perfectionist: How to Manage Perfectionism-Driven Anxiety Using Acceptance & Commitment Therapy* notes that "behaviors are the things we can control the most." We can't conjure thoughts or feelings as if from a genie's lamp. But we can control our actions. Ong gives an example: "I can't really control having loving feelings toward myself. But I can definitely drink coffee in the morning and give myself time to do that." Another reader emailed me with specific actions she takes to be kind to herself: "I take good care of myself with a healthy diet, exercise (nothing intense), relaxation, and gardening." Another chimed in: "I am allowed to do things that bring me joy."

Most appropriate to self-critics, self-compassion can be permission *not* to do things. Permission to rest. Permission to slow down. Permission not to meet our unrealistic expectations, even despite, as one reader put it, "my overactive conscience poking at me." As another reader put it, "I have realized that I really cannot do all the things I expect of myself. Self-kindness can be admitting this from time to time." Yet another: "Not imposing impossible standards on myself." A fourth said: "Saying what I *can't* do. Maybe even—gasp—asking for help."

Having high standards and expecting a lot of ourselves isn't necessarily a bad thing—who doesn't want to be capable, reliable, and get stuff done? But it means there's a perpetual fire under us to do what we "should"—that old internal cattle prod. Granting ourselves some grace and respite from all the shoulds is warm, generous, considerate, and yes, compassionate to ourselves.

All in all, self-compassion doesn't need to be grand, perfect, or polished. It can be an acknowledgment that we make sense, a single word, a caring hand on our bellies, taking time to read a novel with a mug of hot chocolate, or permission not to cook dinner. A little kindness and understanding goes a long way.

As for Eunice, midway through our work together, my family and I moved across the country, and I left Eunice in the capable hands of a colleague who shifted self-compassion into high gear. When Eunice and I reconnected nearly four years later, she reported that while she still can't run and still binges once in a while, she's much happier. What's changed is her magnanimity toward herself.

As we talked, I was struck by her understanding and generosity toward her own behavior. The lessons of self-compassion had softened her self-criticism. Now she tries to be kind to herself when she noshes. She validates herself: *It makes sense that you're turning to it.* She's kind to herself for wanting to make her pain go away: *I get what I'm doing. Even if it's not serving me long term, it sure does work short term.* When she waits out a binge urge, self-compassion has also helped her accept the very real costs of not bingeing. She tells herself: *It makes sense you still feel bad—you didn't nosh—nothing works as well as that nosh. It's a loss not to nosh. Anyone else would feel conflicted, too.* Most importantly, she's kind to herself for being who she is: *Given how my brain works, this makes sense.* As a bonus, she no longer lambastes herself via text to Felix, who is now her husband. "Being kind to Felix is something I have under my control even if I screw up sometimes," she says. "Being mean to myself made me less present with Felix. Plus, it made me like myself less."

Here's the picture-it-in-all-caps take-home: Eunice's feelings, urges, bingeing behavior, and mobility didn't change all that much. Like all of us, she still feels bad and stressed sometimes. She still binges occasionally. She still can't go for a run. But her *response* to all these things changed. As Eunice puts it: "Even if I can't walk and I still nosh, my life is so much better."

TRY IT OUT: Notice when you're being hard on yourself. Your signal might be a feeling like frustration or hopelessness. It might be a behavior, like opening a social media app as a distraction or heading to the kitchen for a binge. It might be an urge, like a temptation to procrastinate. Or it could be the classic: a self-critical thought. Whatever it is, notice it and dispense some kind understanding:

> *This reaction makes sense.*
> *I'm trying to keep myself safe.*
> *A lot of people would probably feel the*
>   *same way.*
> *This is understandable.*

Again, you're not trying to stop the self-critical thoughts, hype yourself up, or give yourself a pep talk. Instead, you're being kind and validating to the oh-so-human person who is on the receiving end of all those critical thoughts: you.

Play with the Thoughts

Julie works as a community liaison to a hospital in Boston, helping patients and families navigate the arcane and twisting world of American health care. She wears braids and an impressive collection of arty necklaces; I see them rotate through every week on Zoom. She comes from a family of peacemakers and do-gooders, who imbued in her a strong sense of ethics, fairness, and social justice, but also a strong sense of self-criticism.

Julie was quick to find herself lacking. When her wife complained about a mutual acquaintance whom Julie found funny and likable, Julie's first thought was, *Well, I do have distorted views of people.* When we worked on her public-speaking anxiety, she chastised herself for small details—occasionally saying *um* and forgetting to restate questions asked of her by the audience. "I should be better at this by now," she fretted. When she was up for promotion, she felt guilty listing all her skills on her résumé: "I should really be more humble."

Together, we looked at her collection of self-judgments. From her views of people to her public speaking to her accomplishments, the theme was "I'm doing it wrong." Hundreds of times a day, in hundreds of different ways, her brain told her she was screwing up. *This isn't right. It's my fault.* And it all happened automatically, by habit, in the blink of an eye.

Like Julie, maybe your brain does something similar. If you listed all your self-criticisms in a Google Doc, what would you title it? *I'm Inadequate. Everyone Is Going to Judge Me. It's My Fault. I'm Not Interesting or Fun to Be With. I'm Not Normal Like Everybody Else. What If I Fail?* There are millions of titles in the self-judgment storage cloud.

But this gives us a metaphor to roll with. In your mind's eye, picture your computer screen. Open a blank document for yourself. We're going to write a story of self-criticism. Type out your title. Julie envisioned typing *I'm Doing It Wrong* at the top of her imaginary document.

Okay, are you picturing your title on your screen? Great. Now, change the font. Julie picked Comic Sans.

Next, change the color. Julie chose blue, her favorite color.

Next, change the font size. Adjust it down to four- or six-point font, and then blow it up to thirty-six or forty-eight. Julie played with a variety of sizes.

Finally, ask yourself: What was that experience like? Julie, for one, smiled. "It actually made it a little funny. And it felt more like I was in charge."

Let's shout this through a bullhorn: Julie's self-critical thoughts didn't go away. Julie didn't Select All / Delete the document. The words were still there in blue Comic Sans. But making them go away wasn't the point; suppressed thoughts inevitably pop up again like a game of Whac-A-Mole, anyway. Instead, she played with them. She gained distance, flexibility, even a little irreverence. And with that, the thought's power is diminished. More importantly, there is room to move forward.

This is one of a zillion variations of *cognitive defusion*. All cognitive defusion techniques help us see our self-critical thoughts for what they are: thoughts. The simplest example is putting the phrase *I'm having the thought that* . . . in front of self-critical thoughts. Other variations popularized by bestselling author and acceptance and commitment therapy trainer Dr. Russ Harris include singing a self-critical thought to the tune of "Happy Birthday," picturing the words on a karaoke screen and imagining a ball bouncing from syllable to syllable, imagining the words embroidered on a pillow, or envisioning them as *Star Wars* opening crawl text accompanied by the theme song.

Or maybe your thought isn't words—maybe it's a movie in your mind. No problem. Stick a clown nose on the main character. Replay it in your mind's eye with over-the-top accents and wild gesticulation. Add some disco balls. The point is not to make them ridiculous, per se, but to put some distance between us and our thoughts so we can see them as thoughts rather than truth.*

Our self-critical thoughts are largely automatic; they come at us as instinctually as a reflex hammer to the knee. But this leaves us in a low-power position. Playing with the thoughts, however, confers choice and influence and moves us into a higher-power position. After some practice, Julie had a *Fight Club*–esque realization that she was the one dispensing the criticism. And because the self-criticisms came from within, she could play with them and transform them. And that changed her relationship with the thoughts. Indeed, picturing an air-

---

* My favorite example of defusion comes from Dr. Chad LeJeune's excellent book, *"Pure O" OCD: Letting Go of Obsessive Thoughts with Acceptance and Commitment Therapy*. One of his clients was plagued by intrusive horrific images, including "a penis being sliced," to which Dr. LeJeune, walking the line between compassion and irreverence, asked, "Like a banana into a bowl of cereal?" The client, previously close to tears from the distress of his thought, erupted into laughter.

plane skywriting *I'm Doing It Wrong* made her take the thought less seriously, which kept her from spiraling around it.

TRY IT OUT: What is the title of your self-criticism story? Practice picturing it in your mind's eye, and then changing it: add animations, make each word a different color. Play with the sounds of the words: sing it, say it in the voice of Kermit the Frog or Morgan Freeman. The goal is not to make it go away. Instead, engage with it. Reflect on how this changes your relationship with the self-critical thought.

Accounting for Your Brain

The clean, sharp smell of sagebrush—camphor mixed with pine—rises from the landscape. It's an early midsummer morning in the heart of the Bighorn Mountains of Wyoming, at eight thousand feet of elevation near the Montana border. Eight-year-old Jesse pulls apart several six-packs of Pepsi and, can by can, carefully sinks each one into the small mountain spring he knows will chill the drinks better than any cooler.

Jesse is here, high in the Bighorns, with extended family ranging all the way from his grandfather to a handful of cousins. The group is preparing for a day of work on the land—repairing their cabin, fixing winter-ravaged roadways, tending to the mine—but also some hard-earned play.

As the sun passes overhead and tasks are completed, Pepsis are pulled from the spring and drained. For Jesse and his cousins, the growing stack of empty cans presents an opportunity. Someone grabs the BB gun cases out of the truck, and Pepsi cans are lined up carefully, safely, along rocks where no one will mistakenly wander by. The rocks are some of the oldest in the world, formed billions of years ago, but Jesse and his kid cousins aren't here for the geology. They're spies and cowboys, stalking their imaginary foes.

Jesse's first shots miss the cans entirely. He can tell each BB is going a little to the right, a little too high. This is typical. They're kids' BB guns, after all, so the sight is never quite straight, the aim never quite true. But it's okay—Jesse simply adjusts appropriately. He aims a little to the left, a little farther down. It's trial and error, and soon he's rewarded with a satisfying jump of the can, the *ping* and rattle of the BB rolling at the bottom. Spy mission accomplished.

Why am I telling you this story about Jesse? Since you're reading this chapter, I'm guessing your brain has a proclivity toward self-criticism. Through the genetic constellation of your extended family, your baked-in personality, and your lived experiences from the moment you entered the world, it's just how your brain is wired. It's going to happen. There is no moral judgment on this. Just like some brains are introverted or extroverted, some are optimistic or pessimistic, some enjoy novelty while others are more cautious, your brain is just weighted a little more toward self-judgment. It's what your (and my) brain does.

Now, just like Jesse's BB gun, your brain totally works. In fact, it's exceptionally functional and pragmatic. It's 100 percent capable of hitting the metaphorical soda can. It wants good things for you: do well, reach those expectations, stay humble, stay ahead of things so you don't get blindsided, stay beyond reproach, stay safe. But the resulting self-judgment, as it were, makes us shoot a little to the side.

Eight-year-old Jesse is now Dr. Jesse Crosby, a Harvard-trained clinical psychologist in Boston, a world away from the Wyoming-Montana border. But he still carries the lessons of shooting in the Bighorn Mountains and now applies them to his clients. "I think about that a lot," he says of the parallel, "whether it's my brain or my physical body. It's not that there's something fundamentally wrong that I need to go have treated. If I just calibrate for that a little bit, I'm good."

The idea of behaviorally accounting for our wiring is rooted in a mind-bendingly complicated theory called *functional contextualism*. We'll steer clear of the philosophical rabbit hole, but in essence, functional contextualism assumes that each of us is acting within our own personal, historical, and situational context—heredity, the way we were raised, current situation—and then asks us to take a pragmatic "What would work here?" approach to our behavior. In other words: assume our brains have good reason for what they do, mindfully notice what we're thinking and feeling, and regardless of whatever our brains are lobbing at us, act in line with what's important to us and our goals.

The take-home? We don't have to rid ourselves of self-judgment to move forward. Living our lives is not contingent upon reprogramming our factory settings. We wouldn't want to do that, anyway. Remember, our brains work really well. We just want to adjust for the tendency to self-criticize.

How do we do that? Well, we can't control our tendency toward self-criticism. If we could snap our fingers and stop, we would have done that by now. But what we can control is our actions. We choose what to do. And with our behavior, we can aim a few inches to the left.

Here's one way I've applied this technique. For background, my brain often thinks professional appearances, like presentations or interviews, went poorly. For instance, after *How to Be Yourself* came out, I was invited to be a guest on a podcast with a wide audience. I took the train down to New York and nervously recorded with the host in a studio with a control room that looked like it could launch a satellite. I made a totally-within-reason number of mistakes, losing my train of thought at one point and making an awkward comment at another, all of which would be edited out. Afterward, the producer lavishly complimented me and the host, but I couldn't shake the feeling that I had come up short.

During celebratory drinks with my editor, Joe, and on the train back to Boston, my brain zeroed in on my perceived mistakes: *Why did I say it like that? I squandered this opportunity. I was all over the place. This was not good.*

Now, my brain's disapproval is automatic; it doesn't matter whether the end result is actually good or not. What's more, I value these opportunities—they're intellectually stimulating, helpful to listeners who resonate with the topic, and allow me to continue being a writer.

Over the years, I've ridden this roller coaster enough times to know *This Was Not Good* is just where my brain automatically goes after anything involving a microphone. I used to believe the thoughts, but I don't anymore. It's just what happens. It's not true or personal—it's just part of the script: do interview, think it sucks, usually realize it was actually fine, learn from it when it's not, repeat. Now, instead of getting wrapped up in the story of *This Was Not Good*, I account for my brain, remember my values, metaphorically aim a few inches to the side, and accept the next invitation the comes along. Even if it feels wrong at first, listening to my values rather than my noisy brain is like combing dried paint out of a paintbrush—everything loosens up and works more effectively.

Again, self-judgment is just what perfectionistic brains do. Thinking these thoughts doesn't make us bad. They might send us into a spiral of *feeling* bad, but there's no moral judgment on a brain making thoughts. Just like our hearts beat and our sweat glands perspire, our perfectionistic brains make self-critical thoughts.

For Julie, when she thought, *I'm doing it wrong*, her natural reaction was to work harder and get it right: stop texting the friend her wife disapproved of, futz with her presentation slides long after futzing ceased to be useful, delete superlatives from her résumé. The thought *I'm doing it wrong* wasn't "bad," per se, but it made her *act* in ways that weren't serving her.

But once she got to know her brain and her pattern, just like Jesse and his off-center BB gun, or me and my brain after an interview, she could account for them and decide what to do by consulting her values rather than her self-criticism. We'll talk more about values in chapter 6, "From Labels to Values," but here's a sneak preview: Values are how you want to *be* in the world. They're not a goal, they're more of a direction. Figuratively, going to Boston is a goal—it's a destination; you can check it off on a list. Heading east is the equivalent value—it's a direction; you could always go more "east." You're never "done" living by what's important to you.

Julie valued, among other things, being present with her family, connecting with her friends, being of service to her clients, and being caring—showing kindness and concern for those in her life.

So Julie practiced catching her self-criticisms. Sure enough, much like her heart continued to beat and her sweat glands continued to perspire, her brain kept churning out the thoughts of self-blame. But she started noticing the pattern: "Oh, there's that *I'm Doing It Wrong* thing again." "My brain is telling me it's my fault again." "Hey, it's happening right now."

But then, rather than letting the self-blame guide her behavior, she consulted her values. When she forgot a friend's dairy allergy and brought over a cream-soaked bread pudding topped with custard sauce for a Sunday-afternoon gathering, she started down the road of "I am such an idiot. I've known this for years—maybe I should get my brain evaluated." But then she caught herself. "Normally, I would have kicked myself for a long time and missed out on the conversation, or I would have kept apologizing until she got annoyed at me." Instead, Julie reported, she realized what was happening, remembered that this friendship means a lot to her, and refocused on the reason she was there: connecting and catching up with her friend. "The *I am such an idiot* thought didn't go away," she said during our session the following week, "but I paid attention to my friend, and we had a nice visit." In other words, Julie aimed a few inches to the left and hit her mark.

In a meta-move, your brain might even criticize you for trying to use self-compassion. *You can't be kind to yourself—you don't deserve it. You'll go down a slippery slope of entitlement and laziness. Being nice to yourself is indulgent and undisciplined. You have no real problems—people who have actually suffered deserve kindness more than you.* Guess what? All these are just thoughts, too. We can use the same techniques: "Oh, this is just what my brain does. I see what it's doing." Turn the thought into a flickering neon bar sign in your mind's eye, imagine it emblazoned on a coffee mug, or sing it to the tune of "Twinkle, Twinkle, Little Star." And then proceed to take good care of yourself.

It's all part of accounting for your excellent but self-critical brain. In eight-year-old Jesse's case, through experience, he learns, *This one shoots a little high and a little to the right.* So he adjusts his behavior accordingly, by trial and error. Aim a little down and over to the left. It feels weird at first not to aim directly at the metaphorical Pepsi can. But over time, we start to internalize the calibration. It becomes visceral and instinctual: bull's-eye.

> **TRY IT OUT:** What self-judgments does your brain regularly dispense? Consider them a natural by-product of your genetics, upbringing, and/or life experience. What actions might you try, not to make them go away but as a work-around that moves you forward?

After his coding boot camp concluded, I didn't see Adam for a long time. He kept in touch sporadically by email; he was looking for a job, a laborious and frustrating process. He went to interview after interview but never got an offer. "They all want experience," he wrote. After more than a year, he came in for a few sessions after his mother passed away. We mostly talked about how moving on isn't betrayal and how there's no one right way to grieve, but he was also proud to say he had landed a job and was going on two months doing "cloud stuff," as he put it, at an insurance company. There were still days at work when he simmered in frustration and self-judgment, but he kept up his attempts to talk to himself more constructively and treat himself more kindly. He found it much easier to be compassionate to himself while he was grieving. "I hope this sticks," he said of his newfound ability to be gentle with himself. Best of all, he said, he hadn't needed a frustration walk yet. "Worst-case scenario, I just go get a cup of coffee and annoy my coworkers by quizzing them about the Bruins." A far cry indeed from stomping among the fit-and-flare dresses.

The Outer Critics
Us and Them

I must also have a dark side if I am to be whole.

—Carl Jung

"WHAT'S WRONG WITH you?" Steve Jobs asks Sarah, his twelve-year-old niece, over a family dinner at a restaurant in Palo Alto. "You can't even talk. You can't even eat. You're eating shit." He continues: "Have you ever thought about how awful your voice is? Please stop talking in that awful voice."

In her book *Small Fry: A Memoir*, Steve Jobs's oldest daughter, Lisa Brennan-Jobs, recounts her father's evisceration of Sarah for failing to live up to his unspoken expectations, leaving her sobbing into her half-eaten burger. As a final kick, he ends with: "You should really consider what's wrong with yourself and try to fix it."

In a 2011 article in *The New Yorker*, Malcolm Gladwell continues the portrait:

He screams at subordinates. . . . He sits in a restaurant and sends his food back three times. He arrives at his hotel suite in New York for press interviews and decides, at 10 p.m., that the piano needs to be reposi-tioned, the strawberries are inadequate, and the flowers are all wrong: he wanted calla lilies. (When his public-relations assistant returns, at mid-night, with the right flowers, he tells her that her suit is "disgusting.")

Gladwell concludes, "Our natural expectation is that Jobs will emerge wiser and gentler from his tumultuous journey. He never does. In the hospital at the end of his life, he runs through sixty-seven nurses before he finds three he likes."

This book is primarily about *self-oriented perfectionism* with its unrealistic standards, overevaluation, and harsh drive of the Inner Critic. However, this chapter touches on the two kinds of Outer Critics: *other-oriented perfectionism*, which is when we're hard on others, and *socially prescribed perfectionism*, which is when we expect others to be hard on us.

Let's start with being tough on others. Drs. Gordon Flett and Paul Hewitt, who originated the theory of the three types of perfectionism, posit that other-oriented perfectionism is driven by beliefs that it is important for other people—usually people close to us like a partner, children, or direct reports—to do no wrong. We expect them to reach our highest expectations. And when they disappoint us, we criticize them, silently or out loud. Steve Jobs may be the ultimate example of other-oriented perfectionism, but even the less demanding among us might keep an intense eye on the tiny Fortune 500 corporations that are our family, children, or employees.

Francesca's husband, whom I never met, but heard plenty about, had overt other-oriented perfectionism. He held himself to the highest standards of professional achievement, fitness, and cooking and looked down upon Francesca's attempts to keep up with him. "This isn't hard," he'd flatly state after Francesca missed a workout or dug through the laundry looking for clean-enough pants for their twin sons. Francesca bent over backward to do things his way, to the point of recording a video on her phone of him pan-frying sole meunière so she could replicate it "the right way." It was no wonder Francesca came in with crushing depression and a habit of listlessly eating M&M's

on the couch. If meeting his sky-high expectations wasn't even hard, what must that mean about her?

Kara's mother had more covert other-oriented perfectionism. According to Kara, she held herself to the highest expectations of homekeeping, hosting, and polite behavior and required her family to follow suit. She was a master of indirect communication, never overtly stating what she expected, but her messages came through loud and clear. Banging the dishes as she washed them meant Kara was supposed to come help. Asking, "Is that what you're wearing?" meant Kara should go change. When she forwarded articles about the danger of heavy metals in dark chocolate, Kara knew it was a comment on her weight. Her mother was mostly a silent martyr, but if Kara dared to question her, she toggled to dramatic overreaction: "How could you?" "What, you don't believe me? You think I'm lying?" "I do this all for you kids, and this is the thanks I get?" After Kara got her own apartment, she was reluctant to come home and visit, and when she did, she walked on eggshells. With no acknowledgment of her needs and wants, and no safe way to talk about them, Kara did the only thing she could: pull away and protect herself.

One of the first to describe other-oriented perfectionism was the great Dr. Karen Horney (say it with German flair: Hor-nigh), an influential psychiatrist and "gentle rebel of psychoanalysis" who dared to challenge sacrosanct tenets of Freudian thought. Horney was spot-on about how the other-oriented perfectionism of Steve Jobs, Francesca's husband, or Kara's mother works. Back in 1950, she wrote, ". . . a person may primarily impose his standards upon others and make relentless demands as to their perfection. The more he feels himself to be the measure of all things, the more he insists—not upon general perfection but upon *his* particular norms being measured up to. The failure of others to do so arouses his contempt or anger."

Indeed, a questionnaire meant to measure other-oriented perfectionism includes items such as: *I think less of people I know if they make mistakes. If I scold others for their failure to live up to expectations, it will help them in the future. An average performance by someone I know is unsatisfactory. I cannot help getting upset if someone I know makes mistakes.*

Yowza. As you might intuit, the whole concept is infused with control, dominance, and passive aggression.

Perfectionism researcher Dr. Joachim Stoeber of the University of Kent notes that other-oriented perfectionism is the only form of perfectionism that isn't rooted in conscientiousness. He dubs it a "dark" form of perfectionism because it's centered on "high self-regard but low regard for others."

This brings us to a dirty word: *narcissism*. Narcissism is a hot potato in psychology—a Disney villain trait. But narcissism exists on a continuum. Healthy narcissism drives self-preservation, entitlement to justice and human rights, protection of one's family and property, as well as squishier concepts that I advocate in this book like self-acceptance, self-worth, and enjoyment. On the unhealthy end of the continuum are the raging narcissists—domineering, demeaning, grandiose yet fragile, quick to gleefully exploit you if it serves their self-interests.

But there's a whole lot of variation in the middle. All of us, people with other-oriented perfectionism included, don't see the world as it is; we see the world as *we* are. As such, people with other-oriented perfectionism are also hard on themselves. They often work long hours, deny themselves pleasures or rest that everybody else gets to have, or constrain themselves to self-discipline that no one else seems to think about. There's often secret pride. *I am not like other people*, they might think with satisfaction. But there's also secret self-loathing: *I am not like other people*, they may also think with shame or fear. A sense of "No one else cares enough to do things right" sits right next to "Nobody can understand me"—a combination of pride, resentment, loneliness, and longing that keeps people with other-oriented perfectionism feeling disconnected. What's underneath all this? Lots of things.

Enter Dr. Thomas Lynch, developer of an empirically supported therapy called Radically Open Dialectical Behavior Therapy. We'll hear a lot from him and his partner, Erica Smith Lynch, throughout the book; they specialize in treating a coping style called *overcontrol* that likes to hang out with perfectionism.

The Lynches note that one of the double-edged swords of overcontrol is *detail-focused processing*—we notice the little things. Lisa

Brennan-Jobs calls her father's famous powers of observation "sensitive and specific as a nerve in a tooth." For example, as nine-year-old Lisa roller-skates with her father on the Stanford campus, he marvels at the detailed stonework of the buildings: faceted, complicated, almost embroidered-looking. "Because he noticed the details and care of the craftsmen who built this place, the way they'd chipped at every block and arranged it, I knew he must be capable of noticing other people, too. Of noticing me," she writes, correctly intuiting his robust evaluation of everything important to him. Indeed, our powers of observation are so keen, sometimes mere mortals can't see what we see—a typo in the slide deck, our kids' insufficiently enthusiastic sportsmanship, a subpar dedication to smiling in the holiday photo—even when we point it out to them.

But our attention to detail isn't the problem. What we notice is accurate—our partner didn't offer our guest a drink, our kid did indeed get an A- instead of an A, the circulated meeting notes are missing some details, our pans aren't hung up in the right order in the kitchen. Instead, when we're struck by a lightning bolt of other-oriented perfectionism, the problem is our reaction.

First is our private, internal, emotional reaction. We get disproportionately frustrated, annoyed, or afraid of the potential consequences when things are not as they "should" be—we should be good hosts, our kid should have gotten an A because he's capable of it, the notes should be comprehensive for people who missed the meeting, whoever put the pans away should know the order because we've shown everyone who lives in this house a hundred times before.

The second problem comes when we turn our internal reaction into behavior—we offer our guest a drink in front of our spouse with an undertone of *Fine, I'll do it myself*, bring up the grade in a pointed tone with our kid at dinner, reply all with unsolicited corrections, or broadcast our annoyance by banging the pans around as we rearrange them. Steve Jobs didn't have a personal connection to the details of the stonemasons' work at Stanford, but he did to everything Apple produced. Therefore, when ads for the 1998 Bondi blue iMac desktop were in development, Jobs went ballistic when he perceived the print color didn't match the product. He shouted at his friend and ad partner Lee Clow, "You guys don't know what you're doing. I'm going to get someone else to do the ads because this is fucked up."

We all get snippy when we're stressed, exhausted, hungry, or triggered. No one responds warmly and empathically all the time. But when we consistently discharge a message of "My way is the right way" both emotionally and behaviorally to the people close to us, it shreds the bonds of our relationships like driving over scattered nails. Consider it a red flag when your kids, partner, or employees grumble in response to your directives, "I can't do anything right," or "No matter what I do, it's not good enough for you."

Next up, empathy. When we're in other-oriented perfectionism mode, evaluating and finding fault, we don't lack empathy, like the clinical version of narcissism, but we momentarily choose to ignore it. We might opt out of *empathic functioning*, meaning we avoid engaging with other people's emotional experiences. We can sense that we're making a partner upset, hurting our kids' feelings, or annoying our colleagues by being intense or critical. But we deliberately choose not to get emotionally involved and instead double down on the logic of our criticism with a cold, dismissive, or intellectual (read: "rational") response. We treat their emotion as unjustified because, after all, we were right. But when we're momentarily blinded by other-oriented perfectionism, we forget that logic and justification don't solve or soothe and instead push us apart.

Indeed, in *Small Fry*, high-school-age Lisa persuades her father and her stepmom, Laurene, to join her in her weekly therapy session. She tells them she feels alone and lonely within the family. Among other things, she wishes they would say good night to her—a simple but meaningful gesture. A long silence passes. Finally, Laurene states dryly, "We're just cold people." Lisa Brennan-Jobs writes, "I had thought I could shame them for being cold and absent. Now I was the one who was ashamed, for ignoring the simple truth." Lisa asked for empathy and was told: *no*.

On a smaller scale, my client Art didn't understand why his direct reports couldn't power through a bout of COVID—he worked from home when he was sick, so they should, too. Art's reasoning?

It's complicated. If we think the struggling person reflects on us—our direct report is being lazy, our partner is acting cringey at the holiday party—their shortcomings become our problem, and correcting the situation takes priority over anyone's feelings. Alternatively, if others' limitations get taken as verification of our own superiority, their failures become evidence we need to highlight. Or, if we're caught up in gunning toward a goal, like getting the grant proposal submitted on time, it can be hard to offer sympathy when our research assistant's ill-timed breakup registers as an obstacle in our way.

I'm Just Trying to Help: Plausible Deniability

It's counterintuitive that our Outer Critic focuses on the people closest to us—our partners, kids, the people we work with every day. We might be generous with strangers or acquaintances, quick to forgive or to focus on positive qualities, but with people close to us, we focus on their flaws and shortcomings.

This puts us in the middle of an internal tug-of-war. On the one hand, we want to get good, correct results out of the people we criticize. On the other hand, we have a sense that being controlling and critical isn't ideal behavior. This isn't who we want to be. Plus, they tell us outright to please chill.

That's why the hidden engine of the Outer Critic is plausible deniability. If we're honest with ourselves, there's usually a little flame of internal knowledge, a tiny inner voice that knows what we're doing. But since being critical and controlling is not how we consciously want to behave, we cover it up by convincing ourselves that's not what we're doing. *It's not that I don't trust them, I'm just showing them how to do it correctly. I'm not being critical, I'm giving advice. I'm not being controlling, I'm just trying to help.*

Plausible deniability goes beyond disguised criticism. Stewing in stony silence while insisting nothing's wrong, humblebragging to flex on our friends, or insulting someone disguised as a joke only works if we convince ourselves it's not happening. But even if we don't realize what we're doing or can pretend we're not doing it, the effects on our relationships are real. We may not be saying the words, but the message of negative evaluation comes across loud and clear.

What we say in other-oriented perfectionism mode	What we really mean	What they hear
I'm just trying to help	I think you're doing it wrong and you should do it my way	You're doing it wrong *or* I don't trust you to do it right
I just want you to do your best	I want you to do *the* best	You're not doing well enough
Just sayin' *or* I'm just putting that out there *or* This is just my opinion, but . . .	You should do it my way, but I'm not going to say so directly	You're doing it wrong
Sure, we can do it your way (in a tone)	But my way is better	Your way isn't good enough, plus I'm annoyed
I don't need help *or* I've got it, thanks	I can do it myself	I don't need you
[Redoing work]	This isn't good enough	You did it wrong

Outer Critics take pride in not being like other people, but that means they are often quite lonely. What helps to knit us back together? In her book *The Dance of Connection*, psychologist Harriet Lerner tells us, "The least helpful thing we can do is to keep focusing on [other people's] problems and trying to be helpful to them. Instead, it would be more helpful for us to begin to share our own problems, limitations, and needs. . . . We diminish people when we don't allow them to help us, or when we act like we don't need anything from them and they have nothing to offer us." Indeed, "I'm just trying to help" and related comments set up a competent-incompetent dynamic that perpetuates separation by transmitting the message "We are not the same." By contrast, disclosing our own vulnerabilities or sharing times we've struggled sets up an equal-equal dynamic which signals we like and trust others and sends the message "We are the same."

Think of the people in your life you're closest to. Do you love them for being right? For showing you how to improve? Probably not. More likely, you love them for how you feel when you're with them: accepted, supported, trusted. Signaling trust is vital. Indeed, the opposite of control isn't being out of control; the opposite of control is trust.

Steve Jobs was lucky. Near the end of his life, as he was dying of pancreatic cancer, Lisa Brennan-Jobs decoded his behavior. During a visit to her father's sickbed, Lisa went into the bathroom and sprayed herself with a lovely rosewater facial mist she found there. She returned to wrap up the visit with a promise that she would be back soon. She gave him a hug. As she was leaving, he called to her:

"Lis?"

"Yeah?"

"You smell like a toilet."

Lisa knew him well enough to intuit it not as an insult but as his version of "honesty." After all, she hadn't realized the rosewater she had sprayed moments before had turned fetid.

Lisa may have figured out how to hear the care at the heart of her father's criticism, but most of us—including the people we love—can't hear that acutely.

Looking Under the Rug of Plausible Deniability

An important note: If you recognized any part of yourself as you read this far, or felt uncomfortable or defensive, you're on the right path. Other-oriented perfectionism thrives in the shadows, and when we realize we're doing it, we can stop pretending we're not doing it, and limit being the Outer Critic to the people we love.

Dr. Thomas Lynch and Erica Smith Lynch, our overcontrol experts, think a lot about plausible deniability. They've developed a technique called *self-enquiry*, which is designed to look squarely at the icky behaviors we wrap in a veneer of acceptability. Indeed, once we admit we can be covertly controlling, it's hard to keep doing it.

Self-enquiry, they write, is a cultivation of healthy self-doubt and self-examination. It starts with what they call "finding your edge." An *edge* is a visceral reaction that separates us from others. It's the thoughts and feelings we're a bit ashamed of. It's where we feel resistant, self-conscious, or defensive if we had to admit, *Yeah, that's how I reacted.* An edge might be a feeling of secret superiority when our partner does something wrong. It might be an urge to lie when someone points out a mistake we made. It might be our tendency to shut down and stonewall when questioned. An edge is where the truth hurts.

Edges are always negative, but not all negative feelings are edges. If someone insults you, of course you're hurt—that's not an edge. If you get ghosted on a date, of course you feel rejected—that's not an edge. With a true edge, we don't want to think about it or admit to it, and we sure don't want anyone to know. Dr. Lynch gives examples of feeling unappreciated when a partner fails to notice that we rearranged their desk for them, ruminating about a look a complete stranger in a restaurant shot at us, or feeling secret pleasure when a friend confesses a misfortune.

What to do? When we find this visceral edge, rather than shoving it under the rug, we need to shine a bright light on it. *What is it that I don't want to admit to or think about? If my shadow side could talk, what would it say—what is it trying to tell me?* And most importantly: *Is there something here for me to learn?*

Focusing on what we can learn—how we can grow—opens us up. This self-enquiry allows us to reflect, update, and consider other options. We can't control our emotional reactions, per se, but reflecting on the messy stuff helps us clean it up. For example, realizing we get hostile with our kids when we feel insecure helps us do it less. Admitting to ourselves that we belittle a partner to feel better about ourselves helps us let it go. Realizing we go into "I'll show them" mode when we feel inconvenienced by our colleagues helps us let it rest.

Why do all this? It's like digging in the trash after accidentally throwing out your retainer. It's aversive and we'd rather not do it, but there's something in there that we need and has great value. When we reflect on how the reactions we're not proud of hurt the relationships that are most important to us, we can strengthen those relationships. When we stop controlling, we start connecting.

TRY IT OUT: Recall a recent reaction you would be ashamed of or defensive about if anyone were to find out. How did it serve you? (It must have been useful in some way or else it wouldn't have happened.) What might it help you understand about yourself? How might you learn and grow from it?

Anticipating Outer Critics: Socially Prescribed Perfectionism

"That shit was in the trash can," remembers Bruno Mars about early versions of "Uptown Funk," his megahit song with Mark Ronson that topped the Billboard Hot 100 for fourteen weeks—a tie for the second-longest run in history—and propelled him to superstardom. "We spent months on that chorus." Chain-smoking in the studio, tweaking variation after variation, he fretted, imagining negative reactions: "Are people going to get off the dance floor because I said something stupid about a dragon?"

After the success of "Uptown Funk," things got downright paralyzing with the follow-up, *24K Magic*. "Coming off the biggest song of my career, it was super-daunting to come in here," Mars said of returning to the studio. He second-guessed everything. "I don't know if people are going to love this shit," he said. "I don't know if radio is going to play it."

Rolling Stone reporter Josh Eells joined Mars in the final months leading up to the album's release. Mars said to him, "We're at the point now where we're losing our fucking minds. My engineer's going crazy; he wants to kill me." Mars played the latest iteration—at last count, the twentieth version—for Eells. It was good, Mars conceded, but something nagged at him about the bridge. "I just have to open it up." Commented Grammy-winning producer Ari Levine, "I've never seen someone so meticulous in my entire life, when it comes to anything."

Welcome to the world of *socially prescribed perfectionism*. Self-oriented perfectionism is internal—our drive comes from inside. But socially prescribed perfectionism is external—it comes from a belief that others will be highly critical if we fail to meet their sky-high expectations.

Bruno Mars traces his intensity to growing up performing in his family's band in Honolulu. He internalized his late mother's high standards of showmanship: "I would watch people just fall in love with her," he says. "She just had this gift." Today, he says, "Every time I mess up onstage, I hear her. 'You're flat!' 'You missed that move!' 'Tell your brother to shave his mustache!' It's all there."

He learned not just to please her but to please everybody: "Because of my upbringing performing for tourists, I had to entertain everyone. Not just Black people, not just white people, not just Asian people, not just Latin people. I had to perform for anybody that came to Hawaii."

Most of us don't come out of socially prescribed perfectionism a pop superstar, but Mars takes it in stride. "I'm confident that she's looking down and smiling, you know?" he says.

I'm not trying to call out Bruno Mars's mom. Socially prescribed perfectionism seldom has just a single person behind it. It's more of a cultural force, like the analogy of asking a fish, "How's the water?" and the fish replies, "What water?" We don't even realize we're swimming in it. But as humans, we react to the context we're placed in. So when we're placed in a post-pandemic, twenty-first-century context of ruthless cultural forces—capitalism, systemic oppression, consumerism—it makes sense that we respond by feeling like everyone is waiting to pounce when we stumble. As Dr. Thomas Curran explains, "Perfectionism is the defining psychology of an economic system that's hell-bent on overshooting human thresholds."

What's more, socially prescribed perfectionism is what researchers dub "interpersonally motivated," meaning we're hungry for acceptance from others, or at least trying to avoid rejection and disapproval. It's a legit reaction to having demanding expectations imposed on us from a parent, partner, or other important person in our life, as well as absorbing assumptions about our capability from the larger culture we float in like specimens preserved in a jar.

As individuals within this culture, there's a pressure always to be our best selves. But our very human foibles, mistakes, and messes get in the way. Researchers call the gap between our perceived standards and the reality of how life plays out *perfectionistic discrepancy*.

So we try mightily to bridge it. Fear that we'll let people down leads to compensatory strategies—a "corrective" process we'll talk more about in chapter 15 called *perfectionistic self-presentation* (and its angsty cousin, *defensive self-concealment*), where we try to look, sound, and act like we've got it all together. Indeed, making a mistake in public is exquisitely mortifying in socially prescribed perfectionism. We keep our vulnerabilities and weaknesses under wraps. We don't talk about that stuff.*

But defensive pretending is exhausting. It's a fast track to predictable results: depression, disordered eating, procrastination, and interpersonal conflict or isolation, which makes us feel worse. We see all the ways

---

* Except maybe in therapy—some folks with socially prescribed perfectionism treat therapy like a parallel universe—the one place they can let their guard down and talk about mistakes and weaknesses. Together, we work on expanding that, disclosing vulnerabilities— whether a little or a lot—to other people in their lives whom they can trust.

we're not being our best selves, and it feels like we're letting everyone down, including ourselves.

Take Eugene. Eugene logged on to our first session one morning in early June. In the background, I couldn't help but notice, were faded Christmas decorations hanging forlornly on the walls. Over the next hour, it all began to make sense as I learned more about Eugene's depression.

Eugene heard "You have to be everything" loud and clear throughout his childhood. His mom was a star local real estate agent—"She's a hustler," Eugene said—who layered on the pressure for him to be great. Eugene never got to decide what to do with his time. He remembers being overscheduled with activities that, over the years, were increasingly honed to get him into Harvard, the Olympics, and the Jet Propulsion Laboratory, though, Mom begrudged, any NASA site would do. Once, he remembers, a Chinese national badminton coach was visiting Boston. His mother finagled a meeting, frog-marched Eugene into the room, and said to the coach, "Make him a star."

At the same time, there were a thousand things he was *not* supposed to be. Mom made it clear he should be less shy, less tongue-tied, less sensitive, less emotional. Eugene's middle and high school years felt like death by a thousand cuts. By the time he left home for college, he had been thoroughly trained to ignore his wants, preferences, instincts, and personality. He didn't trust himself to make any decisions—he had been corrected so many times, he knew whatever he wanted was destined to be wrong.

Eugene was stuck. Most mornings, he would sleep late or scroll through his phone for hours—he couldn't feel inadequate if he was asleep or distracted. He wanted to feel better, but he was so far from where he was "supposed" to be—a rocket scientist, a Harvard graduate, an Olympian—that he felt he didn't deserve to do or feel anything good. "I'm so far behind," he said. "I need to catch up before I can do anything I want to do." He was stuck in the liminal space between "There's no way I can do *anything*—I can't solve climate change or fix society" and simultaneously "Therefore, I can't do anything—I am stuck and incapable."

You Don't Even Have to Do Anything Wrong: Criticism Is Enough

"Sorry to take up your time," mumbled Eugene toward the end of our session, referring to the hour he was paying me for, to do a job I loved. Eugene was sorry a lot: sorry for taking a moment to think before he answered my questions, sorry for not shaving his depression stubble before our session, sorry when a recycling truck rumbled by in the alley behind his house and he worried I could hear it over our Zoom connection.

Eugene's not doing anything wrong. But that's beside the point. A fascinating study led by Drs. Theresa Robertson and Daniel Sznycer with the welp-that-about-sums-it-up title "The True Trigger of Shame: Social Devaluation Is Sufficient, Wrongdoing Is Unnecessary" found that we tend to feel shame when we're devalued by someone else—criticized, judged, excluded—*whether we deserve it or not*.

In the study, each participant played a game that earned them tokens, a percentage of which they could optionally choose to contribute to a pooled token pot—like a tip jar for restaurant staff—that all participants would split at the end. Before they moved on to round two, though, participants went through a *Survivor*-style elimination, voting their fellow players off the metaphorical island by writing brief explanations about why they did or did not want to keep each person in the group. Spoiler: all the feedback was fake, manipulated by the researchers. In half the cases, participants got excluded. They were told they'd been voted off because they hadn't contributed enough to the pot, with feedback like, "I don't like being with people who won't help." But the other half stayed in the group. They were told that everyone wanted to keep working with them, but because they were basically too popular, they would need to work alone for the next round for logistical reasons.

Take note: that means everyone—excluded or included—worked alone for the second round. The only difference was whether their fake evaluation had come back as thumbs-up or thumbs-down. Those who had been excluded, predictably, felt ashamed. Less predictably, they felt ashamed no matter how much they had contributed to the tip pool—even when they had shared 100 percent of their tokens. Perceived rejection, criticism, and other devaluing responses were enough to trigger shame, even when they literally gave everything they had.

The conclusion? Criticism slays us. Devaluation flays us. In Eugene's apologies to me, criticism didn't even have to occur; the possibility was enough for a preemptive "sorry." Ultimately, we can't control other people's (or crafty researchers') feedback. We might get criticized even after doing our best impression of *The Giving Tree* and giving our all. But we'll still try to prevent that devaluation from happening. Which leads us to . . .

People-Pleasing

Lizette and her two housemates had been friends since college. They would have dinner together most days and host movie nights for friends in their apartment above a ramen shop in the "Keep Allston Shitty" neighborhood of Boston. But the roommates would blithely blast their music when Lizette was trying to sleep, "forget" to clean up after movie nights, and invite friends over to stay without consulting her. Lizette couldn't muster the courage to ask them to change their behavior, but when it came time to renew their lease, she also couldn't muster the courage to tell them she didn't want to live with them anymore. She relied on indirect methods like hinting ("Don't you two just want to live together since you both have a nine-to-five schedule?"), pretending ("We all know the landlord is just going to raise the rent beyond our budget, anyway"), and false altruism ("I'm going to let you two get a two-bedroom—there's way more housing availability that way").

Lizette made plans to live with another friend without getting up the gumption to tell her housemates, so when the housemates renewed their lease, she was stuck. She had to tell them she was moving out, which was so distressing to Lizette that she dissociated and can't remember most of the conversation. All she knew is they both gave her the silent treatment until she left. Lizette hadn't wanted to share an apartment for another year, but she hadn't meant to blow up the friendship.

This is people-pleasing. It's a behavioral strategy to influence how others think of us and stay firmly in their good graces, or at least avoid getting voted off the island. It's what's called a *safety behavior*—an action we take to reduce our anxiety and prevent our fears from coming to fruition.

At its most blunt, people-pleasing aims to control other people's reactions and emotions toward us. But people-pleasing doesn't seem "controlling" because the behavior looks like kindness, flexibility, or consideration. In fact, people-pleasing is pretty genius; it not only works hard to prevent dislike but sometimes even gets us smiles of approval. It appears generously selfless, and while that's the appeal, it's also the problem: it renders us self-less. We outsource ourselves to Outer Critics—past, present, and imagined.

People-pleasing, when deployed regularly, diminishes our own volition like an atrophying muscle. For many of us, it's not that we know what we want and deny it. Instead, we read the room and figure out what others want. What they want *is* what we want, because what we want is to get along and avoid the soul crush of all those *d*'s: devaluation, disapproval, disappointment, dislike. What we actually want never really coalesces because we're responding to the force fields of other people.

People-pleasing also snowballs into bigger problems. Even though we're trying to appease, people-pleasing actually burdens other people with things we're supposed to do for ourselves—decide what we like, want, and pursue, and ultimately, how we see ourselves. For example, an international team of researchers found that when we say, "I'm down with anything," we come off as evasive. The decision-maker we're trying to please—say, your friend Marge, who is surveying the friend group about what restaurant to go to—doesn't take your answer at face value. Instead, she assumes you don't want what's already been suggested but are too polite to say so. So Marge then takes on the burden of trying to read your mind, plus she chooses something different from the initial suggestions. In other words, by stating no preference, we make her do mental gymnastics and settle for a second choice, both of which can build resentment toward us.

Even when we know people-pleasing is causing a slow crumbling of our own volition, low-key resentment from Marge, or a dramatic blowup of a relationship like Lizette's, it's hard to stop. It still feels wrong to generate our own force field.

Rolling back people-pleasing can feel wildly selfish and burdensome at first. It's a well-worn neural hiking trail, so when you get up the courage to hack through the overgrown brush with a machete and search for your own needs and wants, it feels somewhere between annoying and criminal. Brain scans back this up. A study in the journal *Frontiers in Human Neuroscience* scanned the brains of people who had difficulty disagreeing with others. The less often they disagreed with others, the more certain parts of their brains* lit up when they actually disagreed, even if they were an expert in the topic being discussed. No wonder Lizette's brain shorted out.

But even if reining in people-pleasing feels like the first step of spiraling into selfishness, it's actually the first step of acknowledging your self-ness. As Emma Reed Turrell writes in her excellent book *Please Yourself: How to Stop People-Pleasing and Transform the Way You Live*, stopping people-pleasing isn't "saying, 'Me first,' it's simply saying, 'Me, too.'"

Start by tuning in to what you need and want—needing to make time for exercise so you have the stamina to keep up with your kids, needing to build in time with friends so you don't get burned out again, wanting to decline the party invitation because you hate parties and only go because you think you'd be letting the host down, or wanting to go to the party even though your partner hates parties and you're scared to leave them stranded. Next, test-drive. Experiment. Say no to your neighbor who only talks to you when he needs to borrow something. Say yes to your boss when she asks you if there's anything you would change about the department.

When we first start to say, "Me, too," we're usually met with one of two outcomes. The first is a big nothingburger. We say, "Me, too," and our feared critic says, "Okay, cool." We might have assumed the worst-case scenario of rejection was a foregone conclusion, but we are

---

* A veritable alphabet soup of the pMFC, AI, and IFG—posterior medial frontal cortex, anterior insula, inferior frontal gyrus—as well as the lateral orbitofrontal cortex and angular gyrus.

surprised with grace, reasonableness, or respect for finally taking up some space.

The second possibility is pushback. People-pleasing "works" for the people being pleased. And when we push against a system, the system pushes back. As Turrell writes, "When they tell you that 'you've changed,' you'll know that what they're really saying is, 'I don't like that you're no longer doing it *my* way.'"

People-pleasing is a form of control, and the opposite of control is trust. It's *not* blindly trusting that no one will criticize you and everyone will like you—that outcome isn't controllable, anyway. Remember, you can donate everything to the tip pool and still get excluded. You can't please everyone, even by doing everything right.

But it *is* trust that you can cope if you don't get a 100 percent pleased and approving reaction. It's trust that you can reach out for support, trust that people are scrappy and can find alternatives to putting everything on your shoulders, trust that people are allowed to have their own reactions without you having to save them from it, trust that you can stand by your right to have needs and limits, and trust that you can muster the resources to deal with disapproval, loss, and change.

Turrell again: "Conditional acceptance is no acceptance at all and the end of a relationship built on people-pleasing is not the wrong result. Rupture in relationship can be repaired if both parties are willing and if it can't be repaired, the relationship was never yours to begin with." The take-home? Of all the people you work so hard to please, be sure to include yourself.

TRY IT OUT: Identify a particular situation or person where you tend to people-please. Honor what people-pleasing is buying you—you wouldn't do it if it wasn't useful. Then reflect on what people-pleasing is costing you. Identify an opportunity to state an opinion, communicate a need, or set a limit that is meaningful to you. Try it out and consider the results. Rinse and repeat.

Shift 2

COMING HOME TO YOUR LIFE

6

From Labels to Values

WHEN CARTER JOINED our Zoom session from his dorm room, his hair was greasy and sticking straight up, the result of holding his head in his hands as he struggled with his linear algebra homework. It was only three weeks into his first semester of college, and he looked as stressed and exhausted as if he were knee-deep into finals.

Carter, the "smart" kid from his crumbling hometown, whom we met in chapter 1, had enjoyed math in high school, so when he got to college, he registered for multivariate calculus. After two weeks of feeling as lost as last year's Easter eggs, he dropped the class and switched to linear algebra, but now he was struggling again.

"The add-drop deadline is today," he told me, "so I'm going to drop linear algebra and add biology." I tilted my head—a silent question; I knew Carter had already taken college-level biology, searching it out at a local community college since his high school didn't offer it at the AP level. After a beat, he added, "I know biology will work out."

Over the next couple of sessions, Carter was able to articulate the effect that the label "smart" had on him: "Okay, if I'm smart, then there're certain things I need to do," he said. "I need to know the answers in math. I need to, like, not have any questions that show I don't understand. I need to basically memorize the study guide so I can do well on the test."

Carter closely tied the label "smart" to his identity. And it was no wonder—doing well academically affirmed his idea of himself and made him feel like he wasn't letting down anyone in his town. But floundering at his math homework late at night shook his scholastic composure and his sense of self. He remembers thinking, night after night as he puzzled over derivatives, *What if I'm not actually that smart?* And that thought, in turn, pulled him away from a genuine interest— math—and toward a safer bet.

We all use labels; think about how you describe yourself. Take the sentence stem "I am . . ." and I bet you can come up with twenty or thirty labels right off the bat: *nice, socially awkward, creative, a weirdo, a father, queer, a nerd, good with kids, Jewish, Republican, not good at relationships, a gardener, a paralegal.* Our labels can become a point of pride: the "rock" of the family is trusted and relied upon. The "supermom" balances work and family with the precision of a rocket launch. Like Carter and his parents, we feel good when teachers write "bright" or "a pleasure to work with" on our childhood report cards.

But when we overevaluate, our labels start to determine our actions. Carter's label "smart" dictates what he has to do or avoid in order to maintain the label. The "mom" of the friend group coordinates the Venmo payments but also abandons her own evening to take care of whoever's had too many margaritas because that's what friend-group moms do. If we're "lazy," we can't possibly be interested in trying ju-jitsu because people like us binge-watch Netflix, right? And if we're an "introvert," belting out a dramatic rendition of "My Heart Will Go On" at karaoke makes your friends turn to each other and ask, "Who is this stranger, and what happened to our friend?"

This all makes sense. We humans like to be consistent. Back when I was learning to be a therapist, a mentor broke my brain with the truism: "People would rather be consistent than happy." Why? Creating a cogent story about ourselves smooths out contradictions and irregularities. Consistency gets us certainty, clarity, control, safety— all fundamentally good things. No one should live in ever-changing chaos.

But the pull for consistency means sometimes labels and behavior start to blur. One client never went to any college parties because he thought his Mormon faith rendered him ineligible, despite longing to own the dance floor fueled by nothing stronger than LaCroix. Another client turned down a promotion despite his colleagues' support and encouragement due to his self-imposed "incapable" label.

Labels can also make others assume certain things about us: All our adult siblings assume that since we're a nurse, we'll automatically be the caregiver for our aging parents. Or our roommate blithely hosts a party the night before we take the LSAT because we're supposed to be "chill."

Social media pours gasoline on this spark. Kids have tried on different labels for years—*Am I emo? Am I an activist? Am I a nerd?* It's part of growing up. Today, especially around mental health, social media posts can be eye-opening and validating in some cases but misleading and confusing in others: "5 Signs You Have Anxiety." "What's Your ADHD Type?" "6 Autistic Behaviors I Do as a Late-Diagnosed Woman." But then, we might start searching for other things in our lives that match up: *Wait, listening to the same song over and over again means I'm autistic? Does that mean I must be socially awkward and have obsessive interests, too?* Especially in young people trying to define who they are, labels can create strictures and rules that define them from the outside in.

In sum, when we try to make our lives consistent with our labels, but our labels tell us what we *can't* do, what we *can't* handle, what we *have* to do, or *have* to be like, then they've boxed us in tighter than an Escalade in a Manhattan parking garage.

What to do? "It's recognizing the chatter about ourselves," says Dr. Michael Twohig, professor of psychology at Utah State University. "And it's okay to follow it; just pay attention to *when* to follow it." Dr. Twohig is one of the bigwigs of acceptance and commitment therapy; ACT* is woven into his DNA. He's the coauthor of the

---

* Overly simplified: ACT is a mindfulness-based, behavior-focused, empirically validated therapy. If traditional cognitive-behavioral therapy aims to change our thoughts and emotions, ACT aims to change our *relationship* to our thoughts and emotions.

insightful *The Anxious Perfectionist: How to Manage Perfectionism-Driven Anxiety Using Acceptance & Commitment Therapy.*

In his own clinical practice, Twohig commonly sees labels that are fundamentally good things: "I'm the planner, I'm the organized one, I'm the caregiver," he lists. "But then it's really hard not to be that," he notes, "because that's how they see themselves." Our labels are what's called *ego-syntonic*, meaning they help us be consistent with our idea of ourselves (there's that darn consistency again).

Thankfully, the answer is more sophisticated than doing the opposite of the label. The point is not to instantly reject the label nor to instantly conform. Should the LDS dancer throw off his Mormon label and start double-fisting a latte and a Miller Light? No way. But he can examine if being LDS is directing his behavior in *unnecessary* ways and making him opt out of a party where he could show off his pop-and-lock skills while downing a Sprite. Or he could opt out of the party not because he is Mormon but because it's not his scene and he'd rather go to the rock-climbing gym with his buddies.

TRY IT OUT: Identify the labels that are most salient to you. How do you identify and describe yourself? How do others identify and describe you? Reflect on how these labels may be determining your behavior: "I have to do [action] because I'm [label]." "I can't do [action], because I'm [label]."

Introducing Values

So what can motivate us instead of our overidentified labels? Our values. Values are the North Star that guides how we want to live our lives. They are what you find meaningful and important in life, and they can be anything: honesty, connecting with your kids, comedy, tradition, hard work, social justice, creating art, being a loving partner, books, generosity, self-care, or any of a million other things.

A true value, as defined by Dr. Twohig and coauthor Dr. Clarissa Ong, has several parts. A value is (1) freely chosen, (2) intrinsically meaningful, meaning you would care about it even if no one ever knew, (3) within your control, meaning it's not contingent upon other people, like being loved or approved of, and (4) continuous—more of a direction than a destination.

The "freely chosen" part is particularly significant. Values are never coercive or obligatory. You freely choose to follow them and are likely willing to tolerate some discomfort or inconvenience to do so. Your values explain why you might volunteer to clean up trash on the beach on a beautiful summer Saturday, let your friend cry on your shoulder after she went back to the partner you just knew wasn't a good match, or sit through your child's squawky middle school orchestra performance, not that I know anything about that last one. If we did any of these things without being driven by our values, we'd feel very different—resentful, exasperated, not to mention in need of some ibuprofen. Labels imply that we "have to" do things. But with values, we don't "have to" do anything. We *choose* to do whatever we do.

The "continuous" part is also important. Just like a pianist can never check off "mastered piano" on a to-do list or a person of faith is never "done" practicing their religion, we're also never done, per se, valuing kindness, sustainability, or our sense of humor. Like we said in chapter 4, values are different from goals. Visiting Australia is a goal—it's a destination. Going west is the equivalent value—it's a direction. You can always go more "west." Therefore, "Make a million dollars" isn't a value, nor is "Travel to see family more often," nor "Write a piano sonata." But the equivalent values might be wealth, financial security, travel, family, creativity, music, or self-expression. You can always move in the direction of your values.

What Are Your Values?

Think of the times in your life you felt the most engagement, meaning, or purpose. Note that I didn't say *happy* or *accomplished*, though that can be part of it. What was happening at the high points of purpose and meaning? What got you through tough times?

By contrast, when did you feel empty, meaningless, coerced, or like you were going down the wrong path? Pinpointing what was missing from your life at the low points can help determine what's most important.

For me, I find deep meaning when I'm connecting with others, making people's lives better, being silly and laughing, feeling awed and calmed by the great outdoors, and cutting through the noise to get to the signal, whether in my writing, the therapy room, or life. But that's right now. Values can change over the course of a life. Your friend who never wears a motorcycle helmet and heedlessly uses ATMs in sketchy neighborhoods at midnight becomes a parent and suddenly starts to value safety. You look through your conservative parents' old photo albums and realize they used to put flowers in gun barrels at anti-war demonstrations.

When clients are thinking about their values, I'll sometimes ask them to list their top five as an exercise, but the actual number and salience varies from situation to situation. In other words, don't get too caught up in getting values exactly right. Our brains are sneaky. It's easy to get perfectionistic when thinking about our values, so be on the lookout for thoughts like *I have to choose the exact right values* or *I must follow my values perfectly*. Rest assured, values aren't carved on a stone tablet—they can simply be a sense of what's important and meaningful to you.

TRY IT OUT: What do you value? What is particularly important and meaningful to you? What brings you a sense of purpose?

Values are meant to be lived, not just held. When we've been driven by "have to" for a long time, it can feel weird and disorienting to shift to freely chosen values. After all, "have to" has served you well. It's certainly served me well.

Shifting from labels to values might mean your actions look significantly different. Dr. Ong gives an example of the shift from labels to values with "I'm a good parent." We might try to fulfill the label of "good parent," with generic actions we "have to" do. "If I'm a good parent, I have to ask my kid repeatedly about their problems and help solve them even if they don't want me to," Ong said.

By shifting to a value of attentiveness to our kid, by contrast, we ask what would work given the particular situation. We become more flexible. Being attentive might mean asking what's wrong and helping solve the problem. But the same value of attentiveness might also mean, "I'm going to give you space right now, because that's what is helpful to you."

On the other hand, shifting from labels to values might mean that your actions look exactly the same on the surface. Only the motivation underneath will be different. Your actions will be the same but will come from a very different place.

For example, Dr. Twohig tells the story of a graduate student he worked with who we'll call Ramon. When Ramon started working with Dr. Twohig, he was productive, but was really driven by, as Twohig calls it, "the beating stick," the sense of "I will keep going because the only acceptable thing to do is be excellent."

Over the five years of his degree, Ramon took his acceptance and commitment therapy training to heart and reoriented his work ethic toward, as Twohig put it, "I'm doing this because I can find meaning in this activity, or I can find meaning in the person I work with, or I want to be helpful, or this will affect the field in a decent way." By the time Ramon graduated, Twohig reflects, "I think it was hard to give up 'if fear is behind me, I'll keep going,' but I'd argue he was more productive than when he got here. And the motivator was truly his values." He was still productive—his surface behavior looked exactly the same after switching to values, but it came from a very different source.

Living your values is possible in any life situation. Dr. Ong gives the example of valuing activism for a cause. If we have money, we can donate. If we have time, we can volunteer. If we have neither, we can have conversations with people in our communities, we can put up signs, we can tell our stories, we can listen with empathy.

In another example, my client Saoirse has a young child with a disability, and she values advocating for him. Right now, he's six, but "advocating for him" will look very different when he's sixteen and different again when he's twenty-six. As their context changes, her actions will change, even as she keeps following the same value.

Biggest important asterisk: *living your values doesn't always feel good.* For example, I value helping people through my writing. But that means I cold-email experts and ask them to volunteer their time for an interview, or I ask my friends to pre-read chunks of a new book—things that don't necessarily help them directly and may even feel burdensome with their busy schedules. I risk making other people stressed in order to follow my values, and that feels illegal to me. Likewise, I value spending time with my family, but sometimes that means I choose to turn down cool projects or say no to friends, and that feels bad, like I'm letting people down. Following my values doesn't always make me feel 100 percent good, but sitting with that discomfort is, for better or worse, part of living a valued life.

"Sitting with discomfort" or "learning to be uncomfortable" is often emphasized in therapy. But let's think about why. The point is not to sit in pain or negative emotions for no reason, or because it's supposed to be good for you, like eating your vegetables. Don't do that. There's nothing inherently commendable about being uncomfortable for the sake of being uncomfortable. Instead, be uncomfortable for a *reason*—to live a life you find meaningful.

Dr. Twohig sums it up: "I often say to my students, if you're saying, 'I *need* to get my dissertation done,' reframe that because you're gonna have to do the work either way. At least find some meaning in the activity. Run toward what you're interested in, what you think you'll like, what is meaningful, and what's in line with your values. As opposed to avoiding: avoiding letting someone down, avoiding failure, avoiding making a mistake."

Rules Pretending to Be Values

We'll talk more about rules in chapter 8, but here's a start. True values are a shepherding guide, not a dictatorial commander. But perfection-ism can morph values into rigid rules.

Here's a simple way to tell when that sneaky conversion has hap-pened: a value has turned into a rule when it feels coercive—*I should, I have to, I can't*—and we have to do it or else. For example, my client Theresa was raised, as she put it, "through a combination of God and my mother," to be generous. But generosity was presented as a require-ment. "If someone asked you for something—a homeless man asked you for a dollar, a friend asked you to babysit—you had to do it," she remembers. But the lack of free will meant it ceased to be a value and became a rule—the very opposite of the spirit of generosity.

Twenty-first-century Western culture hasn't exactly made separat-ing our values from others' expectations easy. In Simone Stolzoff's book, *The Good Enough Job: Reclaiming Life from Work*, he cites a Pop-ulace/Gallup poll that asked respondents how they defined success. A whopping 97 percent of respondents agreed with the following state-ment: "A person is successful if they have followed their own interests and talents to become the best they can be at what they care about most." But when asked, "How do you think *others* define success?" an equally whopping 92 percent agreed that others would think a person is successful "if they are rich, have a high-profile career or are well-known." The implication: if we think we're surrounded by people who only admire wealth, prestige, or fame, it can be challenging to stay true to values that differ.

All that said, your parents, friends, cultural heritage, political system, or religion might influence your values, but they do not define them. Your values are still freely chosen by you. Dr. Twohig talks about values and rules in terms of two yardsticks. The rules yardstick measures: Does this meet the rules? Did I accomplish *X, Y,* or *Z*? The values yardstick is more like: Is this allowing me to live the way I want to live? Is this the person I want to be?

Carter dropped linear algebra and retook biology (which got him the A he wanted), but as we continued our work together, he also reflected on his values, which included a value of learning. When I told Dr. Ong about Carter, she nodded in recognition. "There's all this stuff that comes with 'smart,' which might be in conflict with the value of learning," she said. "We have to ask silly questions to learn. We need to be able to admit we don't know in order to learn. And when we see clients able to make that shift, we'll see it in terms of asking more questions or studying for tests differently, like wanting to know the material rather than memorize the study guide."

Perfectionism is fascinating, she continued, precisely because our surface behavior might look exactly the same after we switch from being driven to maintain our label of "smart" to being driven by the value of learning. "You might still study for three hours, but the intent going into it is different. You're being interested in learning the material, as opposed to 'Oh my gosh, if I don't know this on the test, I'm stupid.'"

Carter is still chipping away at his relationship to "smart," but one session, he reported he had viscerally experienced being guided by values instead of a label. He had gone to visit his girlfriend at her university that past weekend. "On Saturday morning, she started feeling feverish, and by lunch, she was totally sick. We had plans to see some friends, but I chose to take care of her instead of going out. I didn't mind at all." He would have taken care of her regardless, Carter said, but he intuited that if "good partner" had been functioning as a label or a rule—*I have to be a good partner and take care of her*—he might have chafed under the loss of his Saturday. But instead, because fetching Gatorade and tissues was freely chosen, he said, he didn't feel resentful. He was sad not to see their friends, for sure, but both of us were stoked he had experienced choice instead of duty.

7

Our Forgotten Baskets

UCKED NEATLY IN the rolling mountains of western Massachusetts sits Berkshire Community College. One clear Saturday morning in the spring of 2021, the gymnasium, which typically hosts club basketball games, has been transformed. On one side, tables staffed by nurses are neatly arranged with sharps containers, alcohol wipes, and Band-Aids. On the other side, black plastic folding chairs are arranged in strict six-feet-apart rows and columns—the post-vaccination observation area. A steady stream of locals receive their first COVID-19 shots and then settle into the observation area to wait out any immediate adverse reactions.

A trim man with black hair and glasses, wearing a blue surgical mask and a newsboy cap, receives his vaccination from a nurse, pulls his jacket back on, and heads for the observation area. Against a backdrop of blue vinyl wall padding, he takes a seat under the basketball hoop and lays down the large musical instrument case he carries. He opens it. Out comes a cello. He has fifteen minutes to kill, he reasons. He can't leave his treasured cello in the car, so he might as well fill those minutes with music, an offering to the people around him—nurses, volunteers, the newly vaccinated.

As he draws the bow across the strings, the deep, resonant tones rise slowly, and then faster—Bach's "Prelude in G Major." It is spirited yet soothing, an unfamiliar sound in a space accustomed to referee whistles and squeaky sneakers. Some people listen intently, closing their eyes to experience the music more fully, while others glance up and then continue scrolling through their phones. One elderly man drags his chair directly in front of the cellist and, still distanced, leans in, listening keenly. Later, the cellist would comment that the man must have "needed something" that he was delighted to provide. "I'm always happy to respond when people feel like they need some music. That's what I'm here for," said Yo-Yo Ma.

This wasn't the first time Ma had used music to soothe and unite during the pandemic. In the earliest days, he shared and encouraged other musicians to post #SongsOfComfort recordings on social media. His first: Dvořák's "Going Home." As the pandemic progressed, he and his longtime friend, the pianist Emanuel Ax, played pop-up concerts for bus drivers, firefighters, nurses, and other essential workers.

It hadn't always been this way—playing music to connect and support. Ma remembered his priorities had been very different in years prior. He used to focus squarely on technique, accuracy, and precision. "At one point I had the audacity to think I could play a perfect concert," he remembered. "I came to the concert and I started playing. I was in the middle of the concert and I realized everything was going perfectly well," he said. "And I was bored out of my mind." He questioned his goal of the perfect concert. "Is that what I'm trying to do? Am I trying to get it right? Or am I trying to find something?" That was the moment, Ma remembers, "I made a fateful decision that I was actually going to devote my life to human expression versus human perfection." Today, he says, music, whether offered in a packed Carnegie Hall or a distanced community gymnasium, is "how I explore the world around me; it's how I connect to other people; it's how I express myself."

Yo-Yo Ma is onto something. Trying to get it right kept him on track for many years but was ultimately unsatisfying, like a fogged-in summit at the end of a steep hike. Few of us are world-class cellists, but many of us face a similar dilemma: trying to get it right (or more accurately, trying not to get it wrong) has been our guiding light, but it lit the way to a place of dissatisfaction, loneliness, or disconnection. We know something is off, but we can't put a finger on what it is or how to change it. We feel like a stranger in a strange land.

There are many slices in the pie of dissatisfaction, but one of the biggest is our outsize focus on performance. We conflate what we do with who we are, defining ourselves by how well we perform. We tend to, as psychologist Dr. Don Hamachek described it, "over-value performance and under-value the self." We put all our eggs in the basket of performance.

This is *overevaluation*, or when our self-worth, both overall and moment-to-moment, is too dependent on how we perform, what we accomplish, or how hard we work. It's possible to stake our worth on a dizzying array of things: the number on our paycheck, our job title, how faithfully we stuck to our healthy diet (or didn't), being a "good mom," a "good friend," our reflection in the mirror—the list goes on and on.

Overevaluation comes from a good place. Of course we're proud of our accomplishments. We want to do things right because we care deeply. Meeting our expectations makes us feel recognized and valued. Research shows that working toward goals boosts happiness.

But we cross the line from identifying with our performance—incorporating our performance and achievements into our larger self-concept—to overidentifying with it when our goals start to control us. We outsource our self-worth to our performance results. We hold zero tolerance for error because mistakes mean something is wrong with us.

Remember Gus, the "overdrive or park" cookware designer from chapter 1? This was exactly his challenge. Gus put a premium on getting it right in all areas of life. Specifically, he told himself he should come across as über-competent—a good team leader, an insightful thinker, a knowledgeable friend. Without continually superb performance in work and life, he feared, he'd be revealed as incompetent and be sidelined. He put such pressure on himself that before his last quarterly review, he endured a sleepless night. He felt that his review was a referendum on *him*, not just his work. When he opened the email, he scanned the review frantically, searching for reassurance that no one had found him lacking.

Likewise, with friends, Gus tried hard to radiate what he saw as competence—choosing tasteful craft beers, suggesting cool restaurants, steering conversation toward stuff he had read in *The New York*

Times. So his brain always short-circuited a bit when his buddies would do Yoda impressions or toss around dumb name suggestions for his friend Jason's new dog* because, in a maddening paradox, he felt incompetent at acting stupid. "Nobody wants to be the guy who can't hang," he explained. But you can't work at playing.

In both work and life, Gus wanted to be able to use his usual toolbox: try harder, work at it, get better. But like Yo-Yo Ma pre-revelation, he felt unsatisfied and disconnected. When I suggested that we approach his life with metrics other than performance, he looked at me quizzically. "But what else is there?" he asked with genuine puzzlement.

There are at least two answers to Gus's question: connection and enjoyment. To come home to our lives—to shift away from overvaluing our performance—we'll move some of our proverbial eggs from the basket of performance to the baskets of connection and enjoyment.

From Performance to Connection

Let's start with connection. Gus's story—as well as Yo-Yo Ma's—reminds us that perfectionism may look like a personal problem, but it's really an interpersonal problem. A focus on performance outcomes—*Am I doing this right? Did I avoid mistakes? Does this look okay to you?*—comes at the expense of connecting with the other humans in our lives.

All of this is unintentional. We don't set out to focus on goals and tasks instead of connecting. But our genetics, experiences, and cultural messages all combine to create a mindset so common, researchers have a phrase for it: "agency over communion." For example, we might earn successive karate belts but forget to enjoy the camaraderie of the dojo. We might decorate our living room so carefully our guests are afraid to sit down. We might be considered one of the greatest living musicians and realize mid-concert, as Yo-Yo Ma remembers thinking, "'You know, I could actually just stop and walk off the stage and not feel a

---

* Mister Meatball and Chicken Nugget were the leading contenders.

thing' because I had separated the act of doing something from the act of being present."

Paradoxically, we emphasize agency *because* we're searching for communion. Like every human on the planet, we want to feel accepted, but we've somehow absorbed the message that to gain acceptance, we have to perform to the best of our abilities. If we can *perform* well enough, whispers a deeply buried part of our brains, we'll *be* good enough. But our deepest wish is to be accepted without having to perform.

What perfectionism forgets to tell us is that getting it right doesn't make us part of a community. Gus didn't lack contacts, but he did lack connection. He had access to a network of colleagues and even a friend group, but he didn't feel truly a part of either.

It can be hard to break away from performance because it buys us a facsimile of belonging. When we focus our energy on getting it right (or at least avoiding getting it wrong), we often do get it right. And that can yield acclaim. But being impressive has an unintended side effect of being isolating—admiration singles us out, but getting singled out means we're alone.

In mind-bending irony, our drive to find acceptance through performance begins because we already feel separate or different. The author Thomas DeLong, in his book for perfectionistic high achievers, *Flying Without a Net: Turn Fear of Change into Fuel for Success*, notes that pretty much every high-achieving person experiences a "gravitational pull to feel left out," meaning that we "reflexively look for signs and signals that tell you you're being excluded or not wanted." There's a sense we don't belong, even in groups we're already part of.

For Gus, shifting from performance to connection meant doing some things differently. Ever the behaviorist, I asked Gus to do some mental time travel into a future when he felt connected. If he felt accepted, what would he be doing? "I'd be listening rather than rehearsing what to say ahead of time," he said. "I'd probably share more about myself. I'd ask my team and my friends for advice." I had nothing to add. Gus had a great plan.

He tried sharing project updates with his team before they were completely polished and, moreover, asked for their input. The next time Gus gave a presentation, rather than silently reviewing his slides at the podium as people filed in, he greeted people by name as they entered. When he gave the presentation, he focused on sharing his knowledge with the energy of "Look at this cool rock I found!" rather than trying to perform his slides as Gus the Impressive Expert. He prepped for meetings but stopped short of rehearsing beforehand and instead simply focused on what was being said in the moment. With friends, instead of trying to be "good" at hanging out, he tried to tune in and participate when they mused about topics he felt unprepared for, like how zombies never seem to take public transportation.

What really blew Gus's mind, he told me later, was that focusing on connection was easier than focusing on performance. Work was less draining, he said, and he didn't have to zone out on YouTube to settle his nerves after a friend hangout anymore.

For Gus, moving from performance to connection meant doing some things differently. But for Deema, all her actions stayed exactly the same. The only thing that changed? Her mindset. When I worked with her, Deema was studying cello performance at a local conservatory. The previous semester, she had been asked to substitute in an ensemble when the original cellist broke her wrist falling on an icy Boston sidewalk. The youngest student in the ensemble, Deema had been super intimidated to rehearse with master's and doctoral students; she spun with angst all semester, pressuring herself to practice so she wouldn't let anyone down, yet procrastinating practicing all the hard parts, especially her solo. But she got through the winter recital, held her own on the solo, and wiped her brow with relief when none of the other musicians seemed to hate her at the after-party.

Fast-forward to May. Deema logged on for our session and reported that she had been getting lunch in the dining hall when two master's students from the ensemble—Lucas and Caleb—recognized her and called her over. "What's good, Deema! It's been a minute! Sit with us," they said, emanating friendly golden retriever energy. Deema told me she had momentarily stood still with her tray of pasta bake, confused. "But they haven't heard me play since December."

Maybe we feel an equivalent of Deema's confusion: *They haven't heard me play since December.* We think we need to do things well so people like us. *I need to spruce up my living room before I can have people over. I need to lose some weight before I start dating again. I need to kick butt in these rehearsals so these ensemble members like me.* Underlying it all: We have to perform well before we have the right to belong.

She joined them for lunch, Deema told me, but found herself working hard to be funny. She agreed with their opinions. She showed excitement about the things they were clearly excited about. It was fun to have lunch with them, she said, but there was an underlying current of pressure and an urge to prove herself.

Over Zoom, I asked Deema what she might do differently if she approached Lucas and Caleb with connection in mind rather than earning her place through performance. Deema thought for a moment. "I would probably still be funny, but just because I'm funny, not because I had to be," she said. "I would probably still agree with a lot of their opinions, but just because we have pretty similar outlooks. And I would probably get excited about what they were excited about, because that's just part of friendship," she finished. In other words, on the surface, she wouldn't do anything different. But her mindset would be different. Her approach would be different. Connection would come from a place that was less obligatory, more freely chosen, and more authentic.

The next time Deema saw Lucas and Caleb, she put her intention into action. "It was hard. I feel more vulnerable," she reported to me. "Now I have to trust that they like me for me. It's not about my cello performance or how hard I worked at rehearsal or how much I agree with them. It's just me. So if they reject me, that makes it more personal." She paused. "But it felt more genuine," she said. "Hanging out was simpler."

Belonging isn't the only thing we think we have to earn. Here are some other things tough-on-themselves clients have assumed they had to earn through good performance: rest, the right to state their needs, support, understanding, sleep, a break, a hug, some tender loving care.

For both Gus and Deema, this wasn't a one-and-done. The urge to perform still followed them around like an ever-wispier, but still present, rain cloud. But remember: hearts beat, sweat glands perspire, brains make thoughts. *You have to perform so people like you* is going to pop from our brains like cracking open a can of biscuit dough. But, like Gus and Deema, we can choose how much to listen to it.

> **TRY IT OUT:** If you didn't have to prove you belong, what would you be doing? What would you do more or less of? How would you participate and connect?

From Performance to Enjoyment

Jon Bon Jovi looks out on a packed room at a philanthropy conference. He's perched on a stool, holding his guitar, a microphone stand in front of him. "I'm more nervous now than I've been on stadium stages," he tells the enthusiastic audience. He gestures to the white-haired, bespectacled man sitting next to him. "But Mr. Warren Buffett and I are going to perform for you."

Buffett grins. "This has been described as a once-in-a-lifetime experience, and you'll understand why: once will be enough in a lifetime," he quips. The room erupts in laughter.

With Bon Jovi on guitar and Buffett on ukulele, the two break into a duet of Benny Goodman's "The Glory of Love." Buffett warbles the first verse, strumming and serenading the room. He and Bon Jovi swap lead vocals back and forth, and then harmonize, grinning at each other, for the finale.

Is Buffett any good? Arguably not. Does he seem to care? Not on your life. He's clearly having a ball. His love for the ukulele is all over the interwebs, playing Sinatra's "My Way" on CNN, "Red River

Valley" at the annual Berkshire Hathaway shareholders meeting, even coaxing Bill Gates into a duet of "I've Been Working on the Railroad" as they tootle around a conference in a golf cart eating Dairy Queen ice pops. Apparently, billionaires goof off and eat junk food as much as the rest of us.

This is enjoyment all the way. The enjoyment basket is deceptively simple. It's filled with pleasure and satisfaction. Here, we do things purely for the good feelings they give us. If we're used to focusing on performance, focusing on enjoyment might feel vaguely illicit. At the extreme, enjoyment isn't allowed because it doesn't contribute to productivity or progress, or it's something to be atoned for later through more work: *I went and saw a movie, so now I need to study for the equivalent amount of time.* When we're hard on ourselves, joy is suspect. When we're focused on performance, a lot of our enjoyment comes from doing things well—getting a good quarterly evaluation, turning out a gravity-defying soufflé, ripping a PR dead lift off the floor, making everyone laugh during a night out with friends. But then our enjoyment is contingent upon the outcome, or worse, other people's reactions to the outcome. Plus, if we're focused on closing our rings, we miss out on enjoying the movement of our limbs. If we're painstakingly following the recipe, we may not realize the kitchen smells amazing. If we're striving to be a scintillating conversationalist, we might miss the point of enjoying a night out with a friend.

Unpopular opinion: we don't have to be good at something to enjoy it. This took me a very long time to figure out. For example, I've finally accepted that I'm a mediocre baker. I don't know how to frost properly, and everything comes out vaguely asymmetrically. Paul Hollywood would send me home on the spot. But I love how the house smells when there's an almond cake in the oven, and remembering there's leftover banana Nutella bread on the counter has gotten me out of bed more often than I'd care to admit. So let's shout it from the rooftops: you don't have to be good at something to justify doing it. You can be mediocre at skateboarding and still feel drawn to the skate park. Sing off-key notes with your whole chest. Write cringey poetry that moves you to happy tears. Dance like a middle-aged behavioral therapist (*ahem*). Whatever your thing, *you're doing it right because you like it.*

Where is the value in not being great? Connection. It's hard to relate to experts. They're aspirational, not relatable. As the psychologist Dr. Harriet Lerner writes in *Fear and Other Uninvited Guests: Tackling the Anxiety, Fear, and Shame That Keep Us from Optimal Living and Loving,* "I am neither drawn to, nor inspired by, folks who always seem to be competent and having a good day." Struggles, on the other hand, are entirely relatable. Let someone witness you get passed on the bunny slope by a toddler with a pacifier or cut the burned parts off the chicken you just grilled.* It means you trust them and invites them to trust you in return.

Tune in to where you find pleasure, fun, or satisfaction. You may find enjoyment in type 1 fun, also called *hedonic happiness,* which is pleasurable in the moment—eating a Funfetti cupcake, comfort-watching *Love, Actually* for the fortieth time, or channeling your inner ten-year-old by coasting down a hill on your bike. Or you might find satisfying enjoyment in type 2 fun, also called *eudaimonic happiness,* which is challenging and satisfying—stacking the delicate layers of a Russian honey cake, vacuuming the living room carpet into precise diagonal lines, or the burn of biking up the hill. Home in on your personal enjoyment by asking, "What do I like about this?" aside from being good at it (or not sucking). Tune in to your senses. What beauty, textures, scents, or tastes might you savor? There is no moral judgment on what you "should" like. Do whatever makes your heart sing; remember, we're trying to get away from "should."

That said, watch out for a tendency to expect rapturous bliss. Chasing 100 percent enjoyment will let you down. Enjoyment will be mixed with other emotions—self-doubt, insecurity, some guilt. That's okay. We're trying to get away from all or nothing, anyway. A willingness to reach into the mixed bag of emotions gets us access to the good ones.

As for Gus, when he lessened monitoring how well he was performing—keeping an eye on his cool factor—and started focusing

---

* These examples are entirely hypothetical, I swear.

on having a nice time, he felt conflicted but lighter. "It's weird not to try to prove anything," he said. In fact, a few weeks later, Gus came in and reported that he and his friends had gone to a restaurant over the weekend. "They were being loud and ridiculous, and my first urge was to turn the conversation to something I could be good at, like the universal basic income pilot in our town, or a podcast I just listened to, but then I thought, *Eh, screw it*, and just let myself enjoy their company and be glad I was there." Gus smiled. "When I'm not focused on how well I'm hanging, I can hang."

TRY IT OUT: If no one would ever know how well you did, what would you try? If you couldn't measure, progress, or improve, what would you stop doing? What would you still do? What would you do more of?

Shift from All-or-Nothing Performance to Wiggle Room

But what about that performance basket? It's still there. It's still important. But even in this basket, we can separate out what we do from who we are. Dr. Patricia DiBartolo of Smith College and colleagues found that the phenomenon of "I am what I do," officially called *contingent self-worth*, comes in two flavors.

First is *success-based self-worth*, or worth contingent upon performance (e.g., How much money did I bring in this year? Did I eat clean today? Did I manage to act normal at Julie's birthday party, or was I totally weird?).

Second is *activity-based self-worth*, where worth is contingent upon how goal-oriented and productive we manage to be. When I read DiBartolo's description of activity-based self-worth, a light bulb of recognition appeared above my head. There were so many people with my problem that it had a name.

Contingent self-worth "works" when we hit it out of the park, but it emphatically does not work when we face the inevitable problems and setbacks of life, or, to steal from David Foster Wallace, when we're knee-deep in being "a fucking human being."

Let's take Pieter. Pieter came in because his reluctance to speak up at work was impacting his career. His boss, in Pieter's most recent review, told him, "You need to take more space," which made him realize he couldn't continue hiding in plain sight—people noticed him, and they noticed he was remaining silent.

One problem was that Pieter put immense pressure on himself to be impressive. He entertained fantasies of getting standing ovations at conferences. In weekly meetings, he wished for all the faces around the conference table to beam back at him with expressions of bedazzlement, their worlds rocked by whatever pearls of wisdom he had just dropped.

As a child, Pieter had been bullied for years: for being fat, for being the new kid, for being an immigrant, for being, it seemed to him, simply himself. He was chased, spat at, made fun of—he got the message over and over again that he was inadequate—not good enough to be part of the tribe no matter what he did or said.

Bullying skewers our self-worth with surgical precision because we are told to our face that we are substandard, plus we are socially rejected for it. It's exactly the opposite of the social safety our brains are looking for. With years of bullying in his history, it's no wonder Pieter, four decades later, was looking to colleagues to Uno Reverse the lessons of his childhood and assure him, *Wow, Pieter, you're actually amazing.*

But there were three things working against Pieter. First is that his ultrahigh and overly personalized performance standards not only set him up for failure but also set him up to take those perceived failures way more personally. Because Pieter set his standard for adequacy at "jaw-on-the-floor standing ovation," he felt so pressured he could barely breathe in meetings, let alone contribute a semi-erudite comment. For him, each potential comment was a referendum on his worth. No wonder he stayed silent. When he did manage to speak, the averted gazes and neutral reactions of colleagues who were passively listening or surreptitiously checking email on their phones—in other words, normal meeting behavior—made him think he was a miserable failure.

The second problem was that with contingent self-worth, our worth is never a settled question. Every performance becomes a thumbs-up or thumbs-down referendum on our value. We continually have to prove ourselves anew—prove we're good, prove we're smart, prove we're worthy, prove that we belong here, prove we're good enough, which inevitably leads to anxiety, avoidance, and burnout.

Third, Pieter's goal to be impressive, just like being liked or respected, depended on the reactions of other people. He couldn't control how people saw him. Relying on the reactions of others—or any circumstances beyond our control—puts us in a lower power position. We outsource our worth, letting others determine it. In Pieter's case, that meant everyone from childhood bullies to his colleagues in the Monday team meeting.

By contrast, when we focus on the things that we can control—being helpful, being kind, doing good work for the work's sake—that places us in a higher power position. We can't control others' reactions, but we can control our actions. And by focusing on our own actions—by shooting for excellence for the sake of excellence—the outcome is not only more likely to be good, but ironically, it's more likely to get a positive reaction.

Over several months, rather than aim for admiration, which he couldn't control, anyway, Pieter tried to shift to what he could control: being helpful, lending his knowledge to solve problems, being prepared. It felt precarious. Setting aside his shield of forced impressiveness left him feeling vulnerable, like a childhood bully would leap out from under the conference table and spit in his face. But he tried to stake less on his comments in meetings. There was a subtle but profound difference between "*I* didn't give a good answer" and "I didn't give a good *answer*." We'll talk more about this in chapter 10, "From 'Failure' to the Human Condition," but here's a start: The former is a personal indictment—a conflation of his answer and his self-worth.

The latter is still a disappointment, for sure, but the focus is squarely on the answer—it keeps a healthy separation between Pieter's actions and his worth. That particular answer might have been bad, but that doesn't mean Pieter is bad.

Over time, he found himself able to let go of some of his impression management. Again, we don't have to do a 180—little tweaks and rollbacks are sufficient. When Pieter got positive reactions, he still basked in them—who wouldn't? His standards stayed high—it's not in our DNA to slack—but he tried to reality-check his expectations. He also tried to think about himself differently, creating more wiggle room for the routine mess of life.

Remember Social Anxiety Mad Libs from *How to Be Yourself*? Here's a riff on a similar template that helped Pieter move away from the all-or-nothing choices of *I'm impressive* or *I'm a failure*. Instead of sticking with the label of I'm a [valued trait/quality] person, try this for some well-earned breathing room:

I'm a ___[valued trait/quality]___ person who sometimes ___[exception]___.

I'm a smart person who sometimes doesn't know the answer.
I'm a capable person who sometimes screws things up.
I'm a dedicated person who sometimes doesn't try my hardest.
I'm a peaceful person who sometimes loses my temper.
I'm a fun person who sometimes has a serious moment.
I'm a serious person who sometimes lets loose.
I'm a successful person who sometimes fails.
I'm a disciplined person who sometimes lets myself go.
I'm a healthy person who is sometimes unhealthy.
I'm a creative person who sometimes gets blocked.
I'm a good student who sometimes gets a low grade.
I have good judgment and sometimes make dumb decisions.
I'm a productive person who sometimes blows things off.
I'm a hard worker who procrastinates.
I'm a kind person who can advocate for myself.

I'm a good person with some regrets.
I've arrived and am still seeking.

This template moves us from the all-or-nothingness of contingent self-worth and gets us some much-needed wiggle room. Some much-needed permission. Some much-needed room to be human.

> **TRY IT OUT:** Identify examples you resonate with and/or customize the "I'm a [valued trait/quality] person who sometimes [exception]" template for your own life.

* * *

Let's take stock. Instead of one high-stakes performance basket, we have three nestled next to each other, with a tidy distribution of eggs: performance, connection, and enjoyment. Your life and values may require another—maybe a service basket or a justice basket. A visual or performing artist like Yo-Yo Ma may shift some eggs into an expression basket. But connection and enjoyment will be the cornerstones of Coming Home to Your Life. As Yo-Yo Ma reminds us, we can ask: "Am I trying to get it right? Or am I trying to find something?" Because when we shift from trying to get it right to connecting with our fellow humans and having some fun along the way, we might just find what we're looking for.

Shift 3

FROM RULES TO FLEXIBILITY

8

Rewriting the Inner Rulebook

You should be able to endure everything, to understand everything, to like everybody, to always be productive.

—Dr. Karen Horney, *Neurosis and Human Growth*, 1950

FRANCESCA LOGGED ON late to our session one Thursday. "Sorry," she said breathlessly, her image disappearing briefly from my laptop screen while she ducked down to plug in her computer charger. "I just got home from the grocery store."

Francesca's grocery runs often went long because she closely compared items for value, nutrition, and quality. Produce was time-consuming enough. Organic or local? Preportioned or whole? But her archnemesis was the floral department. Francesca loved cut flowers and easily spent forty-five minutes hovering over the bins, comparing: this one had brown edges, this one was missing a blossom. Her conscious, articulated rule? *I want to get my money's worth.* That was true. But there were also deeper, more personal rules buried in her brain, which we'll get to in a moment.

When I was in graduate school, I remember running some data and struggling with the statistical analysis. Confused, I agonized for hours. When I sheepishly showed the results to my professor, fingers crossed, my numbers were all wrong. She looked at me and said, "Ellen, you don't have to do this alone." In an instant, she articulated the rules I didn't even know were in my rulebook: *I can't ask for help. I have to do it all myself.*

In an extreme example, my client Jason told me about his estranged brother, who made his entire family go vegan and give up all fossil fuels, with no exceptions. "He says we're killing the planet," said Jason. "But his kids are tired of not being able to eat pizza or cake at their friends' birthday parties, his wife is mad because he guilts her into not flying to see her family, and everyone would love to at least take the bus rather than biking when it's raining." The rule was, *I can't hurt the environment, ever.*

All three of us had stuck to our own rules so faithfully that it ended up working against us. It cost Francesca valuable time, me a minor humiliation with a mentor, and Jason's brother the goodwill of his entire family. Our high standards had calcified into rules that made us miss the larger point.

We each have an Inner Rulebook deep inside our brains. It's not standardized—in fact, it's custom-made for each of us by important adults in our childhoods, our life experiences, and the cultural amniotic fluid we float in throughout our lifetimes.

It's important to have some rules: *Be kind. Pay your taxes. Don't be racist.* Our personal rules vary from crystal clear to faint and fuzzy, but our brains get the gist either way. Some of the rules are big—*You should always be working to improve yourself. You shouldn't hurt anyone's feelings, even by accident. If you want something done right, you have to do it yourself.* Some are small: *You should include a handwritten personalized note on every holiday card. You can't mix Play-Doh colors. This is the only way to load the dishwasher. For the love of Pete, don't wear double denim.*

Following the Inner Rulebook buys us a lot: clarity and simplicity, a reassuring sense of control, some nice achievements or admiration (or at least a reduction in criticism), and a solid sense of certainty: *This is how things should be, I'm doing it right.* Rules especially come in handy when they help us know how to behave in situations or with people we're encountering for the first time. All in all, rules are quite helpful. There's no need to throw them all out, abandon your responsibilities, and go feral at surf camp in Baja.

But any rule can backfire if it's unnecessary, rigid, arbitrary, or over-identified with our character.

Wanna do a puzzle? Here are the three rules: (1) draw four straight lines (2) that connect all nine dots (3) without picking up your pen. Go ahead and take some time to try to figure it out—it's more fun to do this experientially.

When I first saw this puzzle, I stared at it for a long time, testing out different solutions in my head. A familiar urge of perseverance—"I will dig in and do this!"—kicked in. I wanted to figure it out by myself. But I couldn't.

When I was shown the answer, I found I had inadvertently assigned myself another rule: (4) without going outside the square created by the nine dots. I had added an extra rule that was unnecessary and, crucially, worked against me. (Insert thinking-outside-the-box joke here.)

This is the nine-dot problem, first introduced by Dr. Norman Maier in 1930 in an article in the *Journal of Comparative Psychology*. The takeaway? Sometimes rules are helpful and necessary, but those of us familiar with perfectionism often add extra rules that are unnecessary and work against us.

Here's the solution, though the handle of the umbrella, or the stem of the mushroom, as it were, can be in any corner:

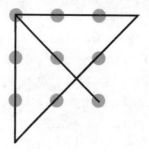

Why are we drawn to rules, even when they sometimes stab us in the back? Rules increase certainty. Anxiety, by contrast, is driven by uncertainty. Situations without clear-cut rules make us anxious because we don't know if we're doing things right or well enough. Therefore, rules, especially self-imposed rules, create order out of chaos.

But it's not just making sense of the world. Following rules helps us make sense of ourselves. Let's go back to contingent self-worth. Since we tend to measure ourselves based on our ability to meet our own high standards, following existing rules or creating highly demanding self-imposed rules gives us standards to strive for. Striving to follow challenging self-imposed rules is a way to prove ourselves. We're doing hard things acceptably; therefore, we are acceptable.

That's why we sometimes go overboard and follow the rules even when they work against us. For example, "I should be nice" works well most of the time. But does that mean we can never ask for a raise because we might make our boss uncomfortable? Or we can't yell, "Leave me alone!" at a stranger harassing us on the street? We follow the rule "be nice" regardless of the situation because it means something about our very character.

The Rules of Rules

As Xavier described his day, I could feel my energy start to ebb. Just listening to his schedule made me want to take a nap under my desk. He ticked his commitments off on his fingers as he talked: "First, I had a technique class, then I had a writing seminar, then I went to my fellowship job and had a meeting with my boss. Next, I signed out a piano practice room, and I tried to work on my homework for composition class. Now I'm here, but after this, I have two rehearsals, and at eight o'clock, I have to record a performance. Last night, I recorded a performance, too, but there were two encores, so I didn't get on the train until eleven, and I tried to grind through my email on my phone, but I fell asleep and missed my stop."

Xavier is a musical theater major at a local conservatory. Both his parents are high-achieving musicians—his mom a jazz singer, his dad a timpanist. All his life, Xavier watched them work long hours, travel for performances and workshops, put substantial energy into staying performance-ready, and devote serious time into mentoring up-and-comers climbing the ladder behind them.

"They're always loving and supportive," Xavier said of his parents, "but they definitely expect me to show up for the hustle." He explained: "Music is an unforgiving field. Jobs are won through audition, but connections often get you the audition in the first place, or other opportunities like independent shows. Summers are super important—there's an unspoken expectation that I should spend all summer at festivals and workshops."

Xavier initially came in because of a serious trichotillomania problem that left him with hard-to-hide bald spots, but we added on perfectionism treatment when he told me, "I always feel like I'm failing."

Xavier's Inner Rulebook was easy to read: *Always be productive. Don't waste time.* Like many people with rigid rules around productivity, he had carved out some preplanned escape hatches, articulating: *I should always be working, except after 9:00 p.m. on Fridays and Saturdays.* During these times, he would allow himself a 180, usually by getting high or drunk. The rest of the week, the rule hung over him. Therefore, whenever he got distracted, took a break, procrastinated, or was inefficient, he broke his rule. No wonder he felt like he was constantly failing. With no margin for error and no room to breathe, there was no way to fulfill "all," so he consistently found himself stuck at "nothing."

Rigid rules have their place. Surgeons should break sterile field 0 percent of the time. Pilots should be sober on 100 percent of their workdays. But more often, like the step-on-a-rake gag, our rigid rules smack us right in the face.

A dead-on description of rigid rules comes from Dr. Karen Horney, the pioneering psychoanalyst we met in chapter 5. Her thinking on perfectionism, which she described as "the tyranny of the shoulds," still hits like a flurry of truth bombs decades later. She puts her finger on three characteristics of rigid rules:

1. Rigid rules disregard feasibility. We aim to follow the rules whether or not they are realistic. We should know, understand, and foresee everything, even though that's not possible. We should know what to do in every situation, even without others' input or complete information. We should be able to overcome every difficulty as soon as we see it. We should take on everything we're asked to do and do it well right away, without warm-up, practice, or mistakes.

This was exactly Xavier's pickle. He didn't truly believe that he should transcend the limitations of a twenty-four-hour day and the human need for sleep, "but it kind of feels that way," he said. He often found himself wishing for more hours in the day. There was a sense that he *should* be able to do everything. Indeed, rigid rules are stronger than logic.

2. Rigid rules disregard context. Whether we were a little kid dependent on a toxic family, an unformed adult in our early twenties, or stuck in an abusive relationship, we believe we should have magically known better and done better. As Horney puts it: "I should have come out of it like a lily out of a swamp." Regardless of what we are dealing with or in how many directions we're being pulled, our outcomes and judgment should be optimal. Doing the best we can doesn't cut it.

3. Rigid rules are contradictory. Collectively, our Inner Rulebook is full of double binds. We should be deeply connected to our friends, families, and partners, yet somehow never feel hurt or annoyed by any of them. We should fully and freely express ourselves, but always control our feelings. We should be fiercely independent and a team player. We should always please everyone and not care what anyone thinks.

Last time I saw my friend Juan, he told me about a weekend trip his family took to Cape Cod with two other families. The Saturday-afternoon sky was blue and full of puffy clouds, and Juan felt inspired. He convinced everyone they should have an impromptu New England clambake on the beach.

They totally winged it. Juan vaguely remembered that a clambake involves a fire in a shallow pit and, somehow, seaweed. Someone went grocery shopping while he and the others experimented, dug the pit, gathered rocks and wood, lined it with seaweed, and built the fire. It didn't work at first, and they had to start over, so around 9:00 p.m., everybody had ice cream for dinner and they put the kids to bed. But they kept working on it, and around 1:00 a.m., the adults feasted on clambake, drank wine, and sang songs under the stars. The next morning, the kids ate corn, potatoes, and sausage for breakfast while running on the beach, the wind in their hair.

I remember listening to Juan's story with my eyebrows up to my hairline. If I had decided to have a clambake, I would have researched it beforehand, applied for a beach fire permit, packed all the necessary ingredients, and followed directions from a reputable how-to article. It would likely have turned out well, in a timely manner. I probably would have timed it to coincide with the sunset, too.

Both methods would yield a clambake with friends. Does that mean my way is the right way? Maybe. But maybe not. I would have turned out a clambake in time for dinner, but I would have missed out on the earned confidence that comes from solving problems on the fly. I would have missed out on the bonding that happens when you're in a pickle with friends. I would have missed out on the experiential reminder that things usually turn out okay.

There are also personal and social costs to insisting on the Right Way. When Susanna hosts a dinner gathering, it is inevitably delicious, beautifully presented, and garners lots of compliments. It takes a lot of time and preparation, so her husband regularly offers to help, but he puts the spices back in the wrong order, his vegetable chopping isn't quite right, and they both get frustrated because Susanna can't articulate her gut-level vision and he can't read her mind. But when she turns down his offers of help, getting all the dishes to the table on time is massively stressful. She's always managed to pull it off, but over the years, it's gotten lonely doing it by herself.

Our rulebooks tell us there is a right and a wrong way to do things. Curiously, the "right way" varies from person to person (spoiler: *our way is always the right way*). There are a million different Right Ways to set the table, practice good hygiene, make coffee, host a party, get an education, raise children, or (drumroll) live a life, which means our individual Inner Rulebooks can be quite arbitrary, despite each insisting they know the golden path.

Why "Good Enough" Feels Wrong

If our Inner Rulebook has all these flaws, why do we follow it? Why don't we ignore the stupid rules, like out-of-date laws no one's bothered to repeal?* Because it's personal. Following our rules means something about our character. *You* should *do your best. You* should *take pride in your appearance. You* should *keep your promises.* Indeed, when we fulfill our rules, they affirm us as a person.

Dr. Roz Shafran of University College London, whose definition of clinical perfectionism forms the basis of this book, along with her collaborators Drs. Zafra Cooper and Christopher Fairburn, assert that clinical perfectionism is "maintained by the biased evaluation of the pursuit and achievement of personally demanding standards." In our conversation, Dr. Shafran remembered giving a talk and asking the audience, "Who would, given the choice, take the easy way out?"

---

* Like the Missouri law that forbids driving on the highway with an uncaged bear in your car. Also, single ladies take note: no parachuting for you on Sundays in Florida.

Most hands went up. Then she asked, "Who would rather do it the hard way?" A few hands went up. She asked each of them to elaborate. "It's the pleasure you get; it means more than if it's handed to you on a platter," said one. Another: "There's a satisfaction in having earned a reward." A third: "It's taking pride in a hard day's work."

A common piece of advice to those of us with perfectionism is "Don't let perfect be the enemy of good." We're told to stop when things are "good enough." But "good enough" doesn't resonate when it's something from which we derive our value. That's why when clients perceive I'm asking them to lower their standards, it goes over about as well as asking them to pull out their toenails. When I first started learning to treat perfectionism, I suggested to one of my clients that he have an 80 percent productive day, which didn't land at all. I might as well have proposed casual shoplifting.

Likewise, Jamila, our overachiever from chapter 1, resisted the idea of a "good enough" contribution to her group project. For her, performance reflected effort, which in turn reflected her moral character. For Jamila, intense effort generally yielded good results, which in turn meant *she* was good. In retrospect, I get it. I know for me, settling for "good enough" work or social behavior feels like settling for a "good enough" brake job on my car.

What's more, we see control, self-regulation, or stress as evidence that we're striving hard enough. There may be a specific process, a level of intensity or effort that reflects on us personally. "Success" includes how hard did I try, how much effort did I expend, how disciplined was I? How many times did I get distracted, end up scrolling TikTok, or stare idly into the middle distance?

Likewise, sometimes we overidentify with the adverse consequences of our efforts, taking them as evidence that our pursuit is sufficiently demanding. The exhaustion is exhilarating; our stress indicates success. It's when getting only four hours of sleep per night is evidence that we're doing our best or not showering for a week means we're serious about midterms. My client Jonathan worked for forty-four hours straight on a report to prove to himself that he had done it justice. But fast-forward a few years. We end up chronically frazzled, sleep-deprived, and lonely. Most of my clients who struggle with perfectionism come in for depression, burnout, social isolation, or relationship problems, a cumulative effect of long-term balls-to-the-wall striving.

So What Do I Do Now?

Thankfully, we don't have to throw the Inner Rulebook out the window and start from scratch, like a medieval monk starting over on an illuminated manuscript with a one-haired brush. Dr. Shafran reminds us that questioning the rules isn't about lowering our standards or betraying our values. Instead, as she says, "it's about giving back control." Editing the Inner Rulebook allows us to have choices rather than merely complying and to be flexible rather than obligated. Sound good? Let's give our Inner Rulebooks a makeover.

After she plugged in her laptop, Francesca told me about her latest tangle with perfectionism. Her twin sons' birthday party was coming up; Francesca simultaneously loved hosting parties—"I really should have been an event planner"—and dreaded them because she got obsessive in both preparation and execution. She told me, "I've walked into parties where the parents didn't do *anything*, and I was like, 'Oh, okay, this is how they do things.' And that's fine, but that's not how *I* do things.

"I spent way too long online last night," she continued. "But I was getting decorations on Etsy, and I wanted to make sure they would match the cake, so I looked at a million different banners and centerpieces. And then I was ordering stuff for goody bags, and I wanted to get the right stickers for each kid. I don't want anyone to be disappointed."

For some of us, customizing goody bags to each kid's personality might seem as extra as wearing a ball gown to work, but for Francesca, it felt like the right thing to do. But she had decided it was costing her too much—by clicking around on Etsy from after dinner until 1:00 a.m., she missed out on reading bedtime stories to her boys and yawned her way through the next day. "I can't keep this up," she said.

Her actions were fulfilling a rule—we just had to figure out what the rule was.

For Francesca, and for all of us, the first step in revision is to **notice and name the rules**. This may be easy. Look for driving thoughts with definitive words like *should, always, never, have to, everyone, must*. It's what the legendary psychologist Dr. Albert Ellis dubbed "musturbation."* *I must overcome any challenge or obstacle. I should optimize time and be as efficient as possible. I have to be calm and centered in every situation. I should always live my best life. I have to meet everyone's needs. Everyone should like me.*

But sometimes naming the rule isn't so easy. Thankfully, we can follow the breadcrumb trail of strong emotion to find our rules. They are tied to the emotional fundamentals of life: feeling good about ourselves, avoiding feeling bad about ourselves, and staying in good standing with our fellow humans.

To find rules that are meant to preserve feeling good about yourself, tune in to when you feel extra sure you're doing things right. When do you feel ultra-confident or a little self-righteous? Francesca's sense of *That's not how I do things* leads us to *I have to be impressive* or *I must win*. Tapping into a feeling of superiority when someone admires your color-coded planner might lead to *I should always be on top of everything*. Feeling super-insistent and a little prideful that you don't need any help building those raised beds in your backyard leads to *I have to do things myself*.

Also tune in to where you feel judgmental or concerned. Where are *other* people not doing it "right"? Karim remembers being genuinely concerned for friends in college who blew off studying to play video games during the week and uncovered a rule of *You should always be doing something productive*.

For avoiding feeling bad about ourselves, tune in to where you feel resentful or obligated. Where do you feel trapped into doing the generic "right thing"? Jenna lost interest in a highly recommended book three chapters in and felt resentful as she slogged through to the end:

---

* The uniquely Ellis remedy? "Stop shoulding on yourself."

I have to finish what I start. Isaac went cafeteria-tray sledding with his friends for two hours but then felt obligated to study for two extra hours: *I have to make up for being "indulgent."* Feeling resentful that your partner didn't get you what you wanted for your birthday even though you never mentioned it might uncover *My partner should be able to read my mind.*

For staying in good standing with your fellow humans, tune in to where you feel like you're failing or falling behind. Where are you doing things wrong? *I need to get rid of these love handles—my body isn't what it should be. I should have more money saved by now—I have to keep up.*

You may not think any of these rules consciously, but you definitely feel them, which serves us well when we're trying to notice and name them. For Francesca, tuning in to the feelings that drove spending forty-five minutes comparing flowers at the grocery store yielded the three overarching rules I promised you at the beginning of the chapter: *I can't make mistakes, I have to be my best,* and *I have to make everyone happy.*

Noticing and naming the rules creates space, perspective, and, most importantly, options. Once the rule is articulated, we decide whether or not to comply. The rules *feel* obligatory, but we always have a choice. More on this shortly, but sometimes we'll follow the rule because it's what we want and value, and sometimes we'll choose to ignore it because it's inconsistent with what's truly important to us.

Once you've articulated your rule, notice what happens when you follow it. **What does the rule buy you, and what does it cost you?**

Picture this on a Jumbotron: *Even the costliest rule buys you something.* Honor that your rules have gotten you many good things. You wouldn't have these rules if they hadn't worked extraordinarily well at some point in your life. For me, *I have to do it all myself* helped make me capable and resourceful. But when I've applied the rule automatically, it hindered me by sending a message of "I don't need you" to people who love me, not to mention taking up more time than I'd prefer to think about.

For Francesca, following the rules of *I can't make mistakes*, *I have to be my best*, and *I have to make everyone happy*, whether she was grocery shopping, hosting a party, or simply living her life, bought her social safety: her brain was trying to maintain harmony by being so good she couldn't be criticized. No wonder she kept it up.

The rules paid off, but also cost her. Browsing Etsy past midnight for the exact right decorations wiped out her evening, not to mention her energy levels the next day. Comparing dahlias at the grocery store ate up precious time and made her late for appointments. Long term, her rules kept her feeling inadequate and anxious because she was failing to live up to impossible expectations. She never got the chance to learn that "flawlessly optimized" wasn't the same as "totally sufficient." In more and more situations, the cons had outgrown the pros.

Consult your values—what's meaningful and important to you? Remember the values discussion from chapter 6? Rather than just following the rules, let's focus on doing what matters to you. As Karen Horney writes, "The shoulds . . . lack the moral seriousness of genuine ideals." Therefore, instead of following the shoulds, focus on being the person you want to be, on spending your time on what's important to you, rather than a generic idea of what is correct.

Gentle reminder: following your values might not feel good. Escaping the silken trap of the Inner Rulebook is hard. Fear of the consequences of not following the Inner Rulebook can stir up a lot of emotion around feared consequences: doing things wrong, making a mistake, disapproval, rejection, criticism, letting someone down.

For example, Alejandro followed his values of being active and social by lifting weights with his buddy Nathan. But on his way to the gym, he found himself getting a little grumpy, thinking about his old classic rule: *I should be studying*. But he knew if he spent those two hours in front of a laptop, he would have ended up procrastinating, anyway. He was caught in a no-win liminal space, stuck between feeling guilty and overwhelmed.

For me, on the way home from an early-morning walk with a friend, I passed my local bookstore, which was open (genius—all bookstores should open at 7:00 a.m.). My Inner Rulebook automatically told me

I really should get home and start my workday—*Always be productive.* But my values of self-care, exploring, doing interesting things, not to mention a belief that books are important, all hovered around me. I went in, but I admit it didn't feel good. It felt vaguely wrong, and I was sad that I couldn't enjoy it more. But I knew if I had made a beeline for home, I'd have felt frustrated with myself for skipping out. It was damned if I do, damned if I don't.

Expect this flavor of no-win situation at first. But as I tell my clients: if you're going to feel uncomfortable either way, you might as well feel uncomfortable while following your values.

This discovery was magical for Stevie, who usually found himself guiltily choosing work over his wife and nine-year-old because his work anxiety was so loud and insistent. Once he realized that his loud metaphorical radio would broadcast *You have to prove yourself* regardless of what he did, he experimented with prioritizing parent-teacher conferences and spent the day with his wife on her birthday rather than just buying her a big guilt-driven present. The loud radio was still there, but he was living his values of being present for family rather than letting the broadcast of work anxiety control him. Indeed, living a workable and flexible life isn't always comfortable, but it is better than living under the dictatorial regime of the Inner Rulebook.

Focus on what works given the context. Remember how the Inner Rulebook disregards context and feasibility? Let's take all those into account. *Context* is the circumstances or situation—distant or recent—that set the stage for the present moment, including your own self, history, and mindset. *Feasibility*, along with its more official cousin *workability*, means what works given the context, your goals, and your values. Both context and workability vary over time and from situation to situation.

Context and workability might be external: you'd adjust your expectations of what was workable to have for dinner in the context of a lazy Sunday with lots of time to cook versus a forty-five-minute airport layover. Context and workability can also be internal: the context of sleeping eight hours and feeling like a million bucks will make one kind of workout feasible while the context of having a sprained ankle calls for another (read: none at all). Apropos to this entire book, in the context of psychological flexibility, it's workable to observe our worries with a compassionate curiosity rather than stressing about them as problems to be solved.

Therefore, rather than rigidly following our Inner Rulebook, we can ask, *What would work for my goals and values, given this context?* The goal is to be functional and flexible, to adapt to *what is* rather than "what should be" from our rulebooks.

For example, *Always be polite* might work in most contexts, but not when we're getting scammed, harassed, or taken advantage of. *Be a good mom* could include making our own baby food and breastfeeding for a year in a certain set of life circumstances, but in the context of untreated addiction and living on the streets might mean giving our baby up. We might think that eating thirty hot dogs in ten minutes is a sign that something is wrong, but in the context of a state fair hot dog-eating contest with scholarship money as the prize, it makes more sense.

If you're not sure what might be workable, turn to your trusted family and friends. If you are contending with *Always be working*, survey your work besties about how many vacation days they take each year and to what extent they join Zoom meetings or check email during those vacation days. To give herself more information about *Make everyone happy*, Francesca asked her friends how often they would make custom dinners for each of their kids.

The goal is not to settle on a new rule like *I will rehearse my presentations three times just like my colleague Dilshad instead of over and over until I feel ready* or *The kids need to eat only what I cook for them like Darlene does with her kids* but to see a fuller range and variability. Like Juan and I and our clambakes, there is huge flexibility of what is "right." The goal is discovery: discovery that there is a range of responses, values, and practices, all of which open you up to the possibility of experimenting with doing what works given your goals and values.

Again, the question isn't "Did I follow the rule?" Instead, experiment with: "What works, for this situation, given what's important to me?"

Let's put it all together and **test-drive your new action**. We're not going to know what works—what takes context, workability, goals, and values into account—until we try it out. This is called a *behavioral experiment* and is the favorite clinical technique of Dr. Shafran. Behavioral experiments are exactly what they sound like: experimenting with a new behavior.

Our thoughts and behavior can be independent from each other. Indeed, who among us has not thought, *I should really go to bed*, and continued to scroll through our phone at midnight? Or thought, *I really shouldn't eat all these fries*, as we dig in the bottom of the bag for the bonus fries? The take-home: we can have a thought and act differently. Therefore, we can think, *No one wants to hear what I have to say*, but then speak up in a meeting. We can think, *If I don't give my kid advice on his English project, he'll never get into college*, and then stay quiet until he asks for our help.

We can do the same with the rules. We can think, *I have to lose weight before I start dating again*, notice, "Hey, there's the Inner Rulebook," and then go on a date. Francesca can think, *I have to make everyone happy*, and notice, "Oh, there's that thing my brain does," and then buy one giant variety pack of stickers for the goody bags, trust she'll be able to respond on the fly in the unlikely event that getting trains instead of construction vehicles becomes a problem, and attend to her kids' bedtime routine and going to bed on time herself.

For years, in instances when I was clearly struggling—to analyze data for a professor, to zip up my wet suit, to rest even though I had a fever—my automatic reaction was to politely refuse offers of help: "No, I'm good." "It's okay, I got this." Now, I try to notice my knee-jerk urge to do everything myself as it arises. I'll think, *Here's that* I have to do it all myself *rule*. And then, sometimes I'll decline, but sometimes I'll say, "Yes, I'd love a hand—thanks for offering."

In sum, mindfully notice thoughts and feelings in the present moment while consciously selecting behaviors that work in line with your goals and personal values. It seems like a lot, but it boils down to doing what works and what matters for you.

* * *

How to evaluate the outcome of your behavioral experiment? Ask yourself, "Did my test drive bring me closer to the life I want to live? To being the person I want to be?" That's different from asking, "How did I feel?" Part of living your values is being willing to feel doubt, anxiety, or other negative emotions in order to live a meaningful life. Old rules don't like to be bent or broken. It may feel weird to do something different, but *did it work*, given the context?

For example, Elliot had a rule of *Don't stick out—the nail that sticks up gets hammered down* but experimented with attending a protest given his value of social justice and the context of recent political events. Molly had a rule of *Take care of everybody else* but experimented with coming to therapy and letting me take care of her because she had descended into unworkable burnout. Jessie had a rule of *Respect your elders* but decided to ask her grandmother not to refer to her friends by their race, à la "the nice Mexican girl."

As for Xavier, he decided to test-drive what it might mean to be flexible on his subway ride home. Over several weeks, sometimes he ground through his email at 11:00 p.m. on the train because it was what worked—he had a deadline coming up, his boss was awaiting a reply—but sometimes, there was nothing pressing at hand, and he just put on a playlist he loved. The first time he listened to music on the train instead of answering work emails felt like he was breaking a rule because, in fact, he was, but he liked the idea of deciding for himself. Next, he test-drove taking a walk after lunch some days. It felt wrong at first, like he was wasting precious time, but one beautiful spring day, he thoroughly enjoyed it. Now, he says, "Sometimes it's the best part of my day." One Thursday, instead of buying another espresso, he allowed himself to take a nap in a big cushy chair in the library and realized it was exactly what he needed.

So: notice and name the rules, weigh the pros and cons of the rules, bring in your values, focus on workability in different contexts, and test-drive new behaviors. After all this, we'll still be conscientious. We'll still expect a lot of ourselves. Dare I say, we'll still be perfectionistic. But rather than unnecessary, rigid, arbitrary, and overidentified rules, we'll be more flexible. We'll be willing to tolerate some discomfort in the name of workability and values. We can hold our rules lightly, follow them if that's what works, or do something else if *that's* what works.

As for Francesca, for her twins' birthday party, she consulted her values to see what was important and meaningful to her. She decided it was important to showcase her artsy-crafty skills, but more than that, she wanted to celebrate her boys' sixth birthday and bring her community together.

When it came time to test-drive *What would work, given this context?* at the party—an outdoor event at a local pick-your-own pumpkin patch—Francesca got more of a road test than she bargained for. It was a windy day, and as Francesca tried to set up under the picnic shelter, she had to jettison plan after carefully laid plan. She reported to me the next Thursday, "The confetti blew off the table immediately, all over the parking lot. I had to put rocks—dirty rocks!—on the corners of the tablecloth to weigh it down, I couldn't hang up the HAPPY BIRTHDAY sign, and the balloons were totally tangled. But you know what? I assigned the kids the job of looking for rocks for the tablecloth, and when the napkins blew away, they all ran and picked them up. They loved being helpful. It made them so happy." The kicker, she said, was that in the past, she would have stayed with the cake table making sure everything looked right, but this year, she said, "I went on the hayride, and the boys were thrilled. They cheered, 'Yay! Mommy's here!'"

Why We Turn Fun into a Chore

CLEANING OUT HIS basement, Ben discovered his old art supply toolbox from high school under some lawn furniture. As if in the Hogwarts library, he held it in both hands and blew off the dust. He opened it to reveal long-forgotten pastels, charcoal, and Faber-Castell pencils. *I'd love to get back into drawing,* he thought, remembering happy lunch periods in the high school art room, intently working on portraits of friends or still lifes of his Converse sneakers.

But then, without even realizing it, a snowball of to-dos rolled through his head. *Okay,* he thought. *I should find some drawing exercises to do. Maybe there's a fifteen-minute-a-day routine online. And I need a drafting table or an easel. I'll have to look on Craigslist. And a class—I should take a figure drawing class. I think I have some availability on Wednesdays.* In a split second, his brain had turned a happy discovery into a series of chores.

When I recount Ben's anonymized story to other clients struggling with perfectionism, they nod in recognition. "Oh my gosh, yes," said Camila. "I was on Instagram and I saw a post of a rainbow fridge— when you pre-chop vegetables and put them in Mason jars and arrange them in rainbow order on a shelf in your fridge—and I caught myself thinking, *Ugh, now I have to make my fridge look like that, too.*" She slapped the table between us for emphasis. "And I don't even meal prep!"

I recognize this, too; the last time I was invited to a wedding, my mind naturally turned to following the rules. What was I "supposed" to wear to a winter wedding in Los Angeles? What would be the "most appropriate" gift to give from the registry, and what was the "right" price point to aim for given my relationship to the groom? I wasn't stressed; I wasn't anxious. My brain just naturally floated to how to do it "appropriately."

Demand Sensitivity

What Ben, Camila, and I (and perhaps you) experience is so common it has a name: *demand sensitivity*, which is a heightened sensitivity to perceived requests or demands, both internal and external. This is where we see our superpower of conscientiousness outgrow its metaphorical flowerpot. The "shoulds" of life call out to us. We orient toward rules and tasks. We are quick to zero in on perceived duties and responsibilities.

This manifests as interpreting neutral comments and situations as demands. The tendency is different from thoughtfulness, as it includes a subtle undertow of "should." We all know (or are) someone who, when a family member wonders aloud where their phone is, starts scanning the kitchen for it. We notice a library book in our friend's car and think we should offer to return it since we're headed to the library tomorrow. Our colleague asks the whole room how to spell *minuscule*, and we're the one to look it up. Just the other day, I wondered out loud about a psychology licensing requirement in front of a colleague, and she took it upon herself to look it up and send it to me. It was kind and considerate, but I also felt bad that she had interpreted my thinking aloud as an assignment.

Our sensitivity to demands makes life both easier and harder. It's easier because it creates certainty—we orient toward what we "should" be doing, which is often something helpful or appropriate. But it also makes life harder; because our conscientiousness is overdeveloped, we end up generating a lot of duties and responsibilities for ourselves, and that in turn can make life feel like a people-pleasing grind.

For example, recently I got an offer to contribute to a video lecture series and mused out loud to my own therapist: "I should probably do it. It's a good opportunity." He looked at me and said, "Are you trying to decide whether or not to do it, or do you feel like you have to do it and you're trying to figure out how to make it work?" There was a long pause. "The latter," I admitted.

He had picked up on the same magic word I listen for to pinpoint demand sensitivity. It comes up regularly, loudly, and unmistakably like a chirping smoke detector low on batteries: *should*. Remember Dr. Karen Horney's description of perfectionism: the "tyranny of the shoulds." We go to the party not because it looks fun and we want to check it out but because we should: it's the right thing to do, we don't want to let the host down, or "it would be good" for us to be more social. That same word sneaks in throughout the day: we should get the salad, not the fries. We should sign up to help at the school bake sale. We should stay on top of our email. But then what happens?

Wants into Shoulds

When there is only room for shoulds, there is no room for wants. Here's the kicker: Because *should* is what our brains gravitate toward, we therefore turn our wants into shoulds. As Dr. Allan Mallinger, a now-retired psychiatry professor from the University of California, San Diego School of Medicine, states in his underappreciated 1982 paper on the topic, we turn "the volitional into the obligatory." As I read his paper, I felt a light bulb above my head begin to glow. Turning the volitional into the obligatory was exactly what Ben was doing as his shoulds about art lessons and exercises ricocheted through his head after discovering his old art supply bin.

I recognize this in my life: when I stumble across a movie I'd like to see or a book I'd like to read, I'll jot it down on a running list I have on my laptop. But then it's part of a list. And my life is already full of lists of things I have to do, from the clinic's electronic medical record task list to my grocery list to my calendar. Don't even get me started on email, a.k.a. a to-do list other people make for you, which I am guiltily terrible at keeping on top of. When I pick up the book at the local library and place it on top of the teetering pile next to my desk, or I sit down to queue up a movie on Netflix, it feels like an assignment. And then I lose interest completely.

Many of us do this because, directly or indirectly, we've learned to put our wants and needs on the back burner. Maybe we were taught that indulging in wants was just that: indulgent. Or we were taught to "be strong," which was at least partially conflated with how thoroughly we denied ourselves. Or we were trying to avoid others' criticism by scoping out the rules and following them. We figured out what was expected of us so as not to do anything wrong.

No matter the cause, our "want" muscles stayed underdeveloped, which, despite our people-pleasing, contributes to feeling isolated or lonesome. When I talked to Dr. Mallinger, he noted that we "feel easily influenced by the force fields of other people" and therefore have to keep our distance.

In some cases, we don't even know what we want. My septuagenarian client Dorothy was expected to take care of her three younger sisters throughout her childhood. There was no room for her girlhood wants or, later, her adult wants—she had taking-care-of-others duties to fulfill. Likewise, my twentysomething client Eleanor learned early that her father's wants and needs were the only ones that mattered in her family. She watched her mother subsume her life within his and followed suit. She realized something was off when, in college, she went clothes shopping on her own for the first time and, standing in front of a rack of shirts, had no idea what she liked.

Alternatively, we do know what we like and want, but since "Because I want to" or even "Because it would help me be happy, supported, or fulfilled" isn't a sufficient reason, like Ben with his art box, we turn the "want" into a chore. As Mallinger said, there's a "chaos associated with autonomy and doing what you want to do." It's not safe to say "I want to," so we change it to "I have to": volition to obligation.

Demand Resistance, a.k.a. Compliance Defiance

Sometimes it stops there. We turn "want to" into "have to," and things simply become less fun. But demand sensitivity often morphs into something even thornier: *demand resistance,* which is a negative, defiant opposition to perceived demands.

As our "have to" pile grows, we start to feel resentful, even if the task was something we initially wanted to do. We start to approach both our shoulds and wants with indignation. It takes on the feeling of a burden. We feel coerced.

And then? We balk. We procrastinate. We kick the can down the road. We say we don't have time. And then we get annoyed at ourselves: "This isn't even hard!" "What is wrong with me?" We call ourselves *lazy, disorganized, unmotivated, mentally ill.* It makes no sense why it took two weeks to reply to our friend's text, six weeks to answer an email, or literally a year to accept our doctor's advice that our body can't deal with dairy and we really need to stop eating cheese, not that I've ever experienced any of those things.

But it does make sense; it's demand resistance. All work and no play makes anyone a resentful human. After fulfilling demands—*I have to finish this project by 5:00 p.m., I should eat this broccoli, I have to get through this pile of mail, I have to call the dentist, I have to find the packing tape so I can return that Zappos box, I should meditate because I'm doing that thirty-day challenge*—we find ourselves swiping mindlessly through TikTok as we say out loud, "I should really go to bed."* With demand resistance, any whiff of the word *should* makes our brains dig in their heels.

---

* Not going to bed is so common it has a name: *bedtime procrastination.* Jasper was one of my early clients, back when I was still in training. I remember him because I felt so ineffective. Among other challenges, Jasper couldn't go to bed. He found himself unable to log off or turn off the TV, even when he was exhausted and desperately wanted to turn in. One week, he reported that he caught himself thinking, *I've got to go to bed,* and then promptly signed into AOL Instant Messenger (ah, the mid-2000s). In hindsight, I realize it was the "I've *got* to" that kept him in front of the screen.

And that's just when we resist our own demands. When we resist demands from others, it gets more complicated. No one likes to be given orders. No one wants to feel taken advantage of or bossed around. But with demand resistance, even though we logically know a task isn't out of line, it still rankles us. We *feel* put upon. Mallinger confirmed, "It feels so organic to the person, like gagging on it when there's something they're supposed to do, even if it's something they initially want to do."

When the demand is from a boss or partner, the problem gets supersized. We feel like we can't refuse outright, either because we're getting a paycheck or because we love each other, so instead, we resist by getting passive-aggressive. It's passive because even if we could put our finger on it, we're not exactly allowed to announce, "I'm resisting you to feel some autonomy," but it's aggressive because our actions are driven by a sense of resentment.

Then our grumpy shadow side comes out. If we live with another conscientious person, we might wait it out, because eventually, they'll just do it themselves. If we can't get out of it, we drag our feet. We criticize them. We play it off. "I was going to do the dishes—why are you so impatient?" Then, when we do it, we do it just well enough to be beyond reproach. "Lay off," we say. "I did it—isn't that what you wanted?" But we toss in a subtle twist of resentment. Maybe we're still hosing off the back deck when the dinner guests show up. Maybe we never write those thank-you notes not because we're too busy but because it feels like they're expected. Maybe we'll pull an all-nighter and blame it on the boss rather than our own procrastination. We'll wait until the last minute to buy a present and then spin an intellectual manifesto about how wedding anniversaries are a corporate invention that support the jewelry industry because we need an explanation for resistance that feels inexplicable.

Our resistance bites us in the butt. Jeanie and her boyfriend hadn't had sex for months. She "wanted to want to," but whenever the possibility arose,* she would get stressed and feel pressured, which didn't

---

* Pun 100 percent intended.

exactly set the stage for romance. Her boyfriend was understanding and supportive, but admitted he was getting frustrated. She was as bewildered as he was. "I love him. I trust him. I don't know what's wrong with me."

Why on earth do we do this? The answer: to have a say. Our resistance speaks loud and clear. When we feel like we have to comply with everything, resistance feels like choice, autonomy, and agency. As Mallinger says, "I oppose; therefore, I am."

If we're steeped in demand sensitivity that's morphed into demand resistance, the only way not to feel like we're being exploited, pressured, or controlled is to resist, even if it consists of still being in the shower when the dinner guests arrive, making our boss's hair stand on end by waiting until the last minute to start a work project, or endangering our relationship with a monthslong dry spell. As Mallinger confirmed, "You have to assume if someone is stubbornly oppositional, they are highly demand sensitive."

What can we do about it? Dr. Mallinger notes that demand resistance is one of the most difficult things to change in the quest to be less hard on ourselves. Shoulds, like that '80s Chicago song, are a hard habit to break. But we're good at doing hard things, remember? So let's give it a shot. Our lives and relationships are worth it.

Dare to Be Unproductive

Those of us who are hard on ourselves often feel guilty or dysphoric when we're not doing something goal- or improvement-driven. Our Inner Rulebooks whisper, "I should always be productive," or "I should always be improving," or "Don't waste time." When we flop in front of Netflix after a long day, our Inner Rulebooks reason we "should" watch a documentary. Demand sensitivity is in high gear when we try to slog through a history of the Taliban because we should really know more about modern history.

So. Dare to be unproductive. It's less about the activity and more about: What looks interesting? Where does your mind keep wandering to? When you find yourself with the urge to be productive with your leisure time, instead ask yourself what makes your Spidey sense tingle: *Avengers: Endgame*? Finally getting Korean corn dogs with the friend you've been too busy to connect with? Do you keep glancing at the latest Emily Henry book? We're swapping the filter of "What would be correct?" for "What looks fun/cool/interesting?" Simply put: *What do I want? What do I need?*

Pro tip: You may find yourself justifying non-productivity as productivity at first. This is totally fine because you're still allowing yourself your wants, even if dressed in "should" clothing. It is 100 percent okay to rationalize reading a Beverly Jenkins novel as stealth productivity because "I should relax." Please do justify an evening being stupid with your roommates as "It's good for our friendship" or watching a gross-out comedy as "This balances me out."

When we first started working on Alejandro's depression, we employed *behavioral activation*, which is just psychology speak for doing stuff you enjoy. Alejandro loved going to the skate park but hadn't been in months because "I should be studying." But once it was an assignment, sanctioned as part of therapy, it became permissible, and he went every week. Again, if your brain has to justify fun and relaxation as "good for you" or "being flexible," no problem—you're still having fun and relaxing.

But after some experience daring to be unproductive, you may also find yourself thinking, *I want to do this, so it's inherently okay.* Indeed, attending to needs and wants, assuming you're not murdering baby seals or the like, is important and correct because you enjoy it. Let's say that again: your needs and wants are important for no other reason than you need and like them.*

There is indeed something unsettling about autonomy, a certain

---

* Does this mean your needs and wants are more important that other people's? Not necessarily. Be flexible within your situation. Your need for sleep will get overruled when you have a newborn but can be heeded when you told yourself you'd go to 6:00 A.M. yoga but wake up with a headache. You might overrule your preference for peace and quiet for your friend's once-in-a-lifetime bachelorette party, but heed it when she wants to go clubbing on a random Tuesday.

precariousness in doing what we want. At first, it might feel illegal to state a preference when our friend asks where we want to grab dinner, to rip open the Oreos in the car on the way home from the grocery store, or sketch our Converses with our rediscovered art supplies simply because it's fun, no lesson or improvement required.

> **TRY IT OUT:** Tune in to what looks interesting, cool, or tempting. What are you not supposed to do because it's unproductive or pointless? What happens if you try it, anyway? Make room for all resulting feelings.

Reconnect with Your Values

Maybe letting yourself be unproductive isn't the problem. Maybe too much time is being spent being unproductive because of demand resistance and resulting procrastination. So let's thread the mind-bending needle that is demand resistance. Sometimes we resist things we don't want to do but are necessary evils—washing the dishes, returning phone calls, any task that is part of our literal job. And sometimes we resist things that we initially wanted to do, but we've twisted them into a chore and now are balking.

For example, I shamefully neglect my email, mostly due to demand resistance. When I think, *I should really keep on top of my email*, or *I need to get through my inbox*, I'd have more luck trying to move the Hoover Dam. But when I reframe it and think about it as connecting or communicating with the individual people on the other end of those subject lines, my resistance loosens. It feels like a choice I'm making—I want to get back to them because those individual people are important to me.

Other examples might include washing the dishes because you value contributing to your household, returning phone calls because it's important to you to be reliable, or, in the case of Jeanie, being neutrally open to cuddling with her partner, with the option to stop at any time, because feeling close to him is important to her and wherever it leads might be fun. Listen closely and we can hear the quietly reverberating echoes of Dr. Michael Twohig from chapter 6: "Run toward what you're interested in, what you think you'll like, what is meaningful, and what's in line with your values."

Super-important asterisk: We can't fake this. We're too smart to gaslight ourselves into believing that a "have to" is now—ta-da!—a want. "Want," when it stems from our values, is inherently a freely chosen, intuitive, personal, subjective gut reaction. As Dr. Clarissa Ong describes, we'll know we're at "want" because "the quality of the experience will shift" in a way we can't reason or analyze our way into.

Another super-important asterisk: Will you suddenly like everything you're doing? Will you race toward aversive chores, stay in a job that exploits you, or smile through a relationship where you're being treated poorly? Big honkin' no. As Dr. Mallinger writes, when you feel internal or external pressure, "the decision to comply or not is entirely yours."

I apply this to the actual wants that my brain twists into chores. Reading, for example. I love reading and always have. Each of the books in the foot-high stack next to my desk started as excitement: *Ooh, that looks super cool!* But thanks to demand sensitivity and resistance, the stack has become a chore—layer after layer of sedimentary deposits to sift through. This is where some playfulness and curiosity and not taking myself so seriously come in—I can tap into the initial excitement that got buried under a layer of shoulds. *Ooh, what would I like? What looks cool?* Will I magic my way into reading the whole stack top to bottom? No. That's not the point. I will read what I'm drawn to and let the rest be.

The larger point is, as Dr. Mallinger writes, "Don't let the ownership of your life slip away."

TRY IT OUT: Identify a task, event, or interaction you are inexplicably resisting. What part of it might you find interesting? What is cool, meaningful, or important about it? Reflect on whether and how this changes your willingness to approach it.

Shift 4

MISTAKES: FROM HOLDING ON TO LETTING GO

10

From "Failure" to
the Human Condition
Releasing Past Mistakes

I'VE NEVER TOLD anyone this before."

At work, whenever I hear this phrase, especially when it's paired with welling tears or averted eyes, I gear up for anything: an admission of addiction relapse, a past sexual assault, a confession that they have feelings for me.* But way more often, it's not at all what I expect.

Văn confessed that in the last few days of his final semester of college, a kind sociology teaching assistant gave him a provisional passing grade so Văn could take part in the graduation ceremony, with the promise that Văn would hand in his final paper the next week. Văn collected his diploma and never turned in the paper, a betrayal that has shamed him for two decades.

Brigita carried the shame of a no-win situation. Years ago, Brigita had an out-of-town friend visit her to celebrate her birthday. But Brigita's local friends also planned to celebrate Brigita's birthday by going out.

---

* This happens not because of anything about me but because of the unique nature of the therapeutic relationship. When vulnerable disclosure is met with unconditional acceptance, of course our brains respond with endearment and affection. It's part of being a totally normal, deep-feeling human.

The out-of-town friend made it clear that she didn't want to go out, so Brigita did both: she hung out with her out-of-town friend at home before and after, but also went out with the group, leaving her friend alone at home to entertain herself. Brigita's mother was horrified: "You did *what*? You left her *alone at your house*?" The shame has stuck to Brigita like a burr ever since.

In a moment of desperation, Libby forged her boss's signature on a supervisory report, which ended up blowing up in her face. She didn't get fired, but the incident went to a monitoring board comprised of experts in the field Libby had one day hoped to network with for a job.

None of these are high crimes. In Brigita's case, I questioned whether she had done anything wrong. But whether or not we've done anything objectively wrong—ethically, emotionally, socially, societally—we've all had experiences like Văn's, Brigita's, or Libby's, where we feel like we've (*peeks through fingers*) *failed*.

Fail. Oh, that word. It gives us the heebie-jeebies. But let's define it. "Failure" means not meeting our own or others' expectations. Sometimes expectations are objective and universal—laws, social norms, basic common sense. But those of us who are hard on ourselves do two things to complicate matters: one, our expectations are often subjective, rigorous, and self-imposed. We set the bar for adequacy at "personally demanding high standard." Two, we adopt a zero-tolerance approach to errors, do-overs, or struggles. In that context, we set ourselves up to transgress our personal standards a lot. And when we do, it's a big deal. We react strongly.

Consider the lowly peanut. When someone without a peanut allergy eats a peanut, things go smoothly. By contrast, when someone with a peanut allergy eats a peanut, there's a big reaction: the peanut triggers hives, swelling, diarrhea, even anaphylaxis. Those of us who are hard on ourselves have a metaphorical peanut allergy to mistakes. When someone without perfectionism makes a mistake, it's not a big deal. They might feel a little embarrassed, exclaim, "Oh, my bad!" and, if needed, offer an apology.

But when *we* make a mistake, objectively or subjectively, we have a

big reaction. Our errors register exponentially higher on our personal
Richter scale than people without perfectionism. Even small failures—
losing track of time and missing an appointment, recommending a
restaurant that ends up being lame—stick to us like a tongue to a frozen flagpole. For me, running ten minutes late is an adrenaline-filled
stress fest. Calling someone by the wrong name, inadvertently hitting
Reply All, forgetting our friend's birthday hit us with powerful shame:
a small bee with a big stinger.

Our shock waves can emanate outward: we might get defensive,
blame others, or double down on logic and reason. Or the big reaction
can go inward: harsh self-criticism, shutting down, a stomachache,
procrastination.

Why do we feel our errors so deeply? Overevaluation. We conflate
our screwups with our character. We mistake the inevitable problems
of life for personal wrongdoing. And public failure? Forget it. We'd
rather read our online banking terms of service agreements in full. At
the DMV.

Our wiring makes it worse because we naturally focus on flaws.
Indeed, in 1965, Dr. M. H. Hollender, one of the first clinicians to
describe perfectionism as a disorder, wrote that each of us who is hard
on ourselves is "constantly on the alert for what is wrong and seldom
focuses on what is right. He looks so intently for defects or flaws that
he lives his life as though he were an inspector at the end of a production line."

For someone with perfectionism-driven social anxiety, an awkward
pause in yesterday's conversation still rankles, while for someone without, it might not have even registered. For someone whose body image
never feels good enough, a pound gained eats up mental bandwidth
until it's dieted away, while for someone else, it's not even on the radar.

We also take our standards very seriously; we have what's called
high moral certitude, which means we have a strong sense of what's
right and wrong, what we should and shouldn't do, and what should
be rewarded or punished.

Finally, when we tend to view ourselves harshly, we view our pasts harshly, too. When we look back, we focus on the lowlights, the missteps, the could-have-been-better efforts. With our stringent standards, we don't allow ourselves a lot of rock-solid successes. I think this is what the researcher Dr. Martin Smith meant when he said that those of us who are hard on ourselves look back and see a string of failures. With regrets filling our rearview mirrors, we start to think of ourselves as failures, impostors, or losers.

Cringe Attacks

"Hello?"

"Hello, I'm calling with the Department of Embarrassing Childhood Memories. Do I have Sara?"

"Yup."

"Great. We want to discuss something that happened to you in the fifth grade. So according to our files, you ran up to your older sister's friend, who you thought was very cool, and you gave him a hug, but he squeezed you so tight he popped every bone in your back and caused you to release all the air in your lungs as well as let out the most massive fart you've ever done in your life?"

(Awkwardly long, horrified pause.) "Uh-huh."

"And this was in a room of about fifty people?"

"Uh-huh."

"Great, and then immediately after all that air was expelled out of your body, did you crumple to the floor?"

"I did."

"Did everyone surround you?"

"Yup."

"And then did he yell out, 'She's fine—she just farted!'"

(Eyes closed, painfully nodding in embarrassment.) "That's accurate."

"Perfect. That's what we've got!"*

---

* So goes a viral TikTok recounting a cringe attack by Sara Hopkins (@sayhopkins).

* * *

A special breed of mistake is fodder for the cringe attack, which is when our brains, without asking, decide to sucker punch us with a flashbulb memory of a past humiliating or awkward moment. Cringe attacks come out of the blue, usually when we're alone and doing something mindless, like showering or folding laundry. It's physical— a wince, the need to squeeze our eyes shut, a reflexive shake like a wet dog. Carter, our small-town college student, gets repeatedly slapped with the memory of a negative comment from a respected teacher. He has to close his eyes, hang his head, and whisper to himself: "Fuck!" For me, whenever my brain decides to recall the time I innocently reintroduced myself to a woman I had previously interacted with *to the point that we had exchanged phone numbers*, I physically shudder as if I'm swallowing something bitter, which, metaphorically, I suppose I am.

The cringe attack memories I've heard from other clients are equally embarrassing—throwing up in front of the whole class, attempting to dance provocatively and seeing an expression of horror on a crush's face, failing to hide an erection in middle school math class. In Melissa Dahl's book *Cringeworthy: A Theory of Awkwardness*, one woman confesses that, at a Halloween party, "I did ecstasy and made out with two guys on the same improv team," a sin that might be construed as oddly endearing but to her is so embarrassing that when the memory hits while brushing her teeth, she yells at her reflection in the bathroom mirror, "Oh my god oh my god oh my god why did you do that?"

Those of us who are hard on ourselves seem to be more prone to cringe attacks than most. Our brains don't let us forget when we've transgressed the Inner Rulebook: *I should always do the right thing, I should always have good judgment, I should never make a fool out of myself*—the list goes on. Speaking of which . . .

It's Not You, It's Your Expectations

The tough-on-yourself brain is all or nothing. We either meet our expectations or fail. Let's remember that our standards are rooted in a good thing: conscientiousness. But sometimes they're so high, they're impossibly inhuman. Many of the following examples are from Dr. Thomas Lynch, the treatment developer of the empirically supported Radically Open Dialectical Behavior Therapy whom we met in chapter 5. We might not hold these expectations word for word, but the essence is accurate.

I expect I . . .
. . . will always do the right thing.
. . . will always be kind and considerate.
. . . will always make optimal decisions.
. . . can control how others see me.
. . . can know the best course of action.
. . . can control others' emotions, experiences, and reactions.
. . . am able to predict what will happen in the future accurately.
. . . can know the intentions of others.
. . . can overcome any obstacle or solve any problem, no matter where or how they may appear.

The verdict? It's not us; it's our expectations. No one always does the right thing. No human can accurately predict what will happen in the future. Despite the tenacity imbued by our never-give-up culture, we cannot overcome every obstacle or solve any problem. As they say, no one gets out of here alive. In short, when we fail, we blame ourselves, but the problem isn't us—it's the yardstick we use to measure ourselves.

The solution is to rethink our expectations. We regret losing our temper at a friend? Apologize for sure, but also release the conviction that we will *always* be kind and considerate. We regret giving up our dream grad school for a relationship that didn't work out? Challenge the expectation that we *always* make the right decision, as well as the expectation that we can, with the accuracy of a crystal ball, predict what will happen in the future.

When I suggest rethinking expectations to clients, sometimes they look at me as if I just proposed evicting old ladies from their homes. They feel like I'm asking them to lower their standards. That's not what we're doing. I'd argue we're keeping the same high standards: be kind and considerate, make good decisions, think about the future. But we're allowing some flexibility—some wiggle room. We're recognizing that we can't go through life expecting to make *zero* mistakes, have *zero* lapses in judgment, or encounter *zero* insurmountable challenges.

Mistakes are part of the package deal of being alive. Regrets are the tax we pay for having human relationships. We've all dropped the ball. We've all hurt people we care about. We've all done dumb things. We can still have high expectations, but we can learn that failing to meet them doesn't render us failures—it simply means we're living the human experience. And that connects us to every human that's ever existed.

This can be disheartening. It's disappointing to realize we are fallible. It's sad to let go of the idea that we can't see, much less control, the future. It's a loss to give up the idea that we can make and execute flawless, regret-free decisions.

But that's kind of the point. Feeling sadness and disappointment at the loss of our unrealistic expectations is an important step toward self-acceptance. Grief is the emotional response to loss. In fact, Dr. Lynch teaches that just like we can grieve the loss of a person or a pet, we can grieve the loss of our all-or-nothing expectations and convictions. We regret making out with two guys in one night: we grieve the expectation that we always have optimal judgment. All we wanted was to flirt with a crush, but we end up ripping an earthshaking fart in front of fifty people: we grieve the belief that we can accurately predict what will happen, or that nothing embarrassing will ever happen to us.

Feeling the loss is important because when we try to avoid "feel," we often end up at "think." And then? We worry, ruminate, and dwell; we get trapped in what we "should" have known or done.

This is not same-day delivery. Grieving the loss of expectations—even unrealistic expectations—takes time. Let go again and again of the expectation that you never do anything embarrassing, stupid, or wrong. Embrace the idea that mistakes are not personal failings but part of the package deal of being alive.

This is hard. I got you. Next, let's move on to those perceived mistakes you can't seem to let go of.

Making Room for Past Mistakes

One of my favorite methods for handling regret and other negative emotions comes from Dr. Russ Harris, the bestselling author of *The Happiness Trap*. He calls it *physicalizing*, and it begins with imagining negative emotion as a physical object within your body.

Here's a test drive: Bring your mistake to mind. The feeling of regret, guilt, shame, or remorse will likely trigger some sensation in your body. Maybe it's a pressure behind your eyes, a ball in the pit of your stomach, a tightness in your chest, or the proverbial weight on your shoulders.

Next, imagine the feeling as a physical object within your body. Drill down on the details. What color is it? What shape and size? Is it transparent or opaque? Solid, liquid, or gas? Is it in motion, or is it still? Heavy or light? If you could run your fingers over it, what texture would you feel?

For example, Justin pictured his regret of dropping out of school as a waterlogged black sponge—heavy, dripping—lodged at the center of his chest, under his sternum. Kara pictured her anxious regret of a friendship lost to miscommunication as a red, glowing web just beneath her skin. Rachel imagined her deep sadness of years lost to estrangement from her mother as a square matte silver box nestled deep in her gut.

Once you've got it placed and pictured, next comes the most important part. Make some room for this object within your body. Inhale and imagine your breath slowly inflating the area, creating space around your object. Picture in your mind's eye some room opening up around it, allowing it to be there.

Notice that I am not saying, "Let it go." This isn't *Frozen*. This is the Beatles: "Let it be." Letting go implies trying to get rid of it, but suppressed thoughts come back like a boomerang. Instead, we are making room for the mistake. When we make room for feeling bad, we often feel less bad. By allowing it, it often diminishes.

This is acceptance. It may feel wrong at first. Making room for regrets sounds about as appealing as making room for a hippopotamus taking a dump in the middle of your living room. But don't make room for regret because you "should." There are enough shoulds in your life. Make room for regret and sadness and grief to move forward, to do what's important to you, to be the person you want to be.

Justin's willingness to make room for his dropping-out-of-school sodden sponge allowed him to speak up at work rather than always feeling like an unqualified impostor. Kara's willingness to make room for the glowing red web of lost friendship she pictured under her skin allowed her to build some burgeoning friendships. Rachel made room for her silver box of estrangement regret so she could let herself love her own child as fully as she could.

Self-Forgiveness and Why It's So Hard to Let Go

Fifteen years ago, when Gabby was in her midtwenties, her mom was diagnosed with advanced lung cancer. Gabby, a nurse with Energizer Bunny energy, became her mom's caregiver, rarely leaving her side. She dove deep into every aspect of her mom's care, from keeping track of medications to doing the dishes to spending hours on the phone with the insurance company.

Months in, Gabby's boyfriend urged her to take a break. "Just few days," he said. "You need some rest. Plus I never see you anymore. We have to water our garden if it's going to live." Gabby felt resentful at the pressure. *He* wasn't dying—couldn't he see this was more important? But her mom encouraged her to go. Gabby's brother could step in and handle things for a few days.

The day before her flight, Gabby took her mom to an appointment. The doctor prescribed a new medication, which Gabby picked up at the pharmacy on the way home. She walked her brother through the routine and handed him a manila folder of lists, schedules, and written directions. "I've got it, Gab," he said. "It's okay—we'll survive without you." Gabby didn't feel right, but everyone, including her mom, told her to go enjoy herself. So she went.

Twenty-four hours later, while she was walking on a palm tree–lined beach hand in hand with her boyfriend, her phone rang. It was her brother. Her mom had had a bad reaction to the new medication and was agitated and confused, totally out of character for the rock-solid, stoic woman they knew. Gabby could hear her in the background—"Why are you here? Where *is* she? I didn't ask for this."

An epic fight with her boyfriend followed. Gabby wanted to fly straight home, but he wanted to stay. Her brother and the care team would figure it out, he said. Gabby couldn't do anything the doctors couldn't do. So she stayed, tearfully and reluctantly. When they got home, her mom was calmer but still foggy and confused. She looked at Gabby with uncomprehending eyes. Her mom lived a few more weeks, but Gabby never saw her lucid again.

Fifteen years later, Gabby still carries the weight of that time. "I'm not a good daughter," she stated simply. "I made the wrong decision. Everyone was telling me to go on vacation, but I knew in my gut that I shouldn't. I should have pushed back, but I didn't, and my decision hurt her." Gabby wishes she had never left her mom's side. "I know she wouldn't have lasted forever, but I might have bought her a few more months."

Of course Gabby wishes things had been different. Of course she carries weighty emotions from that time. Those are normal human reactions. But Gabby also feels like she made a huge mistake. Her shame, guilt, and regret still consume her fifteen years later.

Enter *self-forgiveness*, a positive shift in our feelings, actions, and beliefs about ourselves after a self-perceived transgression or wrongdoing. Self-forgiveness has three parts.*

---

* Or sometimes four. The discretional part—*apologizing and making things right* to the extent possible—is for when we've caused harm. Our guilty conscience drives us to repair and

Paradoxically, the first step of self-forgiveness is **self-criticism** and the guilt, shame, or other negative emotions that go along with it. After all, there's nothing to forgive if we don't think we did anything wrong. This part is easy for us. We beat ourselves up over what we "should" have done. We fervently wish we could rewind time and get a do-over. We either hide our perceived transgression from everyone or compulsively confess. If we confess, we need excessive reassurance. Either way, we crave absolution.

Why do we come down so hard on ourselves? Surprisingly, it's because of our need for human connection. Guilt and its fellow self-conscious emotion, shame, are linked to empathy, honesty, and altruism. As bad as they feel, both emotions have stuck around through the millennia because they help us signal remorse, repair group relationships after a rift, stay part of the tribe, and therefore, survive.

Guilt and shame aren't just for objective wrongdoing. Guilt and shame occur when we perceive we have transgressed a norm or failed to meet a standard, plus we believe the norm or standard was right and binding. It's why your anti-government uncle Gary might blithely cheat on his taxes and feel no shame, but your tween cousin Chloe might spiral with shame after her skinny jeans get called "*so* cheugy" by the middle school's popular girls.

Notice I didn't say "the norm or standard was realistic." Gabby's ethical transgression was built on unrealistic standards: *I should have foreseen the future. I should have stayed by Mom's side without a break for as long as it took. I should have saved her.* Ultimately, whether or not we did anything objectively wrong is less important than the conclusions we draw about transgressing personal or societal standards.

Next is **deconstructing overevaluation**. Remember overevaluation, where we derive our worth from our outcomes? We conflate a negative outcome with our character. My client Xiao, a professor, blamed herself for some students skipping her lectures: "I have to be

---

rejoin the tribe. In a 1983 interview with *The New York Times*, the pioneering psychologist Dr. Helen Block Lewis said, "Guilt is one of the cements that binds us together and keeps us human." She continued, "If it occurs to you that you've done something to injure someone else, guilt compels you to do something to fix it, to repair the bond."

more engaging." She never considered that students might be working, prioritizing other things, or hungover. When Claire discovered her husband had been employing an escort for months, she thought it was because she wasn't enough—wasn't attractive enough, wasn't attentive enough, wasn't appreciative enough. Arthur lost his home during the subprime mortgage crisis and concluded he was a failure in life and business. Gabby conflated her perceived failure with her character: *Because I failed to meet my expectations, I'm not a good daughter.*

Emotion researchers continue to quibble about the exact distinctions between guilt and shame, but Dr. Lewis advanced a significant, commonly accepted difference: guilt focuses on the act, shame focuses on the self, specifically, what researchers call "a negative evaluation of the global self." Gabby concludes she's inadequate, a bad daughter. She condemns her whole person. The classic differential? Shame insists, "*I* did that horrible thing," while guilt says, "I did that horrible *thing*."

Experiment with moving the spotlight from your character to the negative outcome. Test out decoupling the two. We move from "*I* did that horrible thing" to "I did that horrible *thing*," or, as applicable to Xiao's, Claire's, and Arthur's examples, "That horrible thing happened." While it's important to note that guilt isn't "better" or easier than shame—it's not "shame lite"—but it is less personal. Defusing the overidentification defuses shame.*

The last part of self-forgiveness is **fostering positive emotions toward oneself**. This is a tricky one. We can't snap our fingers and feel good about ourselves. But consider this: after taking any necessary responsibility and offering repair, you're allowed to feel good about your overall self. The core of step three is that *failure and positive self-regard are allowed to coexist.*

It's important to point out that feeling better is not contingent

---

* Flashing neon sign: Sometimes we feel ashamed when we're actually angry. Healthy constructive anger looks around and says, *Things should be different.* But if getting angry isn't safe or allowable, it flips to shame. Shame looks inward and says, *I should be different.* In other words, when we dare to say, even in our politest tone, "Um, excuse me? This isn't working, and I would like it to change," shame pushes back and says, "No, *you're* the one who's not working and needs to change."

upon a promise of personal improvement. Since all of us are hard on ourselves here, I repeat: we don't have to promise ourselves, "I'll do better next time to make up for it," or "I'll learn from this and come out of it better." Self-forgiveness doesn't need to be held in escrow, only to be earned by a more deserving version of you. You can simply forgive yourself now.

Self-forgiveness also isn't contingent upon deflecting responsibility. It's not about finding someone else to blame. I'm sure many people told Gabby her brother should have handled it better or insisted her boyfriend should have been more supportive, and she didn't feel any better. Self-forgiveness comes from releasing yourself from your own self-criticism.

One way to feel better about yourself is to do the exact opposite of what shame tells you to do. Shame urges us to hide, to conceal, but that's where it flourishes—in the dark. To make shame shrivel like a vampire in the daylight, do the opposite of concealment: share it with someone you trust. When Văn, Brigita, and Libby shared their stories with people they hoped would understand—despite shame telling them to hide lest they be judged—they were met with support, empathy, and validation, which allowed them to loosen their grip on their guilt and shame.

Bottom line: We've all let other people down. We've all let ourselves down. Give yourself permission to have a full range of human experiences. Allow yourself some grace for past actions your brain finds bad, wrong, dumb, embarrassing, ridiculous, or horrible. You're allowed to feel good about yourself even when your past includes failures. That's called being human.

Self-forgiveness is not instantaneous. It's often gradual and requires multiple rounds. Even if we intellectually understand self-forgiveness, it takes time to sink into our bones. Therefore, in a brain-bending meta-move, forgive yourself for struggling with self-forgiveness.

As for Gabby, she still misses her mom every day. She still feels sad, but she's found some peace. "Guilt doesn't keep me connected to her," Gabby concluded. "I can love her and miss her without beating myself up."

11

From Exam to Experiment
Compassion for
Future Mistakes

Anyone who never made a mistake never tried anything new.

—Albert Einstein

IT WAS TIME. The stagehand opened the backstage door and gestured to thirteen-year-old Tricia Park. The audience's applause ring-
ing in her ears, Tricia made her way past the basses and cellos, her
puffy pink chiffon dress swishing as she walked, to her place beside
the conductor. She could barely see beyond the stage because of the
lights, but that was fine with her—her heart was beating fast enough
without seeing all the eyes on her. She bowed, raised her violin into
position, and launched into a Paganini concerto, with the Baltimore
Symphony Orchestra supporting her. By the end of the piece, it was
clear a child prodigy stood before the audience. It was momentous—
the fruit borne from years of trudging home from school to the violin
waiting in her bedroom, her classmates' screams of delight from the
playground slowly receding.

When Tricia was five and her mom casually asked if she wanted
to play the violin, no one could have predicted the heights to which

her career would soar. She was a natural, blowing through the Suzuki books like a line of falling dominoes. Her talent got the attention of adults. Even as a kindergartener, Tricia, who was painfully shy, figured out that the looks on people's faces when she played meant she was special. Without realizing it, Tricia kept playing the violin because it bought her approval. They liked her because of what she could deliver.

But that meant that every time she picked up the violin was like a final exam. Every performance was a referendum on her value. There wasn't space for mistakes, experimentation, or do-overs. Leading up to her debut in Baltimore, Tricia's teacher conveyed a message that still ricochets inside her brain: "You know, Tricia, when people buy a ticket to come hear you play, they only care about how perfect you are. No one cares whether you are sad or worried or tired, whether you are sick, or whether your dog just died. You have to be consistently perfect no matter what."

Yikes. While not many of us can relate to the pressures of traveling the world as a child prodigy violinist, many of us can relate to the feeling that people are watching and are ready to pounce on any mistake we make. We edit our Instagram captions, then edit them one more time. We don't like to be seen until we've showered and gotten ready—it's not vanity, it's just how we operate. We ask our work bestie if an email looks weird before we send it. With friends, we work hard to add value to every conversation. It feels like the stakes are always high. A lot of life feels like an exam.

In the previous chapter, we looked to the past and forgave ourselves for regrets. In this chapter, we'll look to the future and examine three things we do assiduously to avoid failure in all its iterations. Here's the TL;DR preview. One: back in the early twentieth century, influential psychologist Dr. Alfred Adler regarded perfectionism as a form of overcompensation. And that's exactly what we do to avoid mistakes. We do beyond what needs to be done, creating a buffer that ultimately costs us more than it buys us. Two: we use unreliable indicators to track our progress and tell us when we've done "enough." Three: we try to avoid things we might be bad at. But since learning new things starts with being bad at them, we opt out of activities where we might have to struggle or—*gasp!*—suck. For all of us who feel like life is a big report card, let's walk through all three tactics, plus what to try instead.

Rolling Back Overdoing It

Over the years, teachers told Tricia that what she thought or felt or wanted didn't count—her job was to produce the music as written, as the composer intended it. She was told to focus on the technical execution, the accuracy, the timing. She was expected to do it the same every time, which, given that Tricia was a human rather than a robot, proved impossible. The only solution was to double down: if she practiced six hours and couldn't get the result, she would practice eight hours. And if that didn't work, she would practice ten. "That was the arithmetic," she told me when I interviewed her. In other words, Tricia's solution was to over-practice.

Those of us who struggle with perfectionism might over-prepare, overtrain, overstudy, overclean, overcommit, overexplain, and over-rehearse. We might show up overdressed, be overly friendly, and hold ourselves to overly ethical standards. Indeed, in 1965, Dr. M. H. Hollender, defined it as "to demand of oneself a higher quality of performance than that required by the situation."

After my first book, *How to Be Yourself*, featured medical student Diego who was too distracted by social anxiety to focus on his clinical duties, I received a disproportionate number of requests for therapy from med students in a similar quandary. One of these lovely young people was Kalkidan, a second-year medical student making the transition from textbooks to the clinic. Despite her generally positive evaluations, she felt like every day was a do-or-die performance to keep from getting kicked out of medical school. A worst-case-scenario movie played in her head of being called into the dean's office, seeing her file fanned out on a mahogany desk, covered in red pen marks, and the dean shaking his head in disappointment.

With the sense that every day was a high-stakes exam, Kalkidan overcompensated, working hard to be extra-enthusiastic, extra-helpful, extra-engaged, and extra-attentive to the patients, nurses, residents, everybody. As she tried harder and harder, she got frazzled, and her voice would become high and frantic. It came to light that she was trying to be extra-prepared by memorizing and reciting her presentations word for word, but that meant whenever she deviated from the script in her head, she would lose her place and freeze. Likewise, she was extra-cautious: she spent hours she didn't have rewriting each patient note in her own words so she could never be accused of plagiarizing a colleague's notes. During lectures, she tried to appear extra-engaged— she would tell herself she could only ask questions that showed she was thinking deeply about the topic, but by the time she polished a question to her standards, the moment had passed and she missed what her professor was saying. All the overcompensation was backfiring, with residents and attending doctors raising concerns about her anxiety and poor time management.

When we're scared of making mistakes, like Kalkidan, we might go 110 percent. If we're preparing to talk to someone intimidating, we might write out a script, think of every single question they might ask, and rehearse take after take in front of the bathroom mirror. But then, if the interaction goes well, our overpreparation steals the credit. We don't get the chance to learn that we didn't have to go to such extremes.

Another drawback: overdoing things takes time and energy. There is always a trade-off. Everything we're overdoing is something else we're not doing, whether that's sleeping, connecting with people we care about, or that other project that's three weeks overdue. We pay the price for going full tilt with exhaustion, a resentful partner, annoyed boss, or narrowed life.

Finally, overcompensation implies there is something lacking that requires compensation. Over our lifetimes, much of our sense of self comes from receiving the feedback of other people. So when we use overachievement—school, appearance, competition—to cover our perceived fatal flaws, we never get a chance to learn that our whole selves, perceived "flaws" and all, might be lovable and acceptable just as we are.

Sometimes the expectation of overcompensation comes not from within but from institutions. Garry Mitchell of the Harvard Graduate School of Education studies college prep programs designed to enhance social mobility and balance out inequality by launching Black and Brown students into elite schools and impressive career trajectories. But the programs inadvertently institutionalize the mentality of "twice as good" by holding kids of color to higher standards of behavior and achievement than peers from, say, legacy or donor families, all while costing them community and a sense of identity. Overperformance feels required, getting everything right so no one sees them as undeserving.

Sometimes overcompensating is an understandable strategy. An unequal society can send the unequivocal message that you do, in fact, need to crank out some compensation.

Take *The Best Little Boy in the World*, Andrew Tobias's classic memoir of growing up gay and closeted. Writing under a pseudonym, he draws a direct line from growing up in a stigmatizing culture to doubling down on competition—grades, athletics, elite schools, and employers: "Another important line of defense . . . was my prodigious list of activities. . . . No one could expect me to be out dating . . . when I had a list of 17 urgent projects to complete." Overcompensating buffered him from the criticism and possible rejection that would come from being gay.

Nearly forty years later, Drs. John Pachankis and Mark Hatzenbuehler underpinned Tobias's memoir with data. They looked at two factors: number of years in the closet and degree of codified discrimination in the laws of participants' home states (think Florida versus, say, Vermont) and found both variables predicted the extent to which gay and bisexual young men overcompensated, basing their self-worth on achievement and comparison. Later, Drs. Benjamin Blankenship and Abigail Stewart conceptually replicated the study including queer women, expanding the hypothesis to the Best Little *Kid* in the World, as it were. Shifting one's self-worth out of the control of bigoted law-makers is an understandable move, even with the costs of stress and isolation.

The larger context leaves us with so many questions. How do we know if it's safe to roll back overcompensating? The short answer is we don't always know, and it may not, indeed, be safe. But we can start our experiments with people we think are safe, and then expand outward. In addition, as Garry Mitchell recommends, we can build a sense of community and connection. "That thick sense of cohort can serve as a protective factor," he says.

Thankfully, we're not trying to whip away overcompensation all at once like yanking a tablecloth from beneath a place setting. Despite the inclination of those of us with perfectionism to go all or nothing, Kalkidan doesn't have to flip from over-responsibility to "I don't care what the hospital thinks." Tricia doesn't have to flop from "perfect no matter what" to nothing-matters nihilism. But what lies between the black and white of "Please like me" and IDGAF?

Ultimately, we can roll back overdoing to simply . . . doing. We might roll back overexplaining to simply explaining, being overly polished to simply polished, and so on, with the goal of discovering that we are adequate and capable without the overcompensation. We don't have to save ourselves through overcompensation because, it turns out, we didn't need saving in the first place.

My overcompensation has always been hyper-independence. From moving furniture to navigating friend drama, I did it all myself. For many years, I was reticent to a fault. In my mind, it kept me from being annoying or a burden, but it also kept me separate; by not asking for help, I radiated the message that no one had anything to offer me.

I started rolling back my hyper-independence with the people in my life who felt safe—revealing some of my baggage to friends who were open about their own lives. This felt breathtakingly daring at first. But it also felt like a relief. And it brought me closer to the people I confided in because, to my surprise, they took everything in stride and often confided right back, which brought us closer.

As for Kalkidan, after asking residents and fellow med students for advice on how they handled notes and presentations, she started to experiment with simply being cautious and prepared rather than overly cautious and overly prepared. She still wrote part of her notes from scratch, but allowed herself to copy-paste patient demographics and history. For her presentations, she started holding bullet points in her head rather than an entire word-for-word script, which allowed her to talk as if she were telling a story rather than giving a verbatim recitation. In a pass-fail class, she allowed herself to ask questions as they popped into her head rather than putting them through a quality control inspection before articulating them. It felt wrong and anxiety-provoking at first, like she was imperiling herself, but she was willing to try out methods that had worked for people she respected.

Does Kalkidan still closely monitor how she impacts others? Do I still err on the side of self-sufficiency? Of course—neither of those things are bad. Both of us, as we should, have retained our personality and essential essence, but we've gained something additional: flexibility.

> **TRY IT OUT:** Under what circumstances do you overperform to feel safe? What would it look like to roll back overperformance? What would you do differently? What would stay the same? Consider where you can test out a new approach. Flexibly adjust as necessary.

From the Head to the Heart (and Back Again)

Speaking of flexibility, remember Gus from chapter 7, who wanted to get better at hanging with his friends? You might remember that he's also a dedicated distance runner. He spends many of his Saturday mornings getting up at 4 A.M. to run a casual twenty miles or driving out to Hopkinton or Wellesley to run stretches of the Boston Marathon route. Typically, when Gus runs, he wears a heart monitor and tracks all his metrics with two apps—one for him, one for his coach. The point of his runs was ensuring his speed, stamina, and efficiency were superb—getting a good grade, as it were, on his data and metrics. Over the last few months, Gus had been running less and less. What used to be a joy—the quiet of empty, early-morning streets, the sense of accomplishment—had started to feel like a report card.

On the other hand, my client Timothy is a human resources rep who investigates complaints of discrimination, harassment, and all manner of horrible work experiences. He writes up reports with incriminating emails and screenshots added as appendices. Timothy is aware that his reports make the difference between an accused employee keeping a job and getting fired, as well as workplace justice being served or not. Timothy routinely pulls all-nighters editing his reports, worrying about the effects of his word choices and feeling the weight of people's careers on his shoulders. He hands in his reports only when his deadline forces him to, and sometimes he even pushes several days past that. It doesn't feel respectful to wrap up and hit Send to the HR director until the report feels right. To Timothy, all the agonizing means he's taking his job seriously. It seems like the right thing to do, even if it's making him miserable and exhausted, as well as making his partner resentful when she picks up his slack at home.

Both Gus and Timothy can identify with the "This is an exam" sentiment. But they're using two very different kinds of indicators to strive for a good grade. Gus relies on quantitative or categorical measures to know he's doing things correctly. Let's call this "the Head." The Head is a number cruncher, a data nerd. We maximize our chances of doing well on the "exam" by following the recipe, tracking our points, closing our rings, or completing the three-month training plan for our sprint triathlon to the letter.

Timothy, on the other hand, relies on his gut. He "just knows" when his report is done. Psychologists call this the *felt sense*, a concept first introduced by Dr. Eugene Gendlin, a contemporary philosopher who influenced the legendary humanistic psychologist Carl Rogers. The felt sense, Gendlin writes, is "the body's sense of a particular situation." For example, let's say you're trying to write an important email, but it's just not coming out right. You might feel tense, unsettled, and frustrated. It bothers you. You furrow your brow, jostle your leg up and down, drum the desktop. The felt sense tells you the email is not right. On the other hand, let's say you're trying to write an important email and you're in the groove. You know exactly what to say and intuit it will be well received and appreciated. There is a felt sense of rightness: you lean in, focus keenly on the screen, maybe hold your breath as the words flow. The felt sense of correctness, calm, or satisfaction tells you it's right.

We can feel it in our bodies when we notice crumbs on an otherwise clean counter, spot a crooked picture on the wall, or have a premonition that our friend is mad at us because they haven't answered our text yet. But we also experience it when we know we crushed that job interview, we can tell we're getting a second date, or the house is finally clean. We feel dissonance when we haven't met our standards and concordance when we have.

Let's call this feeling—assurance that standards have been met versus feeling unsettled when they haven't—"the Heart." The Heart just knows—it's intuitive, qualitative, and instinctual.

Both these methods—the Head and the Heart—tell us how we're doing on each exam, but when the costs start piling up, like Gus's deflated enthusiasm or Timothy's marital tension, we can experiment with some flexibility by swapping the Head for the Heart and vice versa.

For example, Gus designed an experiment that swapped his quantitative Head number crunching for some Heart-centered intuition: go on his next run without monitoring anything. Just run and enjoy. This was not without ambivalence. "How will I know when to turn around?" he asked me.

"When you feel like turning around," I replied.

Gus raised an eyebrow. After a pause, he said, "I don't like this, but I'm willing to try."

The following week, I asked how it went.

"It was a little disorienting," he said. "Because I wasn't measuring it, it felt like it didn't count. I wanted credit. But," he continued, "it was also a relief. I felt like I was getting away with something."

Fast-forward: Gus didn't give up his heart monitor or his coach—remember, we're not doing all or nothing and that wasn't the problem, anyway—but he gained some valuable flexibility and remembered the very reason he got into running in the first place: for the fun of it.

Next, it was Timothy's turn. Together, we decided to quantify some limits for him—to use the Head to know when to stop rather than the Heart, which kept him up all night. First, Timothy surveyed his colleagues to ask how many drafts they wrote, how long they spent editing, and how long their reports were. He discovered that he was working more than twice as much as the next most hard-working colleague and that his reports were over 50 percent longer than average. He instituted some limits—hard stop at 8:00 p.m. for kid bath time, no more than five appendices, three-draft maximum. He bent the rules almost immediately, adding six appendices and going through five drafts, but that's fine—compliance wasn't the point. What was? Again, flexibility.

"Okay, Ellen, wait a minute," you might say. "You keep mentioning flexibility." You caught me. Technically, *psychological flexibility* is staying in contact with the present moment regardless of unpleasant thoughts, feelings, and body sensations, while choosing actions based on (1) what will work for the situation and (2) what's important to you (hey, throwback to chapters 6 and 8!). In other words, it's willingness to experience the slings and arrows of life to do what's workable and meaningful to you.

We see flexibility when Gus decides he's willing to go for a run despite a nagging sense that a phone is supposed to tell him when to turn around. It's Timothy's willingness to break for kid bath time despite the urge to crank out one more page. It's my willingness to ask for help despite the roiling sense that I'll be an annoying burden if I can't do it all myself.

Now let's apply some Head-to-Heart and Heart-to-Head swapping to your life. Where are you putting forth disproportionate effort to meet the mark? Where is your inner quality control inspector getting a little too exacting? Imagine this in ninety-six-point font: these are experiments in flexibility, not new rules. Experiment with what works given your situation.

The Heart to the Head Experiments		
	CURRENT HABIT	NEW EXPERIMENT
CLEANING	Cleaning until the kitchen "feels" clean, at the expense of the rest of your evening	Aim for 20–25 minutes of after-dinner cleanup and see how it goes
REHEARSING	Rehearsing a presentation until you feel ready, but losing out on family time for a week	Decide ahead of time to run through 3, 5, etc., times rather than compulsively
APOLOGIZING	Apologizing until you get reassurance that it's okay, but exasperate your friend in the process	Genuinely apologize once, twice max, and then stop
PROVING YOUR POINT	Arguing until your partner disengages or gets angry	Make your point twice and then reevaluate to see if being right or attending to the relationship is more important to you right now
PRODUCTIVITY	Working until you feel like you've done "enough," which never happens	Work 9:00–5:00 (or whatever applies to you) when feasible—the rest will still be there tomorrow

SOCIAL PERFORMANCE	Ruminating about a conversation that felt cringey or awkward	Expect and allow 15% of conversations to be awkward
OPTIMIZING LEISURE EXPERIENCES	Pushing to make the most of every moment	Expect that ⅓–⅔ of leisure or vacation time is planning, setting up, cleaning up, or recovering
EMOTIONS	Always have the "appropriate" feeling or "acceptable" reaction	Allow for the full range of feelings, with or without having to *do* anything about them

The Heart to the Head Experiments		
	CURRENT HABIT	NEW EXPERIMENT
COOKING	Follow the recipe exactly	Experiment, substitute, and add to taste
EATING	Eat a specific number of calories or macros	Eat mostly for your body plus some for your soul
BEDTIME	Go to bed on time	Go to bed when you're tired, whether that's earlier or later
WORKING OUT	Follow the program exactly	Consider whether to push or pull back day to day, given your current energy, sleep, injuries, menstrual cycle, etc.
PUBLIC SPEAKING	Make zero mistakes	Connect with the audience
MUSICAL PERFORMANCE	Make zero mistakes	Express yourself and the composer/songwriter
WEIGHT	Lose, gain, or maintain a certain number	Focus on what your body can do

You Don't Have to Have It All Figured Out Ahead of Time

As Tricia matured, she realized that the advice from her teacher—
"You have to be consistently perfect no matter what"—was toxic and
eating away at her joy, both with the violin and life overall. So in her
thirties, she decided to try something she had never tried before:
improvisation.

Tricia signed up for a fiddle camp, which was heavy on jam sessions
and spontaneous music-making in the hallways at lunch. Tricia remembered, "It was unequivocally awful." It ran counter to everything
she had been taught. More importantly, she was suddenly bad at the
very thing she had given up her childhood to be good at: violin. "In
classical music, vulnerability is not an option," she said. "Progress and
learning and working things out have to be hidden. But in other venues,
like improvisation or jam circles, vulnerability is the only option." She
found herself crying at the end of every day.

By contrast, Tricia had a violinist friend who had been improvising
since he was a kid. He told her he remembered being taken to jam sessions as a preschooler, sitting at the feet of grown-ups making music
together late into the night. "He started by banging on a bowl," Tricia
said. "Then a drum. On violin, he probably started with open strings,
then progressed on his own, and eventually with a group." He learned
gradually, over time, through experience. "Improvising," Tricia concluded, "is a skill."

I agree. Plus, I'll argue that learning anything new is a skill. Take
a look at the following graph. As we learn a new skill or task, the
competence line goes up and down over time. Struggle and setback
are part of the process.

Those of us who are tough on ourselves want the ascending line to
be nearly vertical—we want to master tennis, carry ourselves with easy
social confidence in any situation, get in shape instantly. But that's
part of perfectionism's unrealistic expectations. Pivots, do-overs, and
plain old messing up only feel wrong if you think they shouldn't be
happening.

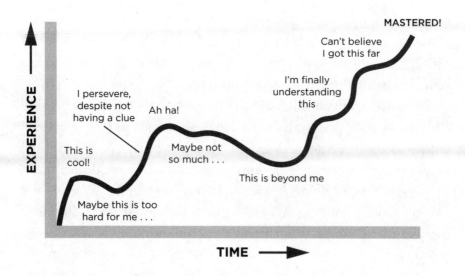

Sometimes the urge to channel our inner Elle Woods—"What, like, it's hard?"—means we prefer to keep the ups and downs of our learning process hidden. This is understandable, so if privacy increases your willingness to try something new, go for it. Frost the cake that no one will see. Do yoga in front of YouTube and your cat. If no one is around to see you fail, did you actually? Tricia did exactly this. After the stress of fiddle camp, she test-drove an interest she had secretly harbored for years, creative writing, and told no one when she enrolled in a creative writing master's program. It was certainly better to try in private than not try at all.

But some things can't be done in private. Fiddle camp. Conversing in a new language. Partner dancing. Team sports. Most of life includes witnesses and activates our peanut allergy to the possibility of mistakes and resulting judgment. But we are adequate even as we do something inadequately. The urge to hide struggle is reasonable, but being willing to let someone see you fall on the bunny slope or taste-test your overbaked brownies signals trust. Struggle, after all, is more relatable than flawlessness.

And what if someone does judge us? It's possible. Probable, even. Judgy people will judge you no matter what you do—ask Dua Lipa about the fallout from her pencil sharpener dance. You'll bust your butt to be respected, then get called pretentious. You'll try hard to be modest, and someone will label it low self-esteem. You'll work hard to follow your ethical standards and get called uptight. You can't win. It's cliché, but you truly can't please everyone, so you might as well follow your values and do what's important to you.

But getting judged still hurts. It's well established that our physical and social neural pain systems overlap, which explains why judgment, criticism, and rejection feel so bad. And if we layer on the cultural expectation not to care what anyone thinks, when we do feel hurt, we conclude we're doing it wrong. Indeed, expecting ourselves not to react to judgment amounts to fighting biology. It's why dozens of compliments don't balance out one criticism: criticism is still a social threat.

What to do? First, those of us who are hard on ourselves tend to default to taking judgment personally. We take others' judgment as proof of a flawed self, especially if we spend time and energy ensuring we're blameless and well liked. But just like the adage "Be yourself," the phrase "Don't take it personally" is simultaneously an eye-rolling cliché and crucially solid advice.

It's helpful for me to remember that habitually judgmental people are usually even harsher to themselves, even if they hide it well. An Outer Critic usually signals an Inner Critic. I read their judgment as an unintended announcement that exposes their inner world. In many cases, this helps me feel compassion for them, and the rest of the time, well, there are worse crimes than a bit of schadenfreude.

That said, the key to "Don't take it personally" doesn't mean defensively finding someone else to blame. It means accepting that criticism is part of life and making room for it, assuming it falls short of emotional abuse. Judgment is the tax for doing anything in the world—launching into adulthood, finding a partner, making and maintaining friendships, existing on social media, or creating anything from a TPS report to a charcuterie board to a child.

But we can make judgment hurt less by focusing on and affirming what's important to us. Simple reminders of our deepest values can make us feel less defensive and more self-compassionate. The best part? It doesn't even have to be related to the criticism at hand. For example, if your academic performance gets panned, you don't have to tamp down defensiveness by focusing on all your past academic triumphs. Instead, wounds can be healed indirectly by focusing on things you know to be unquestionably true about yourself: "I know I'm a really good mom," "Reading books and making art make my world go round," "I was put on earth to help the less fortunate," "Dance is my passion," "I have wicked awesome style," or anything else you genuinely hold dear can shore up the story of yourself and thicken your skin, buffering against threat.

As social psychologists Drs. Geoffrey Cohen and David Sherman explain in their 2014 review of values affirmation interventions, "The goal is not to appraise every threat in a self-flattering way but rather to maintain an overarching narrative of the self's adequacy. A healthy narrative gives people enough optimism to 'stay in the game' in the face of the daily onslaught of threats, slights, challenges, aggravations, and setbacks."

> **TRY IT OUT:** Not to rip off Oprah, but what do you know for sure about yourself and your life? When you're feeling judged or criticized, write out one (or more) deeply held convictions. The judgment or criticism will still be there, but so will your truths.

All in all, we can move our thinking from "This is an exam" with an eye on mistake prevention to "This is an experiment." Whether our activity is as fluid as learning to improvise on the fiddle, as concrete as learning to code, or as amorphous as making a friend, we can approach our journey as a series of let's-see-what-happens-if-I-try-it-this-way steps. In other words, rather than approaching a task as if we have one shot, we can approach it as if we are trying out the next step.

After a lifetime of high-stakes "exams" in front of teachers and worldwide audiences, Tricia is learning to approach life as a series of experiments. Today, Tricia tries to let herself do things just because she feels like trying them out. It's not intuitive—the years of intense pressure are hard to counteract. But she's making it happen. After keeping her creative writing under wraps at first, Tricia did something different. She launched a blog and a podcast, both titled *Is It Recess Yet?* about growing up a child prodigy. Blogs and podcasts are, by their very nature, public and required learning in full view of a growing audience.

Tricia also revisited improvisation and learned that one wrong note on its own might be perceived as a mistake, but deliberately repeated, it could become part of a new phrase or theme. Unlike in classical music, she didn't need to aim for one outcome—there could be a whole range of outcomes. Now when she plays classical pieces, she says, "I think about the character, the art." Classical music, her original genre, "is more of a pleasure *because* I veered away." It's not always an easy road, though. "The second things get pressurized, old habits come back."

These days, when she struggles on the violin, rather than punishing herself with more hours of practice, she might work on some blog writing, do some reading, and then turn back to violin. The other day, Tricia told me, she was working on a notoriously difficult Paganini caprice. But this time, when she got stuck, she put it down and turned to some K-pop arrangements just for fun. She added embellishments and enjoyed the rhythm. When she turned back to the Paganini, she had a fresh infusion of perspective. It wasn't an exam. Instead, it was a pleasure.

FROM PROCRASTINATION TO PRODUCTIVITY

It's Not About Time Management

Tomorrow at 9:00 a.m., you have an interview for your dream job. It's exactly what you want to do, the pay is almost double what you're making now, plus you get amazing benefits and a bunch of perks. You're too excited to sleep and keep tossing and turning as you lie in bed. Finally, you doze off around 3:00 a.m., visions of a fat paycheck and work you love dancing in your head.

When you open your eyes, you slowly turn over and glance at the clock. You sit bolt upright with a surge of adrenaline. It's 8:30! You must have turned off your alarm in your sleep! You throw on some clothes, jump in the car, and speed off. You realize you're driving too fast, but it's the only way you'll make it on time.

At the upcoming intersection, the light turns yellow. You gun it, and your car speeds forward. Just as you reach the intersection, the light turns red, and as you barrel through, a car pulls out right in front of you. You slam on the brakes, but it's too late. You crash into the side of the car and hear a sickening crunch and smashing glass.

When you come to and blink open your eyes, you're lying on the ground and a group of people are standing over you. You hear sirens in the distance. One of them tells you not to move—help is on the way.

Out of the corner of your eye, you see another group of people gathered around a woman with a small child limp in her arms. You hear her cry out, "She's dead! My baby is dead!"

It's the mid-1990s. You're an undergrad at Case Western Reserve University and you're probably wearing a slip dress over a shrunken white T-shirt, grunge flannel, or Reebok Pumps. As part of your psychology class, your professor has mandated participating in at least one departmental study, so you signed up for this one. A few moments earlier, a pleasant grad student who introduced herself as Dianne Tice sat down with you at a large conference table, handed you a paper on which an extended version of this story was written, and asked you to read it aloud.

"Great, thanks for reading that," said Dianne when you finished. "Can you read it again silently to yourself?"

You nod and read it again. It's clear it's supposed to take you on an emotional roller coaster. You can tell you've guessed correctly when, after reading it twice, she asks you to write a short essay on your emotions to amplify them even more. It's easy: regret, grief, guilt.

But then Dianne does something kind of woo-woo. She produces a big purple candle, slides it to the middle of the table, and lights it with a match. As wax begins to pool around the burning wick, it emits a strong floral scent. "This aromatherapy candle has been shown to freeze your mood," she says. "Whatever mood you are in right now, you are very likely to stay in the same mood throughout the experiment."

Then things pivot again. "Okay, now there's a pop math quiz," she says. You roll with it; psychology experiments are goofy.

"I'll come back in fifteen minutes with a challenging multiplication test—no calculators allowed. The test is designed to reflect your analytical abilities and fluid reasoning skills."

This was getting personal. You had been hoping the study would involve taste-testing cookies or something, not doing three-digit multiplication that doubled as an intelligence test.

Dianne continued, "Most students show significant improvement if they practice for about ten to fifteen minutes, but practice effects level off after that, so we won't go any longer. You should practice for at least some of the time, but if you don't want to practice for the full fifteen minutes, that's fine."

Dianne gestured around the room. "Look," she said. "Here are a bunch of magazines, here's a game, or here are some puzzles. I know these are time wasters, but I like to use them when participants don't show up and I have time to kill."

You wrinkle your brow. Was she kidding? The "magazines" were a stack of yellowed technical journals. The top issue, you can see, is dated 1975. The game was an electronic preschool game, and the puzzles are chunky plastic puzzles designed for toddlers. There's a piece missing from one of them. It's like a poorly stocked dentist's waiting room, but worse.

This is a weird study, you think. Baby-killing stories, mood-freezing candles, lame-o puzzles, multiplication tests.

It was indeed a weird study. But it was also the creative brainchild of Dianne and her colleagues Drs. Ellen Bratslavsky and Roy Baumeister, and it dug straight to the root of procrastination. One element was the same for every participant: everybody got fifteen minutes to use as they pleased before the difficult multiplication test. But there were three twists. First was mood. Participants either got the feel-bad dead child story or the opposite, a feel-good story where they heroically saved a child's life and likely felt proud, happy, and capable. Second was changeability of mood. Some of the participants had their mood "frozen" with the candle while others were told their moods could change over time as moods normally do. Lastly, the distractions varied. Some got the yellowed journals and preschool puzzles while others were offered a video game, popular magazines, and an age-appropriate puzzle.

When Dianne left them alone to brush up on three-factor multiplication, she timed how long they spent doing anything but studying, whether it was paging through *People*, half-heartedly picking at the preschool puzzle, biting their nails, or even staring into space.

If straight up avoidance of an unpleasant task was the driving force of procrastination, Dianne and her colleagues reasoned, it wouldn't matter what the room was stocked with. Anything to avoid the stress or tedium of eighth-grade multiplication.

Likewise, they hypothesized, if mood repair wasn't an option—if the folks with the "frozen" mood thought it was futile to try to feel better—maybe they'd go right to the math rather than try to feel better with a few rounds of *Tetris*.

Who procrastinated the most? The group that (1) felt bad, (2) believed they had the power to feel better, and (3) had tempting distractions on hand. Dianne and her colleagues had cracked the code. The experiment demonstrated that procrastination isn't about time management after all. It's about emotion management. Whether we're procrastinating something as big as a multiyear project or as small as washing that chili-encrusted pot we're just letting soak—honestly!—procrastination prioritizes mood repair.

Before we venture further, let's define procrastination. According to procrastination researcher Dr. Fuschia Sirois of Durham University, *procrastination* is a [insert throat clearing here] "common self-regulation problem involving the unnecessary and voluntary delay in the start or completion of an important, intended task despite the recognition that this delay may have negative consequences." In other words, it's kicking the can down the road even though we know better.

Everybody procrastinates at least sometimes, but over 20 percent of adults and up to 50 percent of college students procrastinate consistently and problematically, meaning it has a measurable impact on our jobs, education, relationships, or health. Indeed, procrastination can have big implications if we put off, say, getting a colonoscopy or a mammogram, ending a bad relationship, or getting out of a toxic job. To make things worse, procrastination has been found to be a lifelong trait; it's in our very genes, with a study out of the University of Colorado Boulder finding 46 percent heritability.

Why is procrastination both so common and so hard to remedy? Aversive tasks require quite a bit of self-regulation; we have to focus, get organized, overcome inertia. And a pile of evidence shows that self-regulation deteriorates under emotional distress—heck, nobody blows up their diet, budget, sobriety, or wedding vows because they feel happy and regulated. Indeed, when our brains have to choose between a small but immediate reward and a larger but longer-term reward, feeling bad will push us toward the former.

Therefore, when a task makes us feel lousy, procrastination steps in as a coping mechanism—and a highly reinforcing one at that. Procrastination is a one-two punch that allows us to both avoid the aversive task that's making us feel bad and immediately replace it with something that makes us feel better, whether that's watching baby whales breach on TikTok, baking banana bread, or tackling virtuous but nonurgent projects like grinding through our email or deep cleaning our apartment.

But then, two things happen. One, we outsource our mood management to an external source—TikTok, baking, inbox zero, enthusiastic use of Pine-Sol. Indeed, in fMRI studies, procrastination is linked to lower activity in areas of the brain that regulate emotion, suggesting ineffective coping with negative emotion. Two, we feel worse—guilty, pressured due to time loss, plus whatever initial emotions we were trying to avoid rebound like a beach ball pushed underwater.

What ends a bout of procrastination? Our negative-emotion seesaw eventually tilts the other way. At some point, feeling bad about procrastinating outweighs feeling bad about the task. Our fear of failing the exam finally outweighs the drudgery of studying.

For those of us who are hard on ourselves, procrastination is stickiest around tasks that include some kind of judgment: we'll get graded, reviewed, reacted to, or open ourselves and our work to the opinions of others. This takes the task to a kryptonite level of aversion, even if we've done it a million times before. That's why we trade tasks laden with possible negative evaluation for tasks that are socially safer—it's unlikely that anyone will disapprove of us digging into a low-stakes, low-pressure, or high-virtue task. Case in point: I once procrastinated writing a negative student evaluation by paying my taxes. Again for those in the back: rather than deal with my own anxiety over the imagined hurt I would cause this student, I chose the tedium of *doing my taxes*. At least Uncle Sam wouldn't be resentful at me.

The Many Layers of a Procrastination Parfait

Procrastination isn't just about the task. For those of us who are hard on ourselves, triggers for consistent and problematic procrastination are as intricate as the Kardashian family tree. We stack additional layers on top, each one adding its own dose of negative emotion that requires repair before we get started.

First is our old nemesis **unrealistic standards**. When we hold ourselves to unrealistically high standards for completing a task—a blow-the-boss's-socks-off presentation, a multi-paragraph handwritten reflection in every birthday card, an annual review for a direct report that somehow lists their weaknesses while making them feel good—we can feel overwhelmed, anxious, unsure, insecure, inadequate: all emotions procrastination works to avoid.

Next is good ol' **fear of failure**—as we remember, those of us who are hard on ourselves selectively attend to failure. We focus on flaws, including possible future flaws, both in outcome and process—our result wasn't good enough, or we didn't stick to a certain standard of procedure. Remember Pieter, who put such pressure on himself to make impressive comments in meetings that he felt paralyzed? Pieter's therapy homework was to make low-stakes remarks in meetings such as "I agree with Issa's point," but he kept putting it off because he was afraid he would feel stressed—to him, a failure of process. Even if he said, "I agree with Issa," feeling his heart pound would mean he had failed in his expectation of experiencing a wink-and-finger-guns level of confidence.

Fear of failure can also explain why we procrastinate "easy" tasks.* For

---

* Not all postponement is procrastination. There is a fine line between deprioritizing tasks that fall into the dead zone of "not urgent/not important" and procrastinating in order to avoid the negative emotion that goes with a task that's a hassle, annoying, boring, pointless, or otherwise aversive. I once had a client who put off recycling old paint cans for two years, which on the surface looked like de-prioritization. But for him, it was procrastination because thinking about it created a feeling of anxiety—he didn't want to do it incorrectly and be criticized by the sanitation workers.

Noah, an unemployed twenty-year-old with symptoms best described as failure to launch, enrolling in one class or filling out an application to work at the local coffee shop was overwhelming. Why? If our approach is all or nothing, low expectations can backfire. From Noah's perspective, if he failed at the "small" things—volunteering once a week, getting out of bed before noon—what would *that* say about him? Lowering the bar is threatening, because what if we can't clear it?

Next is **procrastination-related self-criticism**. Now we're getting meta. Feeling bad about playing *Minecraft* for eight hours or avoiding writing a will for ten years slathers on more negative emotion—guilt, shame, self-loathing—like layers of frosting on a very unpleasant cake. And don't forget our well-practiced **general self-criticism**: we dub ourselves stupid, lazy, incompetent, disorganized, hopeless. The contempt we feel for ourselves carries over to the next task, and the cycle of negative emotion and repair through procrastination begins anew.

Sometimes many layers come together at once. Take Antonio, a first-generation college student with a gnarly case of impostor syndrome. His dad worked as a janitor, and he felt immense pressure to excel and to honor his parents' sacrifices for him. He worried that the admissions team had made a mistake letting him in and pictured a dean dispatching a henchman to explain, sorry, there'd been an unfortunate mistake. To remedy the situation, Antonio thought maybe if he could show the college how hard he worked, how he wasn't squandering his precious opportunity, they'd let him stay.

Therefore, whenever Antonio had to write a paper, he was full of self-doubt. He thought *he* was the problem (general self-criticism).

As I got to know Antonio, it became clear that he expected himself to sit down in a library carrel, calmly and confidently open his laptop, and immediately generate a steady stream of full sentences like water flowing from the tap (unrealistic standards; fear of failure—process). He expected his first draft to be the final draft (more unrealistic standards; fear of failure—outcome).

But due to all the pressure, what would actually happen is that he'd sit down in a carrel, open his laptop, and then proceed to read the news, rationalizing that he should know what's happening in the world. Or he'd swipe through TikTok, telling himself that he just needed a break real quick. Before he knew it, it was time to go to his next class. Antonio would end up cranking out papers at the last minute, cringing as he clicked Turn In, and kicking himself for being in this predicament yet again (procrastination-related self-criticism). Closing his laptop, he'd vow that next time, he'd do better. Be better.

Antonio's zero-tolerance policy toward inefficiency and mistakes kept him paralyzed, as did his assumption that disaster—getting kicked out of school—would follow. The work of Dr. Patricia DiBartolo and colleagues at Smith College backs this up; they found that participants who struggled with perfectionism were significantly more likely to (1) anticipate a horrible outcome and (2) think it was likely to occur, which explained the visions of a grumpy dean in Antonio's head and his resultant TikTok sinkholes.

TRY IT OUT: Take stock to understand your procrastination. What factors do you relate to?

Unrealistic standards: What standards do you expect yourself to reach? What do you expect the quality of your work to be? Would you expect that of anyone else?
Fear of failure (outcome or process): Do you feel overwhelmed or stuck because your outcome might fail to meet expectations, whether yours or someone else's? Along the way, does your procedure, effort, or emotion need to be correct or unerring?

> ***Procrastination-related self-criticism:***
> How do you talk to yourself during or after procrastinating? "Why can't I do what I should be doing?" "I should be more responsible." "No matter how much I try, I still put things off." "Why can't I just get started?"
> ***General self-criticism:*** How do you characterize yourself regarding procrastination? "I'm lazy." "I'll never reach my goals." "I have horrible self-control." "I have to do better."

On the surface, the solution seems simple: just get started! But it's not that easy. Let's look at four ways we can keep procrastination from dragging on longer than an airport security line the day before Thanksgiving.

Get Started and Your Mood Will Catch Up

If procrastination is about avoiding negative emotion, do we have to finesse ourselves into a better mood? Are kindness and forgiveness the golden ticket to never procrastinating again? Honestly, no. We don't have to feel better before we start. We can feel crappy and still get started.

This can feel like a hard sell. It smacks of a drill sergeant with a bulging forehead vein and flying spittle yelling, "I don't care how you feel! Just do it!" But hear me out. Remember those two levers at our disposal: acceptance and change. Let's pull both.

Start with some acceptance. We procrastinators, research shows, don't come by mindfulness naturally. Indeed, a phenomenon called *overidentification with affective states*—if I feel it, it must be true—is pretty much the opposite of mindfulness. Anyone who has ever been hangry and then picked a fight with their partner knows how this works. (Me? Never.)

But instead of getting yanked around by how we feel, we can try watching our emotions like a movie playing out on the big screen of our minds. It's not even a long movie; the intensity of emotion drops in a matter of seconds to minutes. What goes up must come down. We can notice our anxiety, overwhelm, or however we feel without needing it to go far, far away. And then, we can open PowerPoint *while* we feel incompetent, figure out the next step *while* we feel incapable, or crack open the book and start studying *while* we feel stupid.

That's acceptance. Now let's pull the lever of "change."

Peel a Banana: Breaking Tasks Down into Ridiculously Small Steps

It's way easier to mindfully tolerate feeling lousy while starting a teeny-tiny task than to mindfully tolerate feeling lousy while starting a ginormous task. Let's use the classic behavior-change technique of breaking tasks down into small steps—but here's the key: we'll break it down into steps so small we feel no resistance.

Our internal cattle prod doesn't like breaking things down. It prefers all or nothing. It tells us we have to do the whole thing, start to finish, in one sitting, effortlessly. But breaking down tasks also breaks down our aversion. My final year of grad school, I worked on a study for individuals with depression and diabetes. One participant was trying to motivate himself to go to the gym, and while I don't remember his name, I remember his first step, which was literally "Peel a banana." This was the precursor to eating the banana that would fuel his workout. "Find car keys" was one of the subsequent steps, which I found highly relatable.

In her book, *Fear and Other Uninvited Guests*, psychologist Dr. Harriet Lerner writes about a friend who lost 190 pounds. Her friend said, "Never in my wildest imagination could I picture losing 190, but I knew that I could lose one pound. That was doable, achievable, and possible, so I simply lost one pound 190 times."

Nobody has to know how small your steps are. Start with "Peel a banana," "Lose one pound," "Turn on computer," or even "Get more information to figure out first step." Retroactively put smaller steps you've already done on your to-do list just for the satisfaction of crossing them off. If you feel any resistance at all, break it down further.

Most effective is the one-two punch of acceptance and change together: when we break down our task into tiny steps *and* are willing to accept feeling temporarily lousy, it's easier to get started. Do this combo regularly, and we collect a tidy bundle of *mastery experiences*, which are essentially small successes and—guess what—we start to feel better, or at least less bad. Each experience of mastery pumps a little bit of air into the proverbial tire of feeling better, and feeling better shrinks procrastination. So we'll make room for our lousy feelings, do the first ridiculously small step—our own equivalent of peeling the banana—and let the momentum of small successes propel us forward.

> **TRY IT OUT:** What tiny step can you take to get started? If you feel any resistance, make it smaller.

Forgive Yourself for Procrastinating

If the goal of procrastination is on-demand mood repair, let's try out other ways to repair our mood. Procrastination researcher Dr. Timothy Pychyl and colleagues found that undergraduates who forgave themselves for procrastinating while studying for their first Psychology 101 midterms procrastinated less while studying for their second midterms. The reason: "decreasing negative affect." In other words, rather than repairing their moods by procrastinating even more, self-forgiveness provided real mood repair and more motivation to study. Likewise, Dr. Fuschia Sirois ran a meta-analysis that found that the relationship between stress and procrastination can be changed through self-compassion. This tracks: if procrastination functions to make us feel better, talking to ourselves kindly—self-forgiveness, self-compassion—can achieve that same effect.

Antonio did not like this at all. Being kind to himself, especially in the face of procrastination, felt wrong, like he was letting himself off the hook, going soft, or losing his edge. His gut told him to improve, not forgive.

I wish I could say, "And then he tried self-forgiveness, and it worked." But that's not exactly what happened. Instead, when he found himself scrolling through the news or swiping through TikTok, he thought, simply, *Oh well*. It wasn't quite self-kindness, but it was less self-criticism and self-disparagement than he usually subjected himself to. At the end of the day, our goal is to do what works. This was Antonio's version of self-kindness and self-forgiveness, and it let up the pressure enough to feel a tiny bit better. As time went on, Antonio was willing to say to himself after procrastinating, "I must have needed that," or, "Oh, this makes sense—I pushed myself pretty hard yesterday." He inched closer to self-forgiveness.

As for us, we might say, "Expecting myself to clean the whole house was really overwhelming; I see why I put that off. It's okay—these things happen." Or simply, "Grace," or "You're all right." This is not magically completed with a snap of our fingers. Repeat it, be patient with contrary feelings like frustration or insistence, and let it slowly sink in.

Did Antonio stop procrastinating forever? No way. But he did experience the power of loosening his grip. TikTok still had a place, but so did understanding, forgiveness, and compassion.

TRY IT OUT: Reflect on a recent bout of procrastination. How does your procrastination make sense? What makes it understandable? From that place of understanding, can you freely choose to forgive yourself, even partway? This may take more than one try. Forgive yourself for struggling with forgiveness.

Connect with Your Future Self

When we're stressed or tired, we pin our hopes on the future version of ourselves. We reason that our future selves will somehow be less tired, more motivated, and able to jump in with gusto. It's the same reason the most common day of the week to start a diet is "tomorrow."

We naturally experience different versions of ourselves over the course of our lives. I hear this phenomenon from clients a lot: "The person I was before I got sober would never recognize me now." "The way I was in high school seems like a different person." "Post-breakup, this is a whole new me."

Dr. Sirois has found that people who procrastinate feel more disconnected than average from their future selves, even if the future is just tomorrow morning. Neuroscience research backs her up; when participants who felt disconnected from their future selves were asked to imagine their future selves, their brains lit up similarly to when they imagined a total stranger.

Since procrastination centers on mood repair, putting our faith in our imaginary future eager beaver selves makes us feel better right now, not only because we don't have to feel bad by starting our task but also because we don't have to feel bad about procrastinating—our future selves will take care of it!

However, because that future self is so different from how we feel right now (motivated! energetic! disciplined! confident!), we feel disconnected from it, like a stranger. Moreover, kicking the can down the road to an idealized future self who will gladly clean the kitchen, work out, or write that final English literature paper keeps us from fully realizing that our *actual* future selves will probably also not want to tackle that pile of dishes in the sink, go to spin class, or wade through *Ulysses*.

Though we can't time travel, Dr. Eve-Marie Blouin-Hudon came close. She created a "mental imagery intervention to increase future self-continuity and reduce procrastination." In her study, she walked college student participants through a guided imagery practice that asked them to "see" their end-of-semester self from an outside perspective. Some sample sentences:

> Pay attention to your future self's face and body. What is your future self wearing? You notice that your future self is holding a textbook and is opening it to read. Pay close attention to the book. Does it look brand new or has it been used often? You look around and see more textbooks, articles, and notebooks from your other classes stacked around your future self. Are the articles highlighted or left blank? Have the notebooks been used often or do they look unused? You see your future self glance over at a notebook and read the notes for a final written assignment that is due in a few days. Does it look like the assignment is almost finished or is there still a lot to be done? How do you think your future self feels? Is your future self prepared for this time of year?

Notice that the script doesn't mandate visualizing a well-thumbed textbook or imagining feeling prepared for finals. Instead, it's choose-your-own-adventure all the way. The point? Vividly imagining our future selves with lots of sensory detail, both inside and out, can make us feel more empathetic for and connected to our future selves and our goals.

> **TRY IT OUT:** When you're tempted to kick the can down the road, picture your future self. It's less about whether your future self has procrastinated or not. Simply aim for strong personal images that promote a sense of empathy and connection with your future self.

As for Antonio, after a particularly stressful stretch, he procrastinated to the point where he had to ask for a twenty-four-hour extension on a paper from a professor, who promptly replied, "No." It was a bitter pill to swallow, and he handed in the paper late for a grade deduction. Even as he continued to struggle with procrastination, he tried to be kinder to himself while he did so. His expectations for himself stayed high—he wanted to advance his family and do right by their hard work. But he discovered he could do that more effectively when his Inner Critic wasn't metaphorically standing over him, yelling at him to do better. Turns out, excellence could include some self-kindness and even some TikTok.

Shift 6

FROM COMPARISON
TO CONTENTMENT

13

Hardwired but Not Haywire

ALL MY REASONS not to go are ridiculous," said Liz. "I think I need to lose the fifteen pounds I gained during quarantine, and then I tell myself that's insane—literally no one cares. And then I think I'll skip this one and go to the next reunion in five years once I'm happier in my job, but that's what I said about the fifteen-year reunion. Mostly I don't want to show up and tell people I got divorced, but statistically, lots of other people probably have, too." Hearing Liz's worries and reframes was like watching a tennis match from midcourt. Her brain hit the metaphorical ball back and forth: worry, logic, worry, logic.

Liz was agonizing about whether or not to attend her twentieth high school reunion. The deadline to register was fast approaching, and she was already disappointed in herself for missing the last one. But deep in her brain, she couldn't stop comparing: her weight, her job, her relationship status. Before the fifteenth reunion, the same thing had happened: she compared her income, her then husband, her hair, and even his hair to classmates she imagined to be wealthy and happily married, with hair out of a Pantene commercial.

Logically, she knew people would be happy to see her, but she still felt she was coming up short. "I'm just not my best self right now," she said. "I want people to see what I'm capable of."

There may be fifty ways to leave your lover, but there are a zillion ways to compare yourself to others. Back in 1954, the American social psychologist Leon Festinger first published his *social comparison theory*, which proposed that we humans constantly compare ourselves to our peers. Comparison is one of the most basic and ubiquitous ways we learn about ourselves and the world—it begins as early as preschool and can even occur unconsciously. We're trying to discern who we are and how we're doing, but every answer to those questions is relative. We only know if our GPA, 5K time, or bathroom cleanliness standard is "good" if it's compared to those around us. I mean, we can't even tell if we're tall or short without comparison.

Social comparison can also function as what's called a *safety behavior*—an attempt to quell anxiety and keep our fears from coming true. We can think of comparison as a form of checking, like checking just one more time to make sure we turned off the stove, except we're checking our standing: Am I doing okay? Better? Worse? Way worse? It's a method to answer the existential anxiety of *Am I good enough?*

But like all safety behaviors, even if we feel better temporarily ("My post got more likes than Kendra's"), it backfires in the long run because (1) it takes up bandwidth that we'd otherwise use to live our lives, and (2) it steals the credit when we come out on top, which underscores the idea that comparing was necessary and important. But most importantly, (3) it backfires because we're outsourcing our worth; our self-esteem rises and falls with each comparison.

Singular but Separate

One kind of comparison, Festinger postulated, is *downward social comparison*, which is comparing ourselves to those we perceive as worse off. The resultant emotions can be negative and directed toward others: pity at best, contempt at worst. Or it can inspire positive feelings that are directed inward: gratitude, thankfulness.

But deciding we've come out on top can also make us feel a little bit superior; maybe you feel just a *teensy* bit smug that you can outsit your peers in meditation class, are the only one in your organic chemistry study group who stuck to the three-week plan for the final, or are the least basic person in the room.

Sometimes our Inner Critics tell us we have to be exceptional simply to meet the standard of "good enough." We work unnecessarily hard to crank out a superior performance. For better or worse, we can pull it off by turbocharging our self-control, delaying gratification, and over-tolerating distress ("I'm *fine*").

My client Jordan was a college athlete who trained through injury and exhaustion because, after much reflection, she realized it made her feel singular—a songbird among sparrows. Her teammates didn't have a three-year daily workout streak—but she did. Liz Jones, the British editor of *Marie Claire*, suffered from an eating disorder for forty years. She wrote, "That's the thing about being a borderline anorexic: it makes you feel superior, clean, morally unimpeachable." As for me, for a long time, I felt tough and honorable for giving birth to my kids without painkillers, but now I realize I was trying too hard to be exceptional.

Like all safety behaviors, being tough on ourselves, blended with downward comparison, backfires. We feel singular and at the same time singled out, separated from potential community and simple enjoyment, not to mention fielding skeptical eyebrow raises from the obstetrician.

Separate Because We Suck

The other direction, Festinger theorized, is *upward social comparison*, or comparing ourselves to those we perceive as better off. The resulting emotions can drill inward: we feel intimidated or dejected. Or outward—we become resentful when we perceive others are doing better in a sphere we care about, especially if we think they're unqualified or undeserving. Sometimes it's positive: we feel inspired: "If she can do it, I bet I can, too!" But often it's negative, leading to insecurity, hostility, resentment.

Take Conor, a conventionally handsome, Boston-accented extrovert.

The receptionists at the clinic loved him: "Hey, you still making trouble?" he'd flirt, with a wink, whenever he came in. He'd be right at home as part of Ben Affleck's entourage in a movie set in Southie—he even manages a pub. But that persona was exactly the problem.

Conor felt his fun-loving, flirty goofball side had to be on display all the time simply to be good enough. Worse, he got feedback when he wasn't "on"—"Hey, you're quiet today," or "Are you all right?" which made him feel like he wasn't meeting expectations. His inner social comparisons were loud and powerful. If one of Conor's friends told an entertaining story or made everyone laugh while they were out golfing or at a bar watching a Red Sox game, Conor's mind automatically went to, "People would rather be hanging out with him, not me." Even with family, he convinced himself his relatives liked his brother-in-law better than him. Conor was embarrassed to admit all this: "Why can't I just get over myself?"

In the same vein as Conor's question, we might feel quietly resentful of our colleague's promotion, our friend's windfall, or our committee cochair's organizing skills, especially if we think they're not working as hard as we are. And that resentment? Aside from feeling down on ourselves, you guessed it: it separates us from them.

Festinger theorized that social comparison was automatic and inevitable. This means trying not to compare ourselves to others is fighting biology. We can't stop, even if we want to. Since Festinger's initial hypothesis, a host of neural evidence has emerged to back up the theory. Drs. Tobias Greitemeyer and Christina Sagioglou of the University of Innsbruck in Austria scanned participants' brains while they earned money for a simple task—estimating in a split second how many dots appeared on a screen. At the end of the task, participants not only received money for their own performance but also how they performed relative to other participants. On the fMRI readouts, the ventral striatum, a part of the brain that tracks subjective value of stimuli, glowed like a campfire based on *relative* payoff. It was activated by comparison, no matter how much money each participant earned individually. This might explain why billionaires try to one-up each others' yachts.

Whichever direction comparison goes—upward or downward—

Festinger also theorized that we compare ourselves to people who are similar to us, which explains why Liz compares herself not to, say, Jennifer Lopez or Jeff Bezos but more to Jennifer and Jeff from her graduating class.

Why? We are social animals. Because our ancient survival depended on staying in good standing within a group, we keep a close eye on our own behavior, which includes comparing ourselves to others to ensure we're keeping pace and coloring within the lines of acceptability. Comparison has kept us and the group going for eons.

But it is notable that such a primeval tendency has been supersized by the most modern of technologies: social media. By now, we know that social media is designed with surgical precision to make users feel deficient and demoralized using gorgeously styled coffee tables, otherworldly travel destinations, masterful makeup tutorials, and carefully orchestrated displays of how real we can be: #MessyHairDontCare. When the standard is set at "dizzying," we feel a nagging sense that our real-life clutter-strewn table, vacation package to Orlando, middling winged eyeliner abilities, or even our mainstream insecurities just aren't good enough. What results is a sense of *discrepancy*, which is psychology-speak for the difference between how we are and how we want to be. Discrepancy, whether it's from social media or IRL, feeds all sorts of not-good-enough sentiments: status anxiety, social anxiety, FOMO, and #goals.

Sometimes social media creates actual community. We find our people; we're more connected. But sometimes this virtual engagement merely *simulates* the meeting of fundamental needs. Plus, psychologist Dr. Andrew Przybylski of Oxford has found that when our basic human needs are not satisfied—love, belonging, and community—we are *more* likely to gravitate toward social media. This makes sense—when we feel like we're in need of some affiliation, of course we're going to seek out more information about our fellow humans. But we can't fill those needs by lurking. A study led by Dr. Philippe Verduyn found that passive social media use—lurking instead of participating—went along with greater social comparison, usually upward social comparison.

But even though comparison is hardwired, it doesn't have to go haywire. Despite the inevitability, we decide how much to fan the flames. It's not the act of comparison that's the problem—it's the result: outsourcing our self-worth to others.

What can we do? The easiest yet most time-consuming technique for reducing the sting of comparison: get older. A study in *Personality and Individual Differences* found that comparison declines as we age. Social comparison is set to "maximum" when we're young and declines as we live our lives. But we can speed things up a bit.

Apples to Tennis Balls

Social comparison has survived evolutionarily, in part, because of efficiency. What may have started with cavemen comparing their fires to their neighbors' fires has morphed into comparing our job titles to Larry's (*"That* guy is an executive director?") because it's quick. We save precious energy and bandwidth by zeroing in on a subset of information—your fire versus Zog's, your job title versus Larry's—rather than sifting through every variable from kindling availability to possible nepotism. But this reveals a fatal flaw. Social comparison is, at its heart, a lack of information. Therefore, to limit its negative effects, let's get more information.

My client Abby fretted that she was the same age as her boss. "What's wrong with me that I'm not at that point in my career?" she asked. She was comparing based on age, which was apples to apples, and job title, which was apples to apple pie, so we broadened the comparison points until we were comparing apples to tennis balls. There were some comparison points she knew: he had an MBA versus her BA; he'd been working at the company for five years, while she was just starting her second year. But there were also a slew of possible comparison points without data: ambition, work hours, institutionalized sexism, partner support or lack thereof, mental health challenges, and other X factors we hadn't even thought of.

By now, we know that social media is the curated highlight reel of others' lives. But so is everything else we see in public. Your coworker's big house might be worth less than he owes on it. Your friend's new promotion might be inducing stomach ulcers and a secret wish to quit and make artisanal goat cheese.

When we compare ourselves to others, we're really asking, "Am I good enough?" Therefore, the goal is to include so many comparison points, both in quantity and variety, that the answer becomes, "Well, I certainly can't determine that by comparing myself to this person!" The comparison falls apart.

Bonus: Sometimes, getting more information allows us to know our comparison target as an actual person. Inevitably, there will be different personalities, aspirations, mindsets, histories, drives, vices, and downfalls. The point is not to revel in their revealed "weaknesses" or to fuel schadenfreude. Instead, when we get to know the people we compare ourselves to, we see that the picture is complex and comparison, thankfully, is futile.

TRY IT OUT: Reflect on getting to know someone who previously intimidated you. How might this apply to the people you currently compare yourself to?

Purpose: Comparison's Shock Absorber

Hassan came to the clinic as a first-year college student whiplashed by metamorphosing from the biggest fish—he was both valedictorian and prom king—in the small pond of his tiny K–12 school to just another fish among thousands in a big private university. A few months into his first semester of college, he found himself caught up not only in comparing himself to how others were doing but also his past self. Indeed, the common advice of "Only compare yourself to who you were yesterday" was backfiring hard. Old Instagram posts of himself bespangled with medals or wearing his prom king crown triggered anxiety, grief, and sadness. "I'll never be this person again," he said. Hassan alternated between ruminative scrolling and avoiding social media for weeks, thereby missing out on DMs from his friends. "Anything less than this," he mused, nodding to old posts on his phone, "is kind of a failure because I already established that I could do it. So I should be able to do it again." He reminded me of an aging starlet gazing at her old movie stills. "I just want to get back to where I was."

Given that time travel wasn't part of the clinic's repertoire, we focused instead on what it was about his achievements that made him value them. Bonding as a winning team? The sense of mastery that came from doing something well? Representing his family and community?

What we were aiming for was *purpose*, defined as a "self-organizing life aim that organizes and stimulates goals, manages behaviors, and provides a sense of meaning." Purpose is personally meaningful, but it also ripples out beyond the individual, providing a sense of connection. In an illustrative study in the *Journal of Experimental Social Psychology*, Drs. Anthony Burrow and Nicolette Rainone of Cornell University asked study participants to post a selfie to a Facebook dupe site and then gave them fake feedback about how many likes their picture received: low, average, or high. They found that the number of likes people received predictably either fed or dragged down their self-esteem, but the effect *in either direction* diminished for those with a strong sense of purpose in life. In other words, it's not that people with stronger purpose didn't notice likes at all, but they didn't rely on them to feed their self-esteem; their self-esteem was less contingent on social approval.

So Hassan thought: *What do I care deeply about? What would I keep doing even if I never got a medal or prom crown?** By our final session, he was still sad about going from big man on campus to random first-year, but comparing his new self with his old self seemed less relevant when he focused on inspiration rather than decoration.

---

* The answer: hip-hop choreography, biology, and his service fraternity.

TRY IT OUT: Purpose isn't a one-and-done life hack—it's more a mindset—but keep your eye on what matters to you and why you get out of bed.

The Opposite of Envy

We can't control our feelings or our thoughts—don't think about a cheeseburger sitting on top of your head!—but we can control our actions. A classic technique from dialectical behavior therapy is to do the opposite of what our negative emotions are telling us to do. Anxiety tells us to avoid, so doing the opposite means facing our fears head-on and doing exactly what we're afraid of. Stress tells us to rush, so doing the opposite means slowing down.

Social comparison can lead to envy.* Envy stems from perceived scarcity—there's only so much to go around. With Conor and the goodwill of his friends, he thought more for them meant less for him. Behaving opposite to envy meant wishing them well—wishing more for them, whether silently or out loud. Conor test-drove silently wishing for more good reactions for his brother-in-law and his cousins. It felt forced and unnatural, but over time, he found that more jokes meant more fun for everyone, and just as importantly, he didn't have to carry the burden of entertaining everyone on his shoulders. "I'm a fun guy who's allowed to have a quiet moment," he marveled.

Social comparison also brings us shame. Shame tells us to withdraw and isolate, like Liz opting out of the reunion. So doing the opposite of shame can include cooperation. Deep within social comparison is the assumption that other people are the competition. Some people relish competition, but not everyone. A lot of people would

---

* Envy is commonly equated with jealousy, like, "Oh, I'm so jealous of her promotion." Both are complex negative social emotions, but they are technically different: *envy* is wanting something you don't have; *jealousy* is fear of losing something you have.

rather opt out. So instead, make friends. Team up. Get advice. When we compare ourselves, we get caught up in others' lives. But sharing, reaching out, and getting closer enriches ours.

> **TRY IT OUT:** What is envy, shame, intimidation, or comparison telling you to do? Test out doing the exact opposite: get advice rather than bragging, wish others well rather than talking smack.

Comparison will still be there. Again, it's hardwired. When social comparison knocks at our door, it makes sense to answer, but we don't have to invite it in and offer our Netflix password. Comparison can exist as a low drone of background noise as you continue to do what's important to you.

Liz ended up going to the reunion, and though she couldn't shut off her brain's comparisons entirely—*How does Louisa look that amazing after three kids?*—she was glad she showed up despite her hesitancy. Liz felt some surges of envy and insecurity at balayage highlights and diamond-studded wedding bands, but showed some impressive magnanimity to herself, reporting, "I figure we all revert to high school at a high school reunion." Even better, "I'm meeting up with some of them for brunch next month," she said with a smile. "We all agreed we can't wait five more years."

Shift 7

FROM CONTROL
TO AUTHENTICITY

Rolling Back Emotional Perfectionism

Being Real on the Inside

S HE TELLS ME I'm cute or that she loves me or that she appreciates me, and it doesn't really sink in," Carter says. "I'm like, 'Why is she saying this? She's just being nice. Does she want something?'"

Carter, who dropped math in favor of biology in chapter 6, was explaining to me that his girlfriend gets annoyed at him because he never believes her when she compliments him or is earnestly positive.

Here's the backstory: Growing up, Carter's mom put a premium on appropriate behavior. When he went to a high school dance, she expected him not only to be charming to ensure his own date had a good time but to be beneficent by asking the wallflowers to dance and make sure they had a good time, too. He described the "right" way to feel at basketball tournaments: "You're supposed to want to win but also be positive and demonstrate good sportsmanship." And at family gatherings, his only options were to feign interest in his older relatives' stories or to pretend to enjoy taking care of his little cousins. He remembered feeling obligated to perform happiness and gregariousness without truly experiencing either. So he put a smile on his face and faked it.* Without meaning to, he learned that emotions were supposed to match the external situation, not his internal experience.

Carter learned from the best: he watched his parents feign appropriate reactions of delight, excitement, or concern to match the situation—creating as-needed, made-to-order emotions.

Made-to-order emotions sound bad, but they come from a good place. As social creatures, getting along with the group is essential for belonging and, by extension, survival. Modulating our emotions to stay in harmony with the group is a smart strategy to stay connected and accepted.

Furthermore, sometimes made-to-order emotions are appropriate: you feign gratitude unwrapping Grandma's annual hand-knit holiday sweater vest while she looks on. You turn your affability up to ten during a job interview. Four words: *service with a smile.* But when manufactured emotions become a habit, performing them makes us feel fake, empty, or even a little bit dead inside. As Dr. Karen Horney writes, "Feelings are the most alive part of ourselves; if they are put under a dictatorial regime, a profound uncertainty is created in our essential being which must affect adversely our relations to everything inside and outside ourselves." Pretty heavy stuff.

The need to be always appropriate in one's felt or demonstrated emotions is a phenomenon fittingly called *emotional perfectionism.* "Should" extends to our own feelings. Predictably, this goes two ways: either you should feel this way (read: happy, controlled, confident, strong), or you shouldn't feel that way (read: pretty much anything else).

Sometimes I will encounter clients who deny feeling particular emotions altogether: "I don't do anger." "I never cry." But they do report feeling numb, detached, or, when I ask the classic therapist question

---

* This is different from "Fake it 'til you make it." *Fake it 'til you make it* assumes you *want* to be able to do the thing you're faking. It means facing your fears: speaking up in meetings despite social anxiety, getting on a plane with a fear of flying. But Carter never aspired to be Casanova at dances or LeBron on the court—he wanted to be there but got the message that joining in and enjoying himself wasn't enough—he had to fake being exceptional, every time.

"How does that make you feel?" the answer is what they think, what they did, or occasionally, a head tilt and long silence. Other times I meet clients who mistake normal emotions like grief, disappointment, embarrassment, awkwardness, ambivalence, irritation, or boredom as problems to be solved rather than universal experiences to be felt.

Or, when we tend to manufacture our emotions like Carter, we think others do the same, which is one reason it can be hard to accept compliments. Carter assumes his girlfriend is being disingenuous because that's exactly what he learned to do.

For the Carters of the world, we turn, in spirit, to Mr. Rogers. In 1969, President Nixon proposed slashing funding for public broadcasting by half, from $20 million to $10 million. Wisely, PBS sent none other than Fred Rogers to testify before the Senate Subcommittee on Communications about the importance of teaching social-emotional learning on television. Leading the hearing was the famously abrasive Rhode Island senator John Pastore, who had neither seen nor heard of Rogers's show. He listened intently to Rogers's reasoning, including an earnest recitation of the lyrics to "What Do You Do with the Mad That You Feel?" and most importantly, the assertion that feelings are "mentionable and manageable."

After Rogers concluded, Pastore commented, "I'm supposed to be a pretty tough guy." But Rogers's testimony, he said, had given him goose bumps. "I think it's wonderful. Looks like you just earned the twenty million dollars." Applause rang through the chamber.

"Feelings are mentionable and manageable" is simple but profound enough to pull the heartstrings of an acerbic New England senator. Once we know where they come from, feelings make sense and can be regulated or simply experienced.

With that in mind, Shift 7, "From Control to Connection," is made up of two chapters. First, we'll focus on the private life of our emotions: how we feel inside, our *emotional experience*, plus our attempts at managing them, or *emotion regulation*. Chapter 15 will focus on emotions in public: what we show on the outside—how we talk, hold our faces, and act—our *emotional expression* (and its opposing counterpart, *expressive suppression*).

Therefore, for all of us who are told *you should feel this way*, or *you shouldn't feel that way*, read on for permission to feel happy, proud, hurt, insecure, ashamed, or whatever you feel. Straight from Mr. Rogers, this is for you.

Mentionable and Manageable

In Fred Rogers's testimony, "mentionable" meant acknowledging the existence of *all* our emotions. "Manageable" meant emotion regulation— implicit or explicit attempts to modify our own or others' emotions (or simply allowing them to exist—to feel what we feel). But what "manageable" *didn't* mean was "shut 'em down."

There are oodles of ways to manage emotion, some more effective or sustainable than others. We might:

» leave the situation: *exit the room, go to sleep*
» stay in a situation but modify it: *tell a joke to lighten everyone's mood, change the subject: "How 'bout them Red Sox?"*
» change the focus of your attention: *engage yourself in an activity, use mindfulness to pay attention differently, distract yourself on your phone*
» reframe a situation: *"That could have been so much worse," "I didn't want that job, anyway"*
» use overt or covert avoidance: *walk the long way around to avoid talking to anyone, or go the short way but wear headphones and sunglasses*
» worry or ruminate (yes, these are both forms of emotion regulation)*
» suppress: *stress eat, pretend everything's fine, never speak of it again*

---

* Overly simplified: Worry and rumination are cognitive methods of engaging with emotion that keep us in an abstract, intellectual, verbal headspace in an attempt to control and avoid the physiological activation of anxiety. Worry and rumination might feel bad, the worrier's brain unconsciously reasons, but feeling the anxiety feels worse.

While no method is intrinsically "good" or "bad," problems with emotion regulation are at the root of anywhere from 40 to 75 percent of psychological disorders, including 100 percent of mood and anxiety disorders.

Geoff came in for a first appointment three weeks before a major presentation at work. He wanted not only to appear calm and anxiety-free for his big moment but to *be* calm and anxiety-free. He didn't want to feel anxious at all, not one little bit. For him, his tendency to get anxious before public speaking was a personal failing. He came in wanting to "get it taken care of once and for all."

I understand Geoff. It feels bad to feel bad. Nobody wants to meta-phorically blast "Everybody Hurts" at maximum volume. We'd rather bop along to "I Feel Good" or at least "Peaceful Easy Feeling."

But remember overevaluation? Geoff took feeling bad as a sign that something was wrong with him. For Geoff, getting nervous before public speaking was a character flaw. By contrast, feeling cool and confident and having total emotional control meant he was doing well as a person.

How do we end up with emotional perfectionism, this unwilling-ness to feel anything we deem inappropriate? Often, we grow up in a household allergic to negative emotion. We might have learned it's wrong to feel bad: *Put a smile on your face. Suck it up. You're being dra-matic. Stop being so sensitive. There's no reason for that attitude. If you can't say something nice, don't say anything at all. What are you so mad about?*

Stephanie, for example, grew up in a household with a type A mom who was highly sensitive to criticism, but could dish it out like a pro. "She would make comments about my weight under the guise of be-ing concerned for my health," Stephanie remembers. "And she would imply that we were destined to be lazy slobs if we didn't help her clean the house," she says. "The expectation that we help was reasonable, but her cleaning projects were always so involved—I remember once she gave me the silent treatment because I didn't want to help her vacuum the tops of the kitchen cabinets."

Whenever her dad sensed Stephanie was getting annoyed, he would run interference and say something like, "You have the best mom ever," or "Mom is such a fantastic mom." For the most part, Stephanie agrees—her mom provided a stable, pull-out-all-the-stops childhood for her. But after being on the receiving end of "I'm just trying to help" criticism yet again, Stephanie would silently stew for hours. "Long past an appropriate amount of time," she remembers. "I would try to make myself stop by saying, 'I have the best mom ever,' but it never worked."

In short, Stephanie wasn't allowed to feel hurt or angry with her mom. So when she inevitably did, she would feel confused and guilty. "I should let it go," she would tell herself. "I should get over this—it's nothing." But denying emotion works about as well as wearing high heels on the beach, which is to say, it doesn't.

As you might have guessed, emotional perfectionism has a lot of rules attached to it. These rules keep Geoff's fear or Stephanie's frustration from being "mentionable." Let's take a look at three common Inner Rulebook rules that tell us: Don't feel bad. Only feel good.

Rethinking the Rules of Not Feeling Bad

The first rule that keeps us from feeling what we feel? **Endure everything.** This rule was articulated by our old friend Karen Horney. It's a fundamental rule for a lot of us who are tough on ourselves. We were taught to persevere, stay strong, and push to overcome challenges— all good things. But when we're expected to endure everything, of all magnitudes, the rule starts to work against us.

For example, while we were working together, Carter's girlfriend nearly cheated on him. She didn't, but it was a near miss. He was heartbroken, but since she hadn't crossed the line, he didn't feel entitled to feel everything he felt: jealous, betrayed, and despondent. (She also didn't help by adopting a "let's pretend this never happened" attitude.) Trying to forget about it consumed his life for weeks. We eventually figured out "endure everything" was manifesting as *I have to get over this.*

For Carter, feeling upset violated his personal standards. He thought he was supposed to handle the situation with wise, dispassionate benevolence, not the rat's nest of emotion that kept him tunnelvisioned to the point that his friends staged a mini-intervention—"Hey, man, you good?"

Not meeting our demanding standards is perfectionism's definition of failure. So every day that Carter spun with rumination over his feelings of heartbreak was another failure. He was holding himself to the spirit of Winston Churchill's alleged quote: "Never, never, never give up." But what Churchill actually said was, "Never give in except to convictions of honor and good sense." It turns out that reconsidering, gracefully bowing out, or pivoting is very different from failing. Rather than enduring everything, we can know when to quit. When Carter finally gave himself the option of "I *don't* have to get over this" and allowed himself to feel the heartbreak, jealousy, outrage, and sadness—as well as have a series of heart-to-heart talks with his girlfriend—he decided to stay.

A second rule that drives emotional perfectionism: **Feelings need to have a clear and logical cause**. We get this one from our families of origin. We might have grown up hearing, *There's no reason to cry*, *I don't know why you're mad*, or *What are you so grumpy about?* Our feelings were denied unless there was a good reason, and maybe not even then. *It's just a dog. Kids go to new schools all the time. Maybe this will teach you a lesson.* Our families might have shut down emotions that made them uncomfortable. But when we get shut down, we get the message that our feelings are the problem. So we double down on trying to stay in control: we over-tolerate distress, overregulate, or mismatch our outside and our inside.

Once we grow up, we can update what we're allowed to feel. Thanks to Dr. Marsha Linehan, the developer of dialectical behavior therapy, we know there is a difference between *valid* and *justified* emotion. All emotions are valid, full stop. Simply having an emotion renders it valid. A justified emotion, however, is what your parents would call "reasonable." It fits the facts of the situation. Feeling jealous because you have some solid evidence your partner is cheating? Valid and justified. Feeling guilty because you dented the family car? Valid and justified.

However, feeling jealous even though your partner is clearly faithful and devoted? Actually, that's totally valid. That feeling must be coming from somewhere—a friend's relationship experience, a history of being cheated on, watching *Real Housewives* marriages go through the meat grinder. But in this case, it's not justified, and it would backfire to act on it, like going through your partner's phone or obsessively questioning their fidelity.

We can't control our feelings—they don't turn off and on like a light switch. Anyone who has ever tried to banish anxiety before public speaking or grief after losing a pet can attest to this. What we can control, however, is our actions. We can leave the room before we throw a punch in anger, or get up to deliver the best man's speech despite feeling like our internal organs are rearranging themselves, all while feeling our very valid feelings. This may not always work, of course—give yourself some grace. But it can be liberating to change the focus of control from feelings to behavior.

A third and final rule about feeling bad that backfires? The exact wording varies, but the rule views negative emotion as a breach of good form: **Always be appropriate / in control / strong**. Those of us who are hard on ourselves are good at this one. But we can be a little *too* good at managing our emotions—a little overregulated, a little overcontrolled. Geoff, for instance, was very good at turning his attention elsewhere when he felt anxious—organizing his desk, rechecking his email—but that just kicked the anxiety down the road. Stephanie's stewing for hours was rumination, which is a form of regulation. But if you ask either of them if they're okay, you'll get the same answer: "I'm fine."

This is common. Those of us who are hard on ourselves often say "I'm fine" when we're clearly not. Some of this is biological. We have selectively high pain tolerance, or as Dr. Lynch calls it, *distress overtol-*

erance. We can endure certain kinds of stress or discomfort for a long time. It's how we grind out all-nighters, exert swing-for-the-fences effort, and live the edict of "The show must go on." I Am Fine buys us a lot. We're rewarded with "We couldn't have done it without you." We save the day. We are a rock. There's a sense of capability, indispensability, pride, heroism, or rising above it all. *I'm the only one who can get the job done right because of my endurance, commitment, or willingness to go the extra mile.*

But I Am Fine also costs us. Over time, the tendency to downplay, suppress, or ignore our suffering can slide into medical problems or depression. Emotional suppression has even been linked to aggression, which might explain why "I'm *fine*" sometimes gets snarled through clenched teeth. And, paradoxically, like Stephanie stewing after not being allowed to be angry at her mother's criticisms, I Am Fine extends the duration of feeling bad. It takes us longer to bounce back after an insult, conflict, or annoyance. *I should be over this by now.*

Sometimes I Am Fine even crosses the line into martyrdom, arrogance, or bitterness. And then, it isolates us. Even as we say, "I am fine," it's clear to others that's not true. They know something's off, but if we insist all is well, they're hamstrung, not allowed to reach out or help us.

We'll talk more about this in the next chapter, but spoiler: people like us more when we show authentic emotion, even if that emotion is negative. Far from being annoying or a burden, an admission of feeling bad, without lambasting ourselves, falling apart, or blaming others, sends two messages: *I trust you* and *We are equals*, both of which are building blocks of liking and closeness.

Rethinking the Rules of Feeling Good

Emotional perfectionism can also tell us it's bad to feel good. On the surface, that's counterintuitive. But when we look deeper, it makes sense. Being proud of ourselves might feel too close to egotism. The unguardedness of joy might feel out of control. If we grew up in an always-appropriate household, we might have gotten pushback for talking excitedly, dancing exuberantly, or showing unrestrained affection. I still feel uneasy when I receive a compliment, though I've learned not to reject it with the equivalent of "Oh, staaaaahp, this old thing?"

To make things more confusing, Western society holds up the extrovert ideal version of fun. We're supposed to enjoy dancing on the bar, doing donuts in the parking lot, or drunken skinny-dipping. But hear this: it's totally okay to be wired more like Bert than Ernie. Not all fun is created equal. For a lot of us, "feeling good" means effort, satisfaction, and rosy after-the-fact reflections. That's great—no need to change a thing. The problems begin when we bring in the Inner Rulebook and can't relax or enjoy even when we've chosen to do so. Therefore, let's take a closer look at some of the rules of feeling good.

The biggest don't-feel-good rule I encounter with clients is **having fun means I'm out of control**. We might not articulate it so starkly, but the felt sense is there. Carter feels this one acutely. As a first-year college student, most Saturday nights he finds himself outside a frat party, the *untz-untz-untz* of bass rattling the windows. The night settles heavily around him as he anticipates the inescapable.

Carter hates dancing. He feels self-conscious, unnatural, and uncomfortable. He plays it off—"I'm white and majoring in a basic science—what do you want from me?" But when he inevitably gets dragged inside, Carter usually finds a place to sit, which separates him from his friends, or stands with his arms crossed while the crowd surges around him. For him, dancing feels out of control because he can't control whether or not people look at him, or what they think about him. He imagines people are watching and judging him.

When I asked our friend, the overcontrol expert Dr. Thomas Lynch, about Carter, he noted that self-consciousness is a social phenomenon—no one feels self-conscious on their own. We need at least one other person—even in our imagination—who we assume is critically observing our actions. There's an unguardedness to fun.

When we feel self-conscious, we are checking whether we are safe within our group. We can't have fun if we're feeling unsafe.

"He's in a situation where he's a chosen member of that tribe, and he's chosen to be a part of the tribe. And [dancing is] what the tribe is doing," explains Dr. Lynch. When Carter stands on the side with his arms crossed instead of dancing, it makes him stand out even more. "A lot of times, there's a secret hope that nonparticipation will somehow make you feel better." But it doesn't.

Think of other times we fervently wish nonparticipation will make us feel better: we watch from the sidelines while our friends play a lively kickball game, continue politely smiling per usual when the photographer calls for a group "crazy picture," or decline to wear a silly cone hat at a kid's birthday party. We think it will exempt us from what Dr. Lynch calls "critical scrutiny," but paradoxically, our nonparticipation may draw the attention we're trying to avoid. Opting out separates us from both the tribe and, with our self-consciousness, the present moment.

Traditional cognitive-behavioral therapy would prescribe exposures— practicing joining in until it doesn't bother us as much. Dr. Lynch does this in his skills classes for people with overcontrol, but emphasizes not taking things too seriously. You can't work at playing. You can't plan to feel like you belong. In the middle of a class, without warning, Dr. Lynch might stand, announce with a smile, "Everyone stand up! Great! Okay, do what I do!" and proceed to flap his arms like a chicken while turning in a circle, making clucking sounds. He might have the group stand and yell, "Tomato!" in increasingly ridiculous voices and then crouch to the ground, whispering, "Potato." All this takes less than thirty seconds—brevity is key—and ends in warm applause for the whole group. He calls it *participate without planning*, and it smuggles the idea that joining in, even for mere seconds, sends a powerful signal to those around us. We belong. We are part of the group and are willing to participate in order to contribute to the well-being and harmony of the tribe.

Over the weeks, the whole class builds up a storehouse of pleasurable memories of joining in. We learn that the opposite of control isn't being out of control. Once again, the opposite of control is trust. Not trust that no one is judging us or that we'll feel amazing if we just let loose a little—that's naive and misleading. But it is trust that we can handle whatever happens, both internally and externally. It's trust that we can try something out and roll with what happens.

Can we replicate this in our lives? Not as efficiently as in a skills class, but we can join in without overthinking it. Mimicking is key. It reduces the necessity of planning and focuses attention on whomever you're following. Just follow the leader. Get in the conga line at a wedding reception, join in with singing "Happy Birthday," dress up on Halloween, or, consider this:

"Beneath my laid-back college-kid demeanor, I lived like a half-closeted CEO, quietly but unswervingly focused on achievement, bent on checking every box. . . . One proving ground only opened onto the next." After laying out her striver tendencies in her memoir, *Becoming*, Michelle Obama recounts a core memory from her college years: one warm spring day, she and her boyfriend Kevin take a ride in his red compact. They head for a remote corner of Princeton's campus, rolling to a stop on an unpaved road next to a field of winter-dead grass and new flowering green shoots. Kevin opens his door and gets out:

> *"Come on," he says, motioning for me to follow.*
> *"What are we doing?"*
> *He looks at me as if it should be obvious. "We're going to run through this field."*
> *And we do. We run through that field. We dash from one end to the other, waving our arms like little kids, puncturing the silence with cheerful shouts. We plow through the dry grass and leap over the flowers. Maybe it wasn't obvious to me initially, but now it is. We're supposed to run through this field! Of course we are!*

Even if the activity isn't your cup of tea or the point isn't immediately obvious, joining in and being connected with the wedding guests on the dance floor, friends at the birthday party, the neighborhood trick-or-treaters, or your exuberant college boyfriend bonds you to the tribe.

When "should" you join in? Your choice. You decide when it's worth it to tolerate some initial discomfort if it buys you connection with others (hey, that sounds like following your values from chapter 6!). When we chant along with the crowd at a football game, agree to be part of a goofy human pyramid, or participate in Anything but a Backpack Day at school, we deposit our pennies in a bank of joining in. And as the bank fills, we can draw on memories that say, *Hey, that was actually fun.*

Surprise—this is mindfulness. Usually, we think of mindfulness as dispassionate awareness, not yelling, "Tomato!" along with a classroom full of people. But look more closely and we'll find it: we can dispassionately observe, but not necessarily respond to, urges to cross our arms and stand off to the side. We can notice how the urges naturally rise and fall, how they modulate. And then, as we "urge surf," we can turn our attention toward yelling, "Tomato!" or dancing on a Saturday night, or participating in our own lives rather than compulsive planning, rehearsal, or the need to get it right. There is dispassionate awareness in this kind of mindfulness, but there is also passionate participation in community.

> **TRY IT OUT:** Assuming it doesn't go against your values, test-drive (briefly!) joining in with what your group is doing. Observe your urge to separate or sit out. Make room for all emotions—pride, embarrassment—that occur while you're joining in.

The second rule is more felt than articulated: **conditions need to be just right** for us to enjoy ourselves. This pushes our detail-oriented buttons. When everything aligns, we get the "just right" feeling and can enjoy ourselves, but it evaporates when any detail changes: the sun overtakes our comfy shady spot, our thighs start to chafe as we stroll on the picture-perfect beach, or there's an errant fly buzzing around the picnic. The not-quite-right detail discolors the whole experience like a drop of ink in a beaker of water.

Again, mindfulness to the rescue. If your brain naturally spotlights the thing that's going wrong, bring up the houselights and use all your senses to widen your attention to encompass more of what's happening. Expand your attention to include the not-quite-right detail, but also everything else—positive, negative, neutral. Yes, there's a buzzing fly at the picnic, but there are also sweating cups of cold lemonade, crunchy potato chips, the fuzziness of the picnic blanket, our friends chatting, and a guy roller-skating in the background, singing "I Will Survive" off-key. The not-quite-right detail doesn't disappear, but it becomes part of the larger picture rather than front and center.

> **TRY IT OUT:** When a not-quite-right detail distracts you, widen your attention to notice more of the moment—positive, negative, neutral all included. Notice how the wider context affects the detail.

Another fun-stealing rule is the largely unconscious idea that **fun or relaxation is unseemly, indulgent, or not a good use of time,** à la "I love working during the holiday break—no one bothers me. I can get a ton done." Or people tell us to celebrate our accomplishments, but we just move on to the next project.

In a series of studies in the prestigious *Personality and Social Psychology Bulletin*, Drs. Katharina Bernecker and Daniela Becker found that a major impediment to what they call "hedonic success" is intrusive thoughts about long-term goals. After all, they say, it's "more difficult to enjoy an after-work drink with your colleagues if you keep thinking you should have stayed in the office." It's also why we can't enjoy the ice cream if we keep thinking about the fruit cup we "should" have chosen. Dr. Becker sums it up: "Those thoughts about conflicting long-term goals undermine the immediate need to relax."

Our success-driven culture sees fun and relaxation as a failure of self-control—when we choose to get the fries instead of the salad or read a novel instead of chipping away at our email. However, Bernecker and Becker explain, experiencing pleasure is a sign of healthy self-regulation. Just like it's important to receive as well as give, or listen as well as speak, "hedonic goals" are the yin to the yang of longer-term goals. In other words, rather than seeing them as indulgence, fun and relaxation are more akin to kindness, care, grace, or benevolence that fit together with longer-term goals as part of a well-lived life.

While we can't stop the "should" thoughts from intruding when we're trying to relax—our conscientious brains will pump them out faster than gossip spreading in a high school lunchroom—we can call on mindfulness once again. We can notice our inner nun with a ruler telling us to get up and get back to work. We can wave politely to her, then let her be. She'll still be there in the background while we turn our attention spotlight to the chatter of our colleagues, the ice cream, the fries, or the novel.

What can supercharge this? Luckily, our superior sense of self-control. We're good at downregulating bad feelings to power through a task. Use that talent to downregulate the shoulds, tap into the five senses, and be mindful of the moment. Grit and fun don't need to be in conflict. Harness one to experience the other.

> **TRY IT OUT:** Use your superpower of conscientiousness to focus on fun. Go all in—channel your inner dog chasing a ball or cat napping in a sunny spot. Allow thoughts about duty or obligation to simply be there as you use your five senses to tune in to the moment.

As for Geoff, who wanted to feel an aviator-shades-and-bomber-jacket level of confidence before his presentation, it's no spoiler to say that didn't happen—confidence is more tortoise than hare. But the talk went better than he expected.

Over the next few months of working together, true to the theme of this chapter, Geoff allowed himself to feel bad to move forward. In other words, he was willing to experience public speaking anxiety while he practiced a new upcoming presentation for his cat, then his partner, then another psychologist and me in a conference room at the clinic. He disclosed to a trusted colleague that he was nervous about presenting, who responded with, "Yeah, I hate public speaking, too," and then offered encouraging nods from the front row. Rather than trying to get rid of every little bit of anxiety like a case of head lice, Geoff gave himself permission to feel bad, which paradoxically allowed him to feel better.

15

Rolling Back Perfectionistic Self-Presentation

Being Real on the Outside

I T's EARLY SEPTEMBER, your first morning after moving into your college dorm. You wake up in an unfamiliar room with a stranger, your roommate, sleeping in the next bed a few feet away. The bathroom is down the hall, past more strangers' doors. Along with other first-years, all strangers, you troop to the dining hall, to sexual misconduct prevention training, to the inevitable ice cream social. The emotionally and socially intense task before you? Turning at least some of these strangers into friends.

Whether or not going away to college was part of your experience, at some point, you've probably found yourself in a brand-new place surrounded by strangers: moving to a new city, joining the military, starting a new job—many life events involve having to make new friends from scratch.

Those of us who are tough on ourselves often experience a sense of being different from other people, of being on the periphery. We identify with the *Dear Evan Hansen* song, "Waving Through a Window": "On the outside, always looking in." We might think it's something to do with us: we're introverts, we're not from here, we're an outsider. Or we might think it has to do with everybody else: cliquishness, department politics, local culture.

It can absolutely be those things. But here's another potential slice of the pie: humans' impressions of each other fall along two fundamental dimensions—competence and warmth.* *Competence* is being smart, talented, and effective—what researchers call "striving to individuate." *Warmth* is being trustworthy, caring, and sincere—what researchers call "striving to integrate the self in a larger social unit."

Since you're reading this book, your seesaw probably tilts toward competence. Indeed, our genetics, upbringing, and culture put us in a double bind. Even though we're wired and reinforced to focus on competence through individual achievement, warmth is still king. As Dr. Susan Fiske of Princeton puts it, "Although both dimensions are fundamental . . . warmth judgments seem to be primary, which reflects the importance of assessing other people's intentions before determining their ability to carry out those intentions." In short, warmth comes first and carries more weight.

Does our tendency to lean toward competence mean people see us as cold curmudgeons? Not at all—indeed, quite the opposite. In a study led by Dr. Charles Judd at the University of Colorado, warmth and competence in individuals correlated positively—a high score on either dimension predicted a high score on the other. Even when the researchers tried their hardest to make up examples that would score high on competence and low on warmth (this person "wrote a little computer program that solved a tough calculus integration problem") or vice versa (this person "spent hours with a friend after the friend's dog died"), the effect remained.

All that said, as life unfurls, decades focused on competence might mean we collect a lot of social or professional contacts but feel like we're not close to as many people as we'd like. We're good, kind people, but our relationships might be shallower or more distant than we want, and we're not sure how to change that.

---

* The exact names of the dimensions can differ, but the gist is the same: competence and warmth, agency and communion, intellectual and social, respecting and liking.

So, with an eye to keeping our agency while pumping up the communal, how do we take our current friendships to the next level? How do we kick-start new friendships? The answer is in sharing ourselves on many levels: in order to be known, we have to reveal ourselves. There's an adage: "If we don't show much, nobody knows much."

Let's start with sharing our emotions. This is not one of those "I feel . . . when you" exercises, I pinkie promise. You don't even have to say a word.

Instead, let's go back in time—way back, before spoken language. It is theorized that emotions evolved as a form of communication within our earliest ancestral communities. Emotions and their resultant facial expressions and body postures developed to communicate accurate information about our reactions, needs, and aims. Our forebears could broadcast that they were angry, sad, happy, or disgusted without language. They could clearly read how others in the group felt and adjust their behavior accordingly ("Yikes, I saw Zog's reaction after he ate those berries—guess I'll stay away from those"). Expression of emotion, including negative emotion, helped groups communicate, synchronize, and, by extension, survive.

The technical term for the outward manifestation of our inner emotional state is *emotional expression*. It's matching the outside to the inside.

Now, sometimes it's important to keep our emotions secret. Controlling your face is important on poker night, during a high-stakes negotiation, or when escorting a friend to their surprise birthday party. That's when we do what's called *expressive suppression*—effortful control to reduce or eliminate emotionally expressive behavior. It's mismatching our outside and inside like two odd socks.

Expressive suppression can be extremely useful in the right context. We might suppress so we can stay professional, play it cool, maintain honor and dignity, avoid unwanted attention ("Are you crying?"), or keep others from thinking poorly of us ("You're not scared, are you?"). Heck, I'd argue that all customer service is based on emotional suppression.

We might also suppress because we've learned it's not safe or allowable to express certain emotions like anger, fear, or hurt, even around people we love. We might have grown up in a family where we were shut down for being too much: we were too loud, candid, inquisitive, or needy. Or we might have grown up in a family where we were too quiet: we were supposed to join in, not be shy, be more confident. So we learned to hide how hard our little duck feet were paddling underwater to create our smooth glide across the surface.

But therein lies the problem. *Perfectionistic self-presentation* is when we show-and-tell only the good stuff; we don't display or disclose our weaknesses, self-doubts, or problems. And when expressive suppression, as part of perfectionistic self-presentation, becomes a habit, putting on our best face—the one that we think keeps us safe—supplants our actual, authentic face.

According to Dr. Thomas Lynch and Erica Smith Lynch, those of us who are careful about our self-presentation tend to show one of two faces to the world. The first is the *overly agreeable face*, or the *overly prosocial face*, which I'll call the Nice Face. It often looks like a big smile worthy of a flight attendant, combined with a lot of nodding. This face sends the message, "I am competent and nice." Think Truman from *The Truman Show*, or, after a long day of being "on," devolving into the Chrissy Teigen face meme. Women do this most often, but so do other genders. If you've ever come home after an event with aching cheeks, you know what I mean.

The second is what Dr. Lynch calls the *overly disagreeable face*,* which I'll call the Strong Face. It's best described by what we *don't* see: varying expressions, nodding, smiling, joining in when people laugh. Think John Wayne, Professor McGonagall, Bill Belichick, or any given poker champion. This face sends the message, "I am competent and strong." Men do this most often, but again, any gender can project this face. It's not because we're an aspiring nineteenth-century

---

* When I first encountered the term *overly disagreeable*, I pictured a grumpy or serious face. But Erica Smith Lynch explained to me that the overly disagreeable face is polite and well behaved. The term comes more from the tendency to disagree with you—and tell you so—if they perceive you're doing or saying something incorrectly.

English governess—it's because we feel an obligation to look capable, invulnerable, and in control, especially in public.

By design, both public faces keep our true feelings under cover and project how we want to be seen: competent, nice, strong. Neither one reveals much else, and that's the issue.

Our faces and bodies send loud and clear messages. And when we use perfectionistic self-presentation of the Nice Face or the Strong Face, the message we inadvertently send is that we're disingenuous, insincere, arrogant, cagey, or excessively formal, all messages that get in the way of connecting with others and deepening relationships. In her bestseller *Platonic: How the Science of Attachment Can Help You Make—and Keep—Friends*, Dr. Marisa Franco writes, "When we're in self-protection mode, we're in anti-relationship mode."

Expressive suppression is hard on our social lives. Research shows that hanging out with someone whose expression doesn't vary—whether they're all smiles or all business—makes us anxious and uncomfortable. It literally increases our blood pressure. And because it's stressful to interact with someone we can't read, we're more likely to avoid them in the future. It decreases willingness to form a friendship, which leads to ostracism and loneliness. We might say something like the following, all of which I've heard from clients: "No one seems to know what to do with me." "I feel like people don't want me around." "I'm lonely, but people suck."

Not only is overreliance on the Nice Face or the Strong Face hard on our social lives, it's also hard on our actual lives. Overlearned expressive suppression keeps us from wearing our hearts on our sleeves, but it raises our chance of heart disease. It also undermines our memory; we're bad at encoding what we're doing or what someone is saying to us when we're busy suppressing, so we miss out on what's happening in the moment. If that weren't enough, habitual suppressors report lower satisfaction with life, lower self-esteem, less optimism, and, paradoxically, more negative emotion than those who don't suppress.

Here's the whole enchilada: we're trying to keep ourselves socially safe by performing the face we think is appropriate, but being hard to read keeps us separated from the very community and acceptance we want, and then we think we have to earn it back through exemplary performance (hey, chapter 7 callback!). Yowza. That's quite the enchilada.

Let's return to those first days waking up in a college dorm. In a study in the prestigious *Journal of Personality and Social Psychology*, a team of researchers led by Dr. Sanjay Srivastava tracked almost three hundred first-year students over their first semester of college. Before arriving on campus and then again after move-in day, students estimated the extent to which they hid their emotions, rating statements such as, "I keep my emotions to myself," and "When I am feeling negative emotions (e.g., anxiety, sadness), I make sure not to express them."

After the ten-week semester concluded, the research team asked these students, their parents, and their new friends about each participant's social life. The team was careful to account for how much each student socialized and how they felt throughout the semester, ensuring the findings made room for both library-loving introverts and party animal extroverts, as well as students who spent the semester feeling homesick and depressed versus euphoric and energized. In other words, the researchers zeroed in on the signal of expressive suppression rather than the noise inherent in the first semester of college. The results? By the end of the semester, students who reported hiding their emotions felt less socially supported, less close to their peers, and less satisfied with their overall social lives.

That all sounds bad, but interestingly, there was one big bright spot. Expressive suppression didn't affect likability. Even though students who didn't show their feelings struggled more with their social lives than those who showed their emotions more freely, *people liked them just as much*. Therefore, even though the suppressors missed opportunities to form close and meaningful relationships in the first semester, they were just as well liked. This makes sense; even without forming close bonds, others can still think we're pretty cool. That means the

Matching the Inside and the Outside: An Experiment

We use nonverbal signals—body language, posture, and especially facial expression—to read others and determine whether we like and trust them. Other people do the same to us. It works quite accurately; we can pick up a large part of what's being communicated with only non-verbal signals—it's the same reason we can get the gist of a foreign-language movie without the subtitles.

Therefore, try an experiment to see how turning the volume up or down on your facial expressions affects the quality of your social interactions. Have two different conversations—with Phil from accounting, a fellow parent on the sidelines at soccer, or the gym friend you see every Thursday but whose last name you don't know. In the first conversation, inhibit your expressions. Do the Nice Face or the Strong Face. Observe how you feel. How effortful is it to maintain your face? How present and tuned in are you? How engaged are you in the conversation? How connected do you feel to Phil, the soccer parent, or your gym friend?

In the second conversation, preferably with the same person, let your outside match your inside more than usual. Show on your face what you feel, not cartoonishly but perhaps 20–50 percent more than you would normally. If you typically use the Strong Face, use your second conversation to experiment with animating your expressions. If you typically use the Nice Face, try letting your smile vary based on whether or not you actually feel happy. Let your face match your words a little more, even if the emotion is negative. Observe the same things: How much work is this? How present, engaged, and connected do you feel? Essentially, we're experimenting with being genuine.

Clients often find being more real, paradoxically, is *easier*. It doesn't take as much energy to be genuine as it does to monitor ourselves and overregulate.

Does this mean we should be 100 percent genuine all the time? Should we let our raw, unedited words and emotions hang out? Tell our boss to shove it? Lick our lips at the cute barista? Please don't do that. In fact, in Western culture, unrestrained expression of strong

raw materials for close social bonding are still there—there's
ration date on getting closer to friends.

Remember Jamila from chapter 1? She teared up describing the
Someone Great where the character Erin helps her bestie Jenny
a breakup while belting, "You coulda had a bad bitch, none
tal." Jamila wasn't in the college study, but she might as w
been—the findings mirrored her experience perfectly. Jamila
me for depression and lack of direction, but we found a big ice
perfectionism underneath. A college senior, she was burned o
spending the previous three years on a daily conveyor belt tha
ered her from one "should" task to another. *I "should" be wor*
this paper. I "shouldn't" go out on Saturday because I'm behind on m
mer internship applications. She spent most of her time alone. V
asked how her week was, she would answer with a big smile an
tone: "Oh, I don't know. I'm okay, I guess. I'm exhausted. It's
stressful week." Her message hinted there was reason for concer
her expression was bright and happy—the Nice Face all the way

Jamila was just trying to be appropriate and do things righ
just like the students in the study, she felt disconnected and c
ically dissatisfied. She had a circle of friends, but they sometime
her out. "I heard a couple of them talking in our suite," she sai
session, "and I heard them say, 'Jamila does her own thing.'" Sh
lonely, but singing in her underwear with her friends would hav
like squandering precious time—the opposite of a "should."

What can everyone who identifies with Jamila's experience
First, let's talk about the nonverbals: showing our inside on the out
when appropriate, as well as activating and signaling a sense of sc
safety. Then we'll move into the verbal realm. We'll drill down on
nitty-gritty of conversation, how to let others in on your life, and
importance of being vulnerable.

emotions is often seen as undisciplined or unstable. The key is to *be authentic with regard to your situation*. Sometimes suppression comes in handy—a meeting with your most exasperating colleague, teaching Grandma how texting works yet again. And sometimes a more expressive face is what the situation calls for. Your face will show frustration to different degrees with your boss, your toddler, or your ex who cheated on you. Overall, the point is flexibility.

"Okay, Ellen," you say, "that's great, but what if my authentic emotion is social anxiety? Or I don't know what I feel because I'm responding to the force fields of other people? Why do you think I use the Strong Face or the Nice Face in the first place?"

I'm glad you asked. Again, "authentic" doesn't mean unfiltered. Indeed, "authenticity" is how we engage *when* we feel socially safe; in *How to Be Yourself*, I say "yourself" is the self you are without fear. But that doesn't mean we should stuff our fears like one of those snake-in-a-can pranks. It means activating a social safety system so you feel more like yourself. Which brings us to . . .

The Eye(brow)s Are the Window to the Soul

Our feelings and our bodies want to align.* We smile when happy, glower when mad, and pout when disappointed. When we feel in danger of being judged or criticized—in other words, when we sense a lack of social safety—the expression that aligns is the Nice Face or the Strong Face. But we've already established how that backfires over the long term.

Thankfully, the fact that our feelings and bodies want to align means we have a solution; where our faces and bodies go, our feelings follow. To accomplish just this, Dr. Lynch teaches a technique called the Big Three Plus One, which activates a sense of social safety. It's three intuitive

---

* It feels weird and artificial to mismatch the inside and the outside. Try it out. For example, slump and put a frown on your face, but say, "This is the greatest day of my life." Or crack a big smile and clap your hands with glee, but say, "I'm heartbroken with disappointment." This works about as well as an underwater fly trap, which is to say: it doesn't.

ways to arrange your body that signal "I'm relaxed and open," plus one unexpected step that puts a metaphorical social safety cherry on top.

First, position your body in a relaxed manner, whether you're sitting or standing. Try out a little contrapposto, à la Michelangelo's *David*, or a relaxing lean into your chair—think more sinking into a papasan than sitting upright at the office.

Second, take a deep breath in and slowly let it out. It should feel satisfying and relaxing, like looking around at a job well done.

Third, smile halfway. Put a friendly *Mona Lisa* smile on your face.

But then, here's the Plus One. Raise your eyebrows. Just a little wag. It's not a Dr. Evil leer. It's more like a friendly lift—a nice accompaniment to the smile.

"Um, Ellen? *Eyebrows?*"

Yes, eyebrows. The eyebrow wag is a universal signal of "I like you; you're in my tribe." Think of greeting someone with a handshake, a friendly exchange, or when you run into an old friend. Eyebrows are up. It signals liking and openness.

So, put it all together:

1. Sit or stand in a relaxed, open stance.
2. Inhale and let out an exhale.
3. Half smile.

PLUS ONE: Briefly lift your eyebrows.

Adopting a posture and expression of social safety creates two feedback loops. First, it creates a feedback loop to those around us, signaling that we're open and approachable—the very opposite of perfectionistic self-presentation. But it also creates a feedback loop to ourselves. Says Dr. Lynch, "It has the added advantage of affecting how you feel internally. It switches on the social safety system."

"But wait a minute," you say. "You're telling me *not* to be fake with the Nice Face or the Strong Face, but now you want me to do this other fake face?"

Dr. Lynch, after twenty years of clinical work with the Big Three Plus One, assures us that it's not fake. Our social safety system can be genuinely activated through our facial expressions and body postures. It alters how we feel about ourselves and the response we get from the world. Plus, he finds that most clients don't find it fake at all. Says Dr. Lynch, "What's really cool about the eyebrows is you do it, and you don't feel inauthentic. Whereas try and tell a joke or something? That feels inauthentic." Thankfully, a deep breath and an eyebrow wag is a much lower bar than keeping a perma-smile on your face all evening.

> **TRY IT OUT:** Next time you're feeling awkward or out of place socially, test-drive the Big Three Plus One.

Disclosure: Letting Ourselves Be Known

Now that we've covered the nonverbals, let's get into what actually comes out of our mouths.

To connect with others, we have to let ourselves be known. And we can't be known if we hide large parts of ourselves. In *How to Be Yourself*, we talked about revealing what we think, do, feel, remember, and relate to in order to give our conversation partner something to work with. This is called *disclosure*, and it magically transforms your life from black-and-white to Technicolor for the people around you. You become more familiar, relatable, and likable.

Disclosure can feel counterintuitive to those of us who are introverted, socially anxious, or perfectionistic. We keep our lives close to the vest, especially our weaknesses and problems. It feels like we're revealing too much, being a burden, or opening ourselves up for judgment. But then? It's hard for others to get to know us, and we can end up feeling like a stranger in a strange land.

The husband-and-wife dynamic research duo of Drs. Arthur and Elaine Aron found that in order to get closer to someone, disclosure should be *sustained*, *reciprocal*, *personalistic*, and *escalating*. Sustained and reciprocal speak for themselves: disclosure should continue gradually over time, and you should get something back about them. Indeed, reciprocity—I'll show you my life, you show me yours—is the very foundation of friendship: the sharing of lives.

But let's drill down deeper on personalistic.

The Magic of Doorknobs

It blows my mind that some people make a living eavesdropping. But that's exactly what researchers do to learn how conversations occur naturally, in the wild. They find that "socially relevant talk"—conversations about self, people, relationships—makes up well over half of conversation, whether you're strolling down Broadway through Times Square in 1922, an indigenous Zinacantan of southern Mexico in the 1970s, or a man in Liverpool in the 1990s. Indeed, nonsocial topics like sports, work, or politics barely break double digits. That means a lot of conversation is about you and your conversation partners.

Therefore, while *not* talking about yourself might feel safe, unobtrusive, or modest, it can come off as a burden—not putting yourself into the conversation makes others pick up the slack. But sometimes nobody picks up the slack, and then conversation goes like this:

YOUR COLLEAGUE: Good morning—how was your weekend?
YOU: It was great. Yours?
YOUR COLLEAGUE: Good. It was relaxing.
BOTH OF YOU: [awkward silence]

Another way to not talk about yourself is to ask lots of questions. Some of us are experts at drawing people out. Or when a conversation partner gladly takes center stage, the more reticent among us can happily relax. But over time, we can start to feel like no one knows us. We get surprised or upset when no one asks us any questions.

There must be a better way. Enter the psychologist Dr. Adam Mastroianni, who calls the "digressions and confessions and bold claims that beg for a rejoinder" conversational "doorknobs," a method of entry into an ever-deeper inner sanctum. Listen, grasp onto whatever doorknob gets your attention, and enter the door it opens. Doorknobs are whatever piques your interest, reminds you of something else, elicits a question, or is "No way! Me, too!" relatable. You get the point. It can be any part of what's being said—the bar is low.

Here's an example of listening for a doorknob:

YOU TO YOUR COLLEAGUE: Good morning. How was your weekend?

YOUR COLLEAGUE: Great. My partner and I did some work on my dad's place.

You now have a bunch of everyday conversational doorknobs at your disposal. Maybe you heard *partner*, *work*, *dad*, or *place*. Whatever part of that sentence your brain grabbed onto, you can toss it back with a related response:

» "Nice—are you the DIYer, or is your partner?"
» "That's cool—what did you work on?"
» "Oh, nice—I'm thinking of doing some remodeling on my place, but knowing where to start is always a challenge."
» "That's excellent—do you see your dad often?"
» "My dad's place could use some work—he's lived there for forty years, so you can imagine how full the basement is."
» "Oh, cool. Does your dad live locally, or did you have to drive a long way?"
» "That's awesome that you do it yourself—I put caulk around my tub several rental apartments ago, but that's the end of my skills."

Whatever you toss back, offer up a doorknob of your own to grasp onto—what you think, do, feel, remember, or relate to—remember, we're going for personalistic. Telling your conversation partner about yourself sharpens their picture of you with ever-finer pixelation, making you more familiar, more likable, and more trusted. For example, here's how you might offer a doorknob when you're speaking:

YOUR COLLEAGUE: How was your weekend?
YOU: It was great. I . . .

» "took the kids to their volleyball tournament. We were there for, I am not kidding, twelve hours."
» "made my annual pumpkin bread."
» "finished this Steve Martin memoir I've been reading. It was so good."
» "accidentally played *Baldur's Gate 3* until four in the morning."
» "went to the farmers market on Sunday and got some funky blue potatoes."
» "saw a parade of tuba players wearing tutus march by as I got my morning coffee on Saturday."

There. No matter what you picked, you gave them something to work with. Hopefully, they'll expand on what you said, such as . . .

» "Wow, they weren't playing the whole time, were they?"
» "My mother used to make the best pumpkin bread, but then she went paleo, to my chagrin."
» "Oh, perfect! What was the title? I need a recommendation."
» "Ha! I did that back in the '90s with the original *Legend of Zelda*."
» "There is a great farmers market just a couple of blocks from my house—which one do you go to?"
» "Well, that's a new one. I'll have to try your coffee shop."

Then, listen for whatever they've offered and keep going. It's like tossing a ball back and forth. Now, is your conversation partner guaranteed to grasp the doorknob and open the metaphorical door? Maybe not: "Oh." Or, "Cool." Conversation continues to skim along the surface of small talk. Doors stay firmly closed. But that's okay. We let it drop, or we try again later.

Since we all have unrealistically high expectations of ourselves around here, it's important to say that none of these doorknobs have to be fancy, impressive, or extraordinary. Lower the pressure by setting the bar way lower. In a counterintuitive study, *Stumbling on Happiness* author and scholar Dr. Daniel Gilbert and colleagues showed one participant a "four-star" movie and three other participants a "two-star" movie and found that the participant who had had a separate, "better" experience "felt excluded during a subsequent social interaction, and this left them feeling worse than participants who had an ordinary experience instead."

Indeed, aiming for out-of-this-world conversations—when we hold ourselves to the standard of appearing impressive or extraordinary or supersmart—"can make the people who have them strangers to everyone else on earth." In short, when we're used to aiming high, lowering the bar might feel wrong, but it allows more friends and potential friends to clear it and join in.

How to Have Deeper Conversations

Next, disclosure should be escalating.

There are different levels of sharing about your life. What you share with your boss will naturally differ from what you share with your Lyft driver, Angela from marketing, your tennis buddy, the friend you've known for twenty years, or your life partner.

But when we're hard on ourselves, sometimes we get stuck. We want to go deeper in our relationships but feel trapped in the shallows. Below are disclosures in increasing levels of depth:

GREETINGS: Friendly acknowledgments. Everyone keeps walking.

> » "Hey, good to see you."
> » "TGIF!"

SMALL TALK: An exchange or two about traffic, the weather, or your local sports team.

> » "Did you get stuck in that backup before the bridge this morning?"
> » "Looks like it's gonna rain this afternoon, but we need it!"

UNIVERSALLY ACCEPTABLE QUESTIONS AND COMMENTS (NONPERSONAL): More substance, but nothing personal is revealed.

> » "Where'd you get those great shoes?"
> » "That place serves bagels the size of hubcaps."
> » "My kid's orthodontist just bought a self-driving car."

UNIVERSALLY ACCEPTABLE PERSONAL DISCLOSURES: Lets the listener in on a little bit about your life, but largely socially acceptable and nonemotional. Some doorknobs. Flirts with vulnerability.

> » "I signed up to run my first-ever 5K in March."
> » "I took my niece to the aquarium on Saturday and was mesmerized by the penguins. I could have stared at them for an hour."
> » "I went to Costco on Sunday afternoon, and it was so crazy that when I got home, I had to lie down."

PRIVATE PERSONAL DISCLOSURES: Discloses a problem or insecurity, asks for help or support, lets the listener deeper into your life. Lots of doorknobs. Signals trust. Solidly vulnerable.

> » "I'm having trouble with my eight-year-old talking back—I've tried everything and I'm not sure what to do next."
> » "Girl, listen to what our boss just said to me."
> » "I wonder if I'm self-sabotaging this term paper by telling myself I work better under pressure."
> » "I have to give a presentation in twenty minutes, and I feel like

I'm going to throw up. I'm gonna go lock myself in a bathroom stall and breathe for a few minutes."

DEEPER PRIVATE PERSONAL DISCLOSURES: Reveals thoughts or feelings that could result in judgment or rejection, but revealing them signals that you trust they won't. Highly vulnerable.

» "I think I need to quit drinking."
» "I thought losing fifty pounds last year would magically solve all my problems, but I still feel lousy."
» "I really like you."
» "Oh, that honestly makes me so envious."

DEEPEST DISCLOSURES: Reveals deep emotions that may not have been expressed before.

» "I've never said this to anyone before, but . . ."
» "I can't do this anymore."
» "I trust you more than I've ever trusted anyone."

The deepest level is reserved for the closest relationships, like a life partner or best friend of many years, but you may have noticed the depth of the two or three levels before that. This brings us to vulnerability. Vulnerability is willingness to show and express thoughts and emotions that we fear might result in criticism or rejection. Both what we say and how we say it indicate, *Hey, this is stuff I usually keep secret.*

Perfectionism tells us to be impressive rather than real, über-competent rather than communal, which can lead to feeling like we're performing for our friends rather than sharing with them. Perfectionism tells us to be appropriate, to do things right. But getting closer means vulnerability: letting people see some of the mess.

With someone you'd like to get closer to—your partner, your sibling, an established friendship you'd like to take deeper, an acquaintance you think has friend potential—being vulnerable adds richness to your relationship. Vulnerability is the umami of conversation—it makes everything go deeper.

But then there's invulnerability. My client Erin is, by any measure, a success story: She works hard at a day job, raises her kids, trains for two marathons a year, and runs a thriving Etsy shop. She always arrives in perfectly applied makeup, seasonally appropriate fabrics, and tasteful accents of color. She knows where to get the best chocolate croissants, which new restaurants are overrated, and, as she informed me, what hairstyle would look better with my face shape. She knows her opinions can come across as judgmental, but prefers to think of herself as sophisticated or cultured. "I'm a maximizer," she proclaims.

But Erin is desperately lonely. In my office, she questions her place in the pecking order, comparing herself to friends and colleagues. She feels she is barely hanging on, failing at her work, her training, her side hustle, and her parenting. She is so busy that friends have given up trying to break into her schedule. She is so task-driven that there is no slack time for found moments with colleagues or long text exchanges with old friends. She understands that her pulled-together appearance and long list of achievements are intimidating to many, but prickles when I broach asking for help or disclosing vulnerability. "This is me," she says. "If people can't handle it, that's their loss."

The busyness, judgment, comparison, and general invulnerability all add bricks to the wall separating Erin and potential community. Sometimes we have good reason to hold things in or pretend we're fine, but for Erin, the very sophistication that set her apart did just that—set her apart—leaving her feeling distant and disconnected.

So how does vulnerability work? First, vulnerability isn't about the topic, per se. You may know someone who nonchalantly brings up their adultery, their prison sentence, or their addiction in the first few conversations. But if it's easy to talk about, it's not vulnerable. By contrast, other people would rather eat a bag of broken glass than tell you they don't have plans for the weekend or that they had frozen pizza twice this week instead of making dinner from scratch. Vulnerability is about what you find objectionable, embarrassing, or shameful about yourself. It leaves you unprotected. It's what could open you up to ridicule or criticism.

Next, how you disclose something vulnerable is as important as what you disclose. If we try to be vulnerable with a no-big-deal, blasé tone, our conversation partner will take our lead, and we're more likely to get a no-big-deal, blasé response.*

But when we use concordant nonverbal signals of embarrassment or shame—palpable nervousness, a facepalm, an eye roll at ourselves, we out ourselves more effectively. Our signals show, "What an embarrassing thing to admit." For me, I've noticed I put my hands on either side of my face à la *The Scream* when I'm disclosing something vulnerable.

These embarrassment signals are vital because they show two things. First is trust. We're not hiding. When we share our doubts, mistakes, insecurities, or fears with someone without falling apart or blaming others, we signal that we trust them. Second is equality. Vulnerable disclosures show that we are equal in our human fallibility. We are not so special. We're not better or separate. Vulnerable disclosure circumvents the expert-novice dynamic and signals, "You and I, we're the same."

Erin did not want to hear any of this. She was much more comfortable giving advice, or "helping" her friends solve their problems. She didn't see any issue, because she was always loving and supportive, and her advice was often spot-on: "Your cover letter has a better chance of getting read if you address it to a particular person instead of 'To whom it may concern.'"

But giving supportive advice without revealing anything about her own problems signaled that she was a mentor or a coach—an unequal relationship—instead of an equal, relatable friend. What's more, a study out of Harvard Business School found that withholding information,

---

* This can be useful sometimes. The verbal-nonverbal mismatch can handily take away vulnerability. Think of the no-nonsense nurse at your last Pap smear or prostate exam: "Take off all your clothes and put on this gown, please." At the doctor's office, using a straightforward tone communicates, "This is not embarrassing or shameful; let's get it done," which elicits an okay-cool-no-big-deal response from us—we put on the gown and don't freak out.

even about shady stuff—cheating on your taxes, drug use—leads others to judge us more negatively than if we came clean. It's counterintuitive—we'd think sweeping our questionable behavior under the rug would make a better impression, but it comes off as hiding, which is worse. Do we risk judgment disclosing our foibles and weaknesses? Yes. Is the social risk of hiding them even greater? Yes again.

We feel close to people we trust and are equal to. And often, we get similar stories back. Case in point, when one of Erin's friends got ghosted by a promising guy she had been dating, after listening with empathy, Erin decided to disclose she had been ghosted once, too, and how heartbroken she had been. Rather than looking at her with pity, as Erin had expected, her friend opened up about her self-doubt, and they ended up talking more deeply than they had in years. Erin came to her appointment the next week, tasteful outfit and perfect makeup as always, but much happier than usual, and mock-grumbled to me, "Fine, you were right."

> **TRY IT OUT:** Notice what happens when you offer unsolicited advice or feedback. Notice what happens when you listen attentively and then offer a personal or vulnerable doorknob. Notice what happens when you reveal something a little bit more vulnerable than usual, keeping in mind the context of your relationship (e.g., your boss versus your bestie versus a new acquaintance).

Putting It All Together

Here's a challenge for you: Pick one, two, or a handful of people in your life you'd like to get closer to and experiment with pushing a little deeper through disclosure. Dr. Thomas Lynch calls this skill

Match Plus One. Offer a doorknob. Give them something to work with. Mindfully listen to how they respond. Then, essentially say, *I'll see you and raise you.* Match their level of disclosure and then go a little further—this is the Plus One part. If you get something roughly equivalent back—remember, disclosure is reciprocal—keep going as long as you're comfortable. Over time and repeated conversations—remember, disclosure is gradual—together you'll build connection, support, and care.

For example, if you usually stay on the surface with the office receptionist but get good vibes from her and wouldn't mind getting to know her better, test out a small disclosure. If your relationship with a friend you've known for years has plateaued, try out a bigger disclosure than usual. How deep you go with anyone, from a stranger to your spouse, is up to you.

As for Jamila, she'll be the first to tell you she's still working on this. She hasn't danced in her underwear with any friends yet, though she'll also admit that's a high bar. But when she and a study buddy were grabbing a late-night bite after cramming for their Nineteenth-Century Novels midterm, Jamila disclosed she wished she hadn't spent so much of her college career studying. If she could do it again, she said, she'd spend more time being dumb with her friends, goofing off, and eating cheese fries late at night just like they were doing right then. Her study partner replied with her own regrets—an all-consuming relationship that ate up her entire sophomore year, an ill-informed study-abroad semester in Florence that left her lonely and depressed. They ended up talking for two hours, the midterm drawing closer with every minute. But for once, Jamila didn't mind. Cheese fries and a potential friend were more important.

Epilogue

Self-Acceptance for Self-Critics

Tom Junod took the 1998 *Esquire* assignment reluctantly. He was known for writing dark, critical pieces and proudly embraced his reputation to "say the unsayable." His first cover story resulted in a threatened boycott of the magazine and outraged criticism. For him, taking the cover story assignment about Fred Rogers, "the nicest man in the world" was considerably off-brand.

At the same time, at the age of forty, Junod was secretly wondering if his celebrated reputation had cost him his humanity. His grim, cruel stories had taken a toll on him. Junod had been twelve years old when *Mister Rogers' Neighborhood* debuted—too old for Daniel Tiger and King Friday. But when a younger colleague who had grown up watching the show pitched the Rogers profile with evident passion, calling Rogers an American hero, it gave Tom pause. He accepted.

As it turned out, Fred Rogers kept a small New York apartment on Fifty-Sixth Street, just around the corner from the *Esquire* offices on Fifty-Fifth Street. Junod called Rogers up late one afternoon and asked if he could come interview him. "Well, Tom, I'm in my bathrobe, if you don't mind," he said. Rogers was sixty-eight and in the habit of taking an afternoon nap. "But you can come over anytime."

Five minutes later, Junod knocked on the door, and

sure enough, there was Mister Rogers, silver-haired, standing in the golden door at the end of the hallway and wearing eyeglasses and suede moccasins with rawhide laces and a flimsy old blue-and-yellow bathrobe that revealed whatever part of his skinny white calves his dark-blue dress socks didn't hide. "Welcome, Tom," he said with a slight bow, and bade me follow him inside, where he lay down—no, *stretched out,* as though he had known me all his life.

Within twenty minutes, Mr. Rogers had Junod talking about his beloved boyhood stuffed animal, Old Rabbit. At the end of their interview, in which Rogers learned more about Junod than the other way around, Rogers took a photo of him with a brick-shaped Instamatic camera. He wanted to show his wife the person he connected with today. Junod later wrote, "There was an energy to him . . . a fearlessness, an unashamed insistence on intimacy." He remembers, "This was not a dragged-out process. . . . It happened immediately." How did Rogers do it? More than twenty years later, Tom would write of their first meeting, "I've been trying to figure out that for a long time."

Rogers's widely known exacting standards, drive, and consideration of every detail could have easily led him down a different path. Rogers could have used an *Esquire* cover interview to push himself and his work, to put another feather in his cap of accomplishment, or to compensate for some perceived inner shortcoming from his, by all accounts, lonely childhood. He could have tried to impress Junod or give a performance of the Nicest Man in the World. But he didn't. Instead, he ran full speed toward what was meaningful to him: human connection. He demonstrated genuine interest in Tom. Remember Rogers's words to Tom Junod back at the beginning of this book: "Look at us—I've just met you, but I'm investing in who you are and who you will be, and I can't help it."

After Rogers died in 2016, Junod wrote of his longtime friend, "He gave so much to me, so much trust and friendship, without asking me to earn it."

One old friend of Rogers's, Eliot Daley, once reflected on the elusive energy Junod puzzled over for twenty years:

> I would describe him as the ultimate "what you see is what you get," with one exception. What most people couldn't see in Fred was his enormous power. Power. Capital P. Fred is the most powerful person I have ever known in my whole life. . . . I've dealt with a lot of people whom the world regards as powerful. None of them could hold a candle to Fred's power. . . . His power derived from a really unique place. It was his absolute self-possession, which is very different from self-interest or self-satisfaction, or selfishness. He didn't need anything from you or from me. He welcomed it, but he didn't need it.

In other words, he had a sense that he was enough. What's more, he generously bestowed the same sentiment on those around him—they were enough, full stop. During the final moments of one episode taping, while Mr. Rogers took his sneakers off and hung up his sweater as usual, he looked offstage at François Clemmons, the actor who played Officer Clemmons for twenty-five years. Rogers spoke the closing lines: "You make every day a special day just by being you, and I like you just the way you are."

As Rogers walked off set, Clemmons asked: "'Fred, were you talking to me?' And he said, 'Yes, I have been talking to you for years. But you heard me today.' It was like telling me I'm okay as a human being. That was one of the most meaningful experiences I'd ever had."

Even with all his quiet self-assurance, was Fred Rogers 100 percent free of doubts, problems, or self-criticism? Not at all. Remember the angsty all-caps stream of consciousness typing while procrastinating writing an episode script? AFTER ALL THESE YEARS, IT'S JUST AS BAD AS EVER. Very human problems plagued Rogers throughout his life. As a kid, he was overweight, sheltered, lonely, and sickly, enduring, as he put it, "every imaginable childhood disease." He was bullied, running home to taunts of "Hey, fat Freddy! We're going to get you, Freddy!" More challenges emerged over the decades. Despite his virtuosity with small children, Rogers was "mystified" by teenagers, including his own. When his wife, Joanne, caught their teenage sons, Jim and John, growing marijuana in the basement, she was amused by their entrepreneurial spirit, but Fred was furious. When John wrecked his car on an icy road, Fred grew angry enough that they "yelled and screamed at each other for an hour," according to John. Life happened, all the way up to the very end, when a painful battle with stomach cancer included the surgical removal of the organ in its entirety.

But like Rogers, we don't have to get over our self-criticism or magically clear our lives of pain before we, too, run full speed toward what's important to us. We don't have to make any changes at all before we choose to do what's meaningful. We might constantly compare ourselves to others, lug around an Inner Rulebook to rival *War and Peace*, and maintain a perfectly overlapping Venn diagram of self-worth and accomplishments, and we can still decide to focus on connection, like Fred Rogers, or our own equivalents, whatever they may be. As our old friend Dr. Michael Twohig summed it up, "A perfectionistic thought isn't necessarily good or bad; it's what you *do* with it."

As I mentioned in the introduction, the word *perfection* is from the Greek word *teleiōsis*. The root, *telos*, has traditionally meant "goal." But more modern translations have started interpreting it as "purpose."

The old way, "goal," implies "what." What is the end to be achieved? But the new interpretation, "purpose," is "why." *Why* are you doing this? It's the French *raison d'être*, the Japanese concept of *ikigai*, or the universal notion of why we get out of bed in the morning.

Purpose isn't discovered, all at once, like a treasure chest, nor is it something we keep to ourselves, without connection or benefit to others. Instead, it's an ever-evolving sense of what's important to you. Of *who's* important to you. Don't mistake what needs to get done for how you want to live your life.

And what about the inevitable problems that pop up along the way? What about the big and small irritants of life that our focus-on-flaws brains are programmed to see? One of my supervisors advised me to teach clients to treat their problems like a small animal—a fuzzy hamster, a wiggly salamander, or a trilling songbird—to hold them lightly. With a small animal, if we are too firm and rigid, we will make a big mess. But neither can we pretend they're not there. Therefore, take your problems seriously, but not too seriously. Honor them, take care of them, but hold them lightly. Their existence is part of the package deal of being alive.

At the beginning of the book, we contrasted clinical perfectionism—perfectionism that costs us more than it buys us—with adaptive perfectionism, which is perfectionism that buys us more than it costs us. They're not that different, but they're worlds apart. Just a few small adjustments changes our trajectory. Think of Gus channeling the earnest energy of "Look at this cool rock I found" during his presentation rather than rigidly performing his slides with a goal of being impressive. Think of Francesca rolling with the windy day at the pumpkin patch rather than trying to clamp down on the Pinterest vision of the perfect cake table in her head. Think of Carter taking care of his sick girlfriend not because he's trying to fulfill the role of "good boyfriend" but because he finds it meaningful to spend his Saturday dispensing Tylenol and ginger ale. Think of Jamila sheepishly telling her study partner she regrets grinding so hard during college and wishes she had prioritized friendship more, resulting in a two-hour conversation over cheese fries about what they'd do differently if they knew freshman year what they know now. With adaptive perfectionism, we still hit it out of the park, but the ball takes a very different path.

As for me, I am still perfectionistic—I still have high standards and expect a lot of myself. Like I said at the beginning, *How to Be Enough* was the book I needed *now*. And over the course of researching, writing, and trying to live the concepts I was uncovering, I felt my mindset shift toward that of "the package deal" again and again. Mistakes are part of the package deal of trying something new. Awkward miscommunications are part of the package deal of close relationships. Self-criticism is part of the package deal of my brain's wiring, but that doesn't mean I have to listen to it. Always having more to do is part of the package deal of a rich and full life. I don't have to take any of these by-products—miscommunications, mistakes, self-blame, unchecked to-dos—overly seriously, because they are a natural part of what happens while I'm running toward what I find meaningful.

Sometimes old "shoulds" creep in and pull me off course, like a compass near a strong magnet. And sometimes I catch my brain morphing values into rules—"But this is meaningful to me, so I *have* to do it." I'm not getting things exactly right, but paradoxically, that's the point.

And you? You've worked so hard. Let yourself linger over your strengths, honor all that you already do so well, respect the genetics and temperament and life experience that makes you who you are. Thank your 1965 UCLA freshman basketball squad dream team of traits: conscientiousness, deep care, and strong work ethic for what you do so well. There are so many ways you take it to the next level. To mix my sports analogies, you already hit it out of the park.

If you didn't need to do better, didn't have anything to prove, absolutely didn't have to work harder—in short, if you knew you were enough just as you are—what would you be doing with your life? If what happens next were up to you, what would you do?

Guess what? Welcome home to your life. What will you do first?

Acknowledgments

This book was harder to write than *How to Be Yourself*—a global pandemic, a major concussion, and a thornier academic topic were all challenges along the way. I was tremendously lucky to have so many people help me navigate and I am grateful to them all.

We'll start with the team at St. Martin's Press. Executive Editor Anna DeVries worked her magic and made this book so much better. I wish I could skywrite "thank you" behind a plane to Jamilah Lewis-Horton, Sara Beth Haring, Sophia Lauriello, Sallie Lotz, Cassie Gutman, and Laury Frieber. I am grateful to Kathy Doyle for ten years of advocacy.

The all-star team at Aevitas Creative Management was helpful beyond my wildest dreams. My agent, Todd Shuster, is both an indefatigable advocate and a perfect gentleman. The team including, over the years, Justin Brouckaert, Jack Haug, Lauren Liebow, Erica Bauman, and Erin Files kept so many wheels turning and made it all look easy.

Dr. Lisa Smith, Dr. David Barlow, and everyone at CARD: I am truly grateful for your continued support of my less-than-traditional career path.

The talented and generous Diana Howard drew clear, beautiful illustrations for both books. Thank you, thank you!

Huge gratitude to friends who generously served as early readers: Karen Adler, Ali Asgar Alibhai, Julia Altenbach, Aaron Cohn, Naomi Darom, Doron Gan, Noa Kageyama, Pia Owens, Beth Shikatani, and Sharvari Tamhankar. You all have big brains and bigger hearts.

My book buddy Anna Goldfarb served up support, enthusiasm, and love both tough and squishy. Viktoria Shulevich accomplished wonders with her clear-eyed feedback—I will always be so grateful!

Thank you to my mastermind group of six years—Noa Kageyama, Chris Howes, and Jason Haaheim. You are all brilliant and badass. Thank you to my author support group, especially Marisa G. Franco for inviting me to join and connecting me to this community.

I'm grateful to Jade Wu for carrying the torch and her continued teamwork, Naomi Dunford for her spot-on advice, Sadie Hall for her collaboration, and Jesse Crosby for his compassionate acceptance.

Big thanks to the researchers, clinicians, supervisees, and individuals who talked with me at length and lent me their knowledge and experience: Eve-Marie Blouin-Hudon, Jesse Crosby, Josh Curtiss, "Eunice," Angelina Gomez, Andrew Hill, Jennifer Hudson, Thomas Lynch and Erica Smith Lynch, Allan Mallinger, Jennifer Mitchell, Clarissa Ong, Tricia Park, Osiris Rankin, AJ Rosselini, Roz Shafran, Beth Shikatani, Martin Smith, Mike Twohig, and Aleena Hay Wickham.

Some of the examples in this book were drawn from clients seen by graduate students and early career therapists I supervise and who work under my license. The face-to-face, session-by-session credit goes directly to: Kristy Cuthbert, Stephanie DeCross, Liz Eustis, Ally Hand, Peter Luehring-Jones, Elliot Marrow, Danielle Moskow, Maya Nauphal, Osiris Rankin, Stephanie Steele, Nadine Taghian, and Erin Ward-Ciesielski.

Always the library nerd, I say thank you to the Boston University Libraries and the Cambridge Public Library.

I extend my heartfelt gratitude to my clients. While confidentiality prevents me from naming you, please know that your courage, resilience, and openness have deeply inspired me. Thank you for allowing me to be a part of your lives and for teaching me. This book is a testament to your strength and growth.

My parents, Sharon and Dan Hendriksen, and brother, Stephen Hendriksen, make brief appearances in this book but are a steady and supportive presence in life. Suzanne Park has been endlessly generous with her time and home. This book wouldn't exist without the support, love, and silliness of Nicolas Currier and Adrien and Davin Currier. I love you all.

For every reader and listener, from episode one Savvy Psychologist listeners to the brand-new reader, I say thank you from the bottom of my heart. You are the driving force behind every word written. I'm so grateful to make this journey alongside you.

NOTES

Prologue

1 **December evening in 1937:** Neal Gabler, *Walt Disney: The Triumph of the American Imagination* (New York: Knopf, 2006).

1 **bejeweled celebrities like:** Erin Glover, "Opening Night, 1937: 'Snow White and the Seven Dwarfs' Premieres at Carthay Circle Theatre," *Disney Parks Blog*, December 21, 2011, https://disneyparks.disney.go.com/blog/2011/12/opening-night-1937 -snow-white-and-the-seven-dwarfs-premieres-at-carthay-circle-theatre/.

1 **Charlie Chaplin had wired him:** Gabler, *Walt Disney*, 440.

1 **audible sniffling:** Gabler, *Walt Disney*, 441.

2 **Walt hired a small army:** Gabler, *Walt Disney*, 443.

2 **Walt screen-tested:** Gabler, *Walt Disney*, 412.

2 **"Have the hummingbird":** Gabler, *Walt Disney*, 436.

3 **screaming, "We gotta get the picture out!":** Gabler, *Walt Disney*, 440.

3 **he admitted, "I've seen so much":** Gabler, *Walt Disney*, 437.

3 **highest-grossing American film ever:** Wikipedia, s.v. "Snow White and the Seven Dwarfs (1937 Film)," accessed January 7, 2024, https://en.wikipedia.org /w/index.php?title=Snow_White_and_the_Seven_Dwarfs_(1937_film)&ol-did=1194158663.

3 **"appeared to be under the lash":** Gabler, *Walt Disney*, 930.

3 **"Just a hobby":** Gabler, *Walt Disney*, 748.

3 **"I envy you":** Gabler, *Walt Disney*, 749.

4 **RSVP "NO!" in red crayon:** Gabler, *Walt Disney*, 1000.

4 **"It gets lonely around here.":** Gabler, *Walt Disney*, 1001.

4 **reporter who visited the studios:** Gabler, *Walt Disney*, 752.

4 **The popcorn machine:** "Josie Carey Interview, by Karen Herman for The Interviews: 25 Years," Television Academy, July 23, 1999, http://televisionacademy.com/interviews.

4 **"to make it better":** Maxwell King, *The Good Neighbor: The Life and Work of Fred Rogers* (New York: Abrams, 2018), 108.

5 **"I've seen you talk with kids"**: King, *The Good Neighbor*, 144.

5 **Over thirty-one seasons and 895 episodes:** Jonathan V. Last, "Mr. Rogers' Legacy: 895 Episodes of Lessons," *Philadelphia Inquirer*, Just 12, 2011, https://www.inquirer.com/philly/opinion/currents/20110612_Mr__Rogers__legacy__895_episodes_of_lessons.html.

5 **multiple levels of review:** King, *The Good Neighbor*, 179.

5 **He stopped production:** King, *The Good Neighbor*, 179.

5 **"guided drift":** King, *The Good Neighbor*, 117.

6 **the Monday button:** King, *The Good Neighbor*, 193.

6 **"Fred just looked at it.":** King, *The Good Neighbor*, 187.

6 **"Am I kidding myself":** *Won't You Be My Neighbor?*, directed by Morgan Neville (Los Angeles: Tremolo Productions, 2018).

6 **"Fred, of course, was an amazing perfectionist":** King, *The Good Neighbor*, 307.

7 **"There wasn't a spontaneous bone":** King, *The Good Neighbor*, 326.

7 **Ten-year-old Jeff Erlanger:** "Won't You Be My Neighbor? (2018)—Mister Rogers & Jeff Erlanger Scene (8/10)," YouTube video, 3:23, posted by Movieclips, January 10, 2019, https://www.youtube.com/watch?v=USWXF1XW2zo.

7 **Jeff rolled onstage in a tuxedo:** "Fred Rogers Inducted into the TV Hall of Fame," YouTube video, 5:59, posted by Julian Park, April 9, 2012, https://www.youtube.com/watch?v=TcNxY4TudXo.

7 **cooling their feet:** "Won't You Be My Neighbor? (2018)—Officer Clemmons Scene (5/10)," YouTube video, 2:41, posted by Movieclips, January 10, 2019, https://www.youtube.com/watch?v=K6O_Ep9bY0U.

7 **"There was something serious yet comforting":** François S. Clemmons, *Officer Clemmons: A Memoir* (New York: Catapult, 2021).

7 **"Do you know you're strong":** Tom Junod, "Can You Say . . . 'Hero'?," *Esquire*, November 1, 1998, http://classic.esquire.com/article/1998/11/1/can-you-say-hero.

7 **Rogers even connected with Koko:** "Koko the Gorilla Meets Mister Rogers (Mr. McFeely Interview)," YouTube video, 3:44, posted by December 22, 2021, https://www.youtube.com/watch?v=93gCILhqIvA.

7 **"There was an energy to him":** Junod, "Can You Say . . . 'Hero'?"

8 *perfectionism*, **or the tendency to demand:** Marc H. Hollender, "Perfectionism," *Comprehensive Psychiatry* 6, no. 2 (1965): 94–103, https://doi.org/10.1016/s0010-440x(65)80016-5.

9 **from within as a personality style:** Carmen Iranzo-Tatay et al., "Genetic and Environmental Contributions to Perfectionism and Its Common Factors," *Psychiatry Research* 230, no. 3 (2015): 932–39, https://doi.org/10.1016/j.psychres.2015.11.020; Jason S. Moser et al., "Etiologic Relationships Between Anxiety and Dimensions of Maladaptive Perfectionism in Young Adult Female Twins: Twins, Anxiety, and Perfectionism," *Depression and Anxiety* 29, no. 1 (2012): 47–53, https://doi.org/10.1002/da.20890; Martin M. Smith et al., "Perfectionism and the Five-Factor Model of Personality: A Meta-Analytic Review," *Personality and Social Psychology Review* 23, no. 4 (2019): 367–90,

https://doi.org/10.1177/1088868318814973; Federica Tozzi et al., "The Structure of Perfectionism: A Twin Study," *Behavior Genetics* 34, no. 5 (2004): 483–94, https://doi .org/10.1023/b:bege.0000038486.47219.76; Tracey D. Wade and Cynthia M. Bulik, "Shared Genetic and Environmental Risk Factors between Undue Influence of Body Shape and Weight on Self-Evaluation and Dimensions of Perfectionism," *Psychological Medicine* 37, no. 5 (2007): 635, https://doi.org/10.1017/s0033291706009603.

9 **reaction to a demanding environment:** Thomas Curran, *The Perfection Trap: Embracing the Power of Good Enough* (New York: Scribner, 2023); Thomas Curran and Andrew P. Hill, "Perfectionism Is Increasing over Time: A Meta-Analysis of Birth Cohort Differences from 1989 to 2016," *Psychological Bulletin* 145, no. 4 (2019): 410–29, https://doi.org/10.1037/bul0000138; A. Hill and M. Grugan, "Introducing Perfectionistic Climate," *Perspectives on Early Childhood Psychology and Education* 4, no. 2 (2020): 263–76.

9 **In a bold 2019 study:** Curran and Hill, "Perfectionism Is Increasing over Time."

ADDITIONAL SOURCES: "Mister Rogers' Neighborhood Death of a Gold Fish 1101." Vimeo video, posted January 28, 2016. https://vimeo.com/153417661 (page discontinued).

Frank S. Nugent, "The Music Hall Presents Walt Disney's Delightful Fantasy, 'Snow White and the Seven Dwarfs'—Other New Films at Capitol and Criterion," *New York Times*, January 14, 1938.

Chapter 1: How We See Ourselves

14 **something downright magical:** Joachim Stoeber and Kathleen Otto, "Positive Conceptions of Perfectionism: Approaches, Evidence, Challenges," *Personality and Social Psychology Review* 10, no. 4 (2006): 295–319, https://doi.org/10.1207 /s15327957pspr1004_2.

14 **examined almost ten thousand American adults:** Angela L. Duckworth et al., "Who Does Well in Life? Conscientious Adults Excel in Both Objective and Subjective Success," *Frontiers in Psychology* 3 (2012), https://doi.org/10.3389/fpsyg.2012.00356.

14 *conscience,* **our inner sense of right and wrong:** John Wesley, *A Plain Account of Christian Perfection (1777) by: John Wesley* (North Charleston, SC: CreateSpace, 2017); Online Etymology Dictionary, s.v. "Conscientious," accessed October 22, 2023, https://www.etymonline.com/word/conscientious.

14 **conscientiousness can tip over into unhelpful perfectionism:** Douglas B. Samuel et al., "A Five-Factor Measure of Obsessive-Compulsive Personality Traits," *Journal of Personality Assessment* 94, no. 5 (2012): 456–65, https://doi.org/10.1080/00223891 .2012.677885; Nathan T. Carter et al., "The Downsides of Extreme Conscientiousness for Psychological Well-being: The Role of Obsessive Compulsive Tendencies" *Journal of Personality* 84, no. 4 (2016): 510–22, https://doi.org/10.1111/jopy.12177; Raymond Bernard Cattell and Paul Kline, *Scientific Analysis of Personality and Motivation* (San Diego: Academic Press, 1977); Murray W. Enns and Brian J. Cox, "The Nature and Assessment of Perfectionism: A Critical Analysis," in *Perfectionism: Theory, Research, and Treatment*, ed. G. L. Flett and P. L. Hewitt (Washington, DC: American Psychological Association, 2002), 33–62; Paul L. Hewitt and Gordon

L. Flett, "When Does Conscientiousness Become Perfectionism? Traits, Self-Presentation Styles, and Cognitions Suggest a Persistent Psychopathology," *Current Psychiatry* 6, no. 7 (2007): 49–60.

15 **Two core elements lie at the heart:** Roz Shafran, Zafra Cooper, and Christopher G. Fairburn, "Clinical Perfectionism: A Cognitive-Behavioural Analysis," *Behaviour Research and Therapy* 40, no. 7 (2002): 773–91, https://doi.org/10.1016/s0005-7967(01)00059-6; Roz Shafran, in discussion with the author, December 13, 2021.

15 **There are actually three boats:** P. L. Hewitt and G. L. Flett, "Perfectionism in the Self and Social Contexts: Conceptualization, Assessment, and Association with Psychopathology," *Journal of Personality and Social Psychology* 60, no. 3 (1991): 456–70, https://doi.org/10.1037/0022–3514.60.3.456.

16 **this type comes from all around us:** Thomas Curran, *The Perfection Trap: Embracing the Power of Good Enough* (New York: Scribner, 2023).

16 **increasing—no exaggeration here—exponentially:** Thomas Curran and Andrew P. Hill, "Perfectionism Is Increasing over Time: A Meta-Analysis of Birth Cohort Differences from 1989 to 2016," *Psychological Bulletin* 145, no. 4 (2019): 410–29, https://doi.org/10.1037/bul0000138.

16 **the trend is likely to continue:** Gordon L. Flett and Paul L. Hewitt, *Perfectionism in Childhood and Adolescence: A Developmental Approach* (Washington, DC: American Psychological Association, 2022).

16 **twenty-five years of research:** Martin M. Smith et al., "Perfectionism and the Five-Factor Model of Personality: A Meta-Analytic Review," *Personality and Social Psychology Review* 23, no. 4 (2019): 367–90, https://doi.org/10.1177/1088868318814973.

16 **the wheels start to come off:** Andrew P. Hill and Thomas Curran, "Multidimensional Perfectionism and Burnout: A Meta-Analysis," *Personality and Social Psychology Review* 20, no. 3 (2016): 269–88, https://doi.org/10.1177/1088868315596286.

16 **"In a challenging, messy and imperfect world":** Martin M. Smith and Simon Sherry, "Young People Drowning in a Rising Tide of Perfectionism," Conversation, February 5, 2019, http://theconversation.com/young-people-drowning-in-a-rising-tide-of-perfectionism-110343.

17 **meta-analysis of 284 different studies:** Karina Limburg et al., "The Relationship Between Perfectionism and Psychopathology: A Meta-Analysis," *Journal of Clinical Psychology* 73, no. 10 (2017): 1301–26, https://doi.org/10.1002/jclp.22435.

17 **reaches its tendrils into problems:** Joachim Stoeber and Laura N. Harvey, "Multidimensional Sexual Perfectionism and Female Sexual Function: A Longitudinal Investigation," *Archives of Sexual Behavior* 45, no. 8 (2016): 2003–14, https://doi.org/10.1007/s10508-016-0721-7; Kathryn Fletcher et al., "Buffering Against Maladaptive Perfectionism in Bipolar Disorder: The Role of Self-Compassion," *Journal of Affective Disorders* 250 (2019): 132–39, https://doi.org/10.1016/j.jad.2019.03.003; M. M. Antony et al., "Dimensions of Perfectionism Across the Anxiety Disorders," *Behaviour Research and Therapy* 36, no. 12 (1998): 1143–54; Parviz Asgari et al., "Effectiveness of Acceptance and Commitment Therapy on Perfectionism and Resilience in Migraine Patients," *International Archives of Health Sciences* 8, no. 3 (2021): 138, https://doi.org/10.4103/iahs.iahs_115_20.

NOTES | 277

17 **A sobering meta-analysis:** Statewide Suicide Prevention Council, *Alaska Suicide Follow-Back Study Final Report* (Juneau: Alaska Department of Health, 2003), http://dhss.alaska.gov/SuicidePrevention/Documents/pdfs_sspc/sspcfollowback2–07.pdf.

22 **boil down to these very human needs:** R. F. Baumeister and M. R. Leary, "The Need to Belong: Desire for Interpersonal Attachments as a Fundamental Human Motivation," *Psychological Bulletin* 117, no. 3 (1995): 497–529, https://doi.org/10.1037/0033–2909.117.3.497.

22 **more than half of Americans consider:** Jessica Buechler, "The Loneliness Epidemic Persists: A Post-Pandemic Look at the State of Loneliness among U.S. Adults," Cigna Group, accessed October 31, 2023, https://newsroom.thecignagroup.com/loneliness-epidemic-persists-post-pandemic-look; J. Blagden, W. Tanner, and F. Krasniqi, "Age of Alienation: Young People Facing a Loneliness Epidemic," Onward, July 8, 2021, https://www.ukonward.com/reports/age-of-alienation-loneliness-young-people.

22 **tighter social fabric:** Timothy P. Carney, *Alienated America: Why Some Places Thrive While Others Collapse* (New York: Harper, 2020); Charles Murray, *Coming Apart* (New York: Crown, 2013); Robert Putnam, *Bowling Alone: The Collapse and Revival of American Community* (London: Simon & Schuster, 2001).

22 **Social media crushes the souls:** "The Facebook Files," *Wall Street Journal*, September 15, 2021, https://www.wsj.com/articles/the-facebook-files-11631713039.

22 **seismically quieting the planet:** Elizabeth Gibney, "Coronavirus Lockdowns Have Changed the Way Earth Moves," *Nature* 580, no. 7802 (2020): 176–77, https://doi.org/10.1038/d41586-020-00965-x.

22 **agency over communion:** Andrea E. Abele and Bogdan Wojciszke, "Agency and Communion from the Perspective of Self Versus Others," *Journal of Personality and Social Psychology* 93, no. 5 (2007): 751–63, https://doi.org/10.1037/0022-3514.93.5.751.

23 **Drill down on social anxiety:** David A. Moscovitch, "What Is the Core Fear in Social Phobia? A New Model to Facilitate Individualized Case Conceptualization and Treatment," *Cognitive and Behavioral Practice* 16, no. 2 (2009): 123–34, https://doi.org/10.1016/j.cbpra.2008.04.002.

23 **tracked several hundred participants:** Prem S. Fry and Dominique L. Debats, "Perfectionism and the Five-Factor Personality Traits as Predictors of Mortality in Older Adults," *Journal of Health Psychology* 14, no. 4 (2009): 513–24, https://doi.org/10.1177/1359105309103571.

24 **Officially, this is called *adaptive perfectionism*:** Randy O. Frost et al., "A Comparison of Two Measures of Perfectionism," *Personality and Individual Differences* 14, no. 1 (1993): 119–26, https://doi.org/10.1016/0191-8869(93)90181-2; David M. Dunkley et al., "The Relation Between Perfectionism and Distress: Hassles, Coping, and Perceived Social Support as Mediators and Moderators," *Journal of Counseling Psychology* 47, no. 4 (2000): 437–53, https://doi.org/10.1037/0022-0167.47.4.437; Stoeber and Otto, "Positive Conceptions of Perfectionism"; Peter J. Bieling, Anne L. Israeli, and Martin M. Antony, "Is Perfectionism Good, Bad, or Both? Examining Models of the Perfectionism Construct," *Personality and Individual Differences* 36, no. 6 (2004): 1373–85, https://doi.org/10.1016/s0191-8869(03)00235-6.

27 **from the Greek *teleiōsis*:** Wikipedia, s.v. "Christian Perfection," accessed November 12, 2023, https://en.wikipedia.org/w/index.php?title=Christian_perfection&oldid=1184836014; Online Etymology Dictionary, s.v. "Perfection," accessed November 19, 2023, https://www.etymonline.com/word/perfection.

ADDITIONAL SOURCES: Monica Ramirez Basco, *Never Good Enough: How to Use Perfectionism to Your Advantage without Letting It Ruin Your Life* (Ashland, OR: Blackstone, 2020).

Sidney J. Blatt, "The Destructiveness of Perfectionism: Implications for the Treatment of Depression," *American Psychologist* 50, no. 12 (1995): 1003–20. https://doi.org/10.1037/0003-066x.50.12.1003.

Gordon L. Flett and Paul L. Hewitt, eds. *Perfectionism: Theory, Research and Treatment* (Washington, DC: American Psychological Association, 2002).

Sharon Martin, *The CBT Workbook for Perfectionism: Evidence-Based Skills to Help You Let Go of Self-Criticism, Build Self-Esteem, and Find Balance* (Oakland, CA: New Harbinger, 2019).

Ved Mehta, "Casualties of Oxford," *The New Yorker*, July 25, 1993, https://www.newyorker.com/magazine/1993/08/02/casualties-of-oxford.

Martin M. Smith et al., "The Perniciousness of Perfectionism: A Meta-analytic Review of the Perfectionism–Suicide Relationship," *Journal of Personality* 86, no. 3 (2018): 522–42, https://doi.org/10.1111/jopy.12333.

Chapter 2: The Many Salads of Perfectionism

28 **It's based on the research:** Roz Shafran, Zafra Cooper, and Christopher G. Fairburn, "Clinical Perfectionism: A Cognitive-Behavioural Analysis," *Behaviour Research and Therapy* 40, no. 7 (2002): 773–91, https://doi.org/10.1016/s0005-7967(01)00059-6; Roz Shafran, Sarah J. Egan, and Tracey D. Wade, *Overcoming Perfectionism, 2nd Edition: A Self-Help Guide Using Scientifically Supported Cognitive Behavioural Techniques* (London: Robinson, 2018).

30 **some of which are paraphrased:** Patricia Marten DiBartolo et al., "Shedding Light on the Relationship Between Personal Standards and Psychopathology: The Case for Contingent Self-Worth," *Journal of Rational-Emotive and Cognitive-Behavior Therapy* 22, no. 4 (2004): 237–50, https://doi.org/10.1023/b:jore.0000047310.94044.ac; Randy O. Frost et al., "The Dimensions of Perfectionism," *Cognitive Therapy and Research* 14, no. 5 (1990): 449–68, https://doi.org/10.1007/bf01172967; P. L. Hewitt and G. L. Flett, "Perfectionism in the Self and Social Contexts: Conceptualization, Assessment, and Association with Psychopathology," *Journal of Personality and Social Psychology* 60, no. 3 (1991): 456–70, https://doi.org/10.1037/0022-3514.60.3.456; Paul L. Hewitt et al., "The Multidimensional Perfectionism Scale: Reliability, Validity, and Psychometric Properties in Psychiatric Samples," *Psychological Assessment* 3, no. 3 (1991): 464–68, https://doi.org/10.1037/1040-3590.3.3.464; Joachim Stöber, "The Frost Multidimensional Perfectionism Scale Revisited: More Perfect with Four (Instead of Six) Dimensions," *Personality and Individual Differences* 24, no. 4 (1998): 481–91, https://doi.org/10.1016/s0191-8869(97)00207-9.

ADDITIONAL SOURCE: Monica Ramirez Basco, *Never Good Enough: How to Use Perfectionism to Your Advantage Without Letting It Ruin Your Life* (New York: Touchstone, 2000).

Chapter 3: The Beginnings of Things

35 **first-of-its-kind study:** Jennifer H. Mitchell et al., "An Experimental Manipulation of Maternal Perfectionistic Anxious Rearing Behaviors with Anxious and Non-Anxious Children," *Journal of Experimental Child Psychology* 116, no. 1 (2013): 1–18, https://doi.org/10.1016/j.jecp.2012.12.006; Jennifer Mitchell, in discussion with the author, December 20, 2021; Jennifer Hudson, in discussion with the author, November 29, 2021.

36 **instructions designed either to elicit:** Mitchell et al., "An Experimental Manipulation."

38 **In their 2002 analysis:** Gordon L. Flett, Paul L. Hewitt, Joan M. Oliver, and Silvana Macdonald, "Perfectionism in Children and Their Parents: A Developmental Analysis," in *Perfectionism: Theory, Research, and Treatment*, ed. G. L. Flett and P. L. Hewitt (Washington, DC: American Psychological Association, 2002), 89–132.

38 **It's officially called the *anxious rearing model*:** Flett et al., "Perfectionism in Children."

39 **The second family environment:** Flett et al., "Perfectionism in Children."

43 **in fourth and seventh graders:** Deborah Stornelli, Gordon L. Flett, and Paul L. Hewitt, "Perfectionism, Achievement, and Affect in Children: A Comparison of Students from Gifted, Arts, and Regular Programs," *Canadian Journal of School Psychology* 24, no. 4 (2009): 267–83, https://doi.org/10.1177/0829573509342392.

43 **A 2018 *Harvard Business Review* article:** Laura Empson, "If You're So Successful, Why Are You Still Working 70 Hours a Week?," *Harvard Business Review*, February 1, 2018, https://hbr.org/2018/02/if-youre-so-successful-why-are-you-still-working-70-hours-a-week.

44 **Flett and Hewitt call it the *social reaction model*:** Flett et al., "Perfectionism in Children."

46 **Flett and Hewitt call it the *social learning model*:** Flett et al., "Perfectionism in Children."

48 **the specific disorders that coil around perfectionism:** Naomi R. Wray et al., "Genome-Wide Association Analyses Identify 44 Risk Variants and Refine the Genetic Architecture of Major Depression," *Nature Genetics* 50, no. 5 (2018): 668–81, https://doi.org/10.1038/s41588-018-0090-3; Michael G. Gottschalk and Katharina Domschke, "Genetics of Generalized Anxiety Disorder and Related Traits," *Dialogues in Clinical Neuroscience* 19, no. 2 (2017): 159–68, https://doi.org/10.31887/dcns.2017.19.2/kdomschke; Olga Giannakopoulou et al., "The Genetic Architecture of Depression in Individuals of East Asian Ancestry: A Genome-Wide Association Study," *JAMA Psychiatry* 78, no. 11 (2021): 1258–69, https://doi.org/10.1001/jamapsychiatry.2021.2099; Tracey D. Wade and Cynthia M. Bulik, "Shared Genetic and Environmental Risk Factors between Undue Influence of Body Shape and Weight on Self-Evaluation and Dimensions of Perfectionism," *Psychological Medicine* 37, no. 5 (2007): 635–44, https://doi.org/10.1017/S0033291706009603; Toshimitsu Kamakura et al., "A Twin Study of Genetic and Environmental

Influences on Psychological Traits of Eating Disorders in a Japanese Female Sample," *Twin Research and Human Genetics* 6, no. 4 (2003): 292–96, https://doi.org/10.1375/136905203322296647; Rachel Bachner-Melman et al., "Anorexia Nervosa, Perfectionism, and Dopamine D4 Receptor (DRD4)," *American Journal of Medical Genetics. Part B, Neuropsychiatric Genetics* 144B, no. 6 (2007): 748–56, https://doi.org/10.1002/ajmg.b.30505.

48 **growing handful of studies hint:** Federica Tozzi et al., "The Structure of Perfectionism: A Twin Study," *Behavior Genetics* 34, no. 5 (2004): 483–94, https://doi.org/10.1023/B:BEGE.0000038486.47219.76; Carmen Iranzo-Tatay et al., "Genetic and Environmental Contributions to Perfectionism and Its Common Factors," *Psychiatry Research* 230, no. 3 (2015): 932–39, https://doi.org/10.1016/j.psychres.2015.11.020.

48 **a 2015 study in the journal:** Iranzo-Tatay et al., "Genetic and Environmental Contributions."

48 **heritability estimates ranged as high as 66 percent:** Jason S. Moser et al., "Etiologic Relationships Between Anxiety and Dimensions of Maladaptive Perfectionism in Young Adult Female Twins: Twins, Anxiety, and Perfectionism," *Depression and Anxiety* 29, no. 1 (2012): 47–53, https://doi.org/10.1002/da.20890.

49 **"become more individualistic, materialistic":** Thomas Curran and Andrew P. Hill, "Perfectionism Is Increasing over Time: A Meta-Analysis of Birth Cohort Differences from 1989 to 2016," *Psychological Bulletin* 145, no. 4 (2019): 410–29, https://doi.org/10.1037/bul0000138.

49 **"Young people are sifted and sorted more":** "EP 88: Professor Andrew Hill—Perfectionism in Youth Sport," Athlete Development Project, https://athletedevelopmentproject.com/2020/08/ep-88-professor-andrew-hill.

49 **"prizes achievement, image, and merit":** "Why Perfectionism Is on the Rise—and How to Overcome It," Goop, https://goop.com/wellness/mindfulness/why-perfectionism-is-on-the-rise-and-how-to-overcome-it/.

50 **"more or less flat until around 2005":** Thomas Curran, *The Perfection Trap: Embracing the Power of Good Enough* (New York: Scribner, 2023).

50 **We spend one-third of our time online:** Simon Kemp, "The Time We Spend on Social Media," DataReportal, January 31, 2024, https://datareportal.com/reports/digital-2024-deep-dive-the-time-we-spend-on-social-media.

50 **O, the Oprah Magazine published:** Editors of O, *Live Your Best Life: A Treasury of Wisdom, Wit, Advice, Interviews, and Inspiration from O, the Oprah Magazine*, 1st ed. (Birmingham, AL: Oxmoor House, 2005).

51 **Take an expectation like graduating:** Jean M. Twenge, *iGen: Why Today's Super-Connected Kids Are Growing Up Less Rebellious, More Tolerant, Less Happy—and Completely Unprepared for Adulthood—and What That Means for the Rest of Us* (New York: Atria Books, 2018).

51 **the esteemed psychologist Dr. Martin Seligman:** M. E. Seligman and M. Csikszentmihalyi, "Positive Psychology: An Introduction," *American Psychologist* 55, no. 1 (2000): 5–14, https://doi.org/10.1037/0003-066x.55.1.5.

51 **Dr. Jean Twenge shows:** Twenge, *iGen*.

52 **Indeed, a study by Drs. Sharon F. Lambert:** Sharon F. Lambert, W. LaVome Robinson, and Nicholas S. Ialongo, "The Role of Socially Prescribed Perfectionism in the Link Between Perceived Racial Discrimination and African American Adolescents' Depressive Symptoms," *Journal of Abnormal Child Psychology* 42, no. 4 (May 2014): 577–87.

    ADDITIONAL SOURCES: Josh Cohen, "The Perfectionism Trap," *The Economist*, August 10, 2021, https://www.economist.com/1843/2021/08/10/the-perfectionism-trap.

    Sarah Green, "The Hidden Demons of High Achievers," *Harvard Business Review*, May 2011, https://hbr.org/2011/05/the-hidden-demons-of-high-achi.

Chapter 4: Beyond the Inner Critic

57 **There are three ways to ultimate success:** Harris, Lynden (correspondent), "Kindness Makes a Community," *The Chapel Hill News,* February 17, 2013, 1A.

58 **three primary colors of perfectionistic self-criticism:** Raymond M. Bergner, *Pathological Self-Criticism* (New York: Springer, 2014).

59 **Consider these six:** Bergner, *Pathological Self-Criticism*, 46.

59 **a pianist setting out to learn:** Bergner, *Pathological Self-Criticism*, 48.

60 **A grandfather in China:** Jenny Bozon, "Man Runs Sub-3.30 Marathon While Chain-Smoking Pack of Cigarettes," *Runner's World*, November 16, 2022, https://www.runnersworld.com/uk/news/a41969594/chinese-smoking-marathon-runner/.

61 ***excellence* is the realistic, sustainable, healthy:** G. L. Flett et al., "Perfectionism Cognition Theory: The Cognitive Side of Perfectionism," in *The Psychology of Perfectionism: Theory, Research, Applications*, ed. Joachim Stoeber (New York: Routledge, 2018), 89–110; Patrick Gaudreau, "On the Distinction between Personal Standards Perfectionism and Excellencism: A Theory Elaboration and Research Agenda," *Perspectives on Psychological Science* 14, no. 2 (2019): 197–215, https://doi.org/10.1177/1745691618797940; Tracey D. Wade, "Prevention of Perfectionism in Youth," in *The Psychology of Perfectionism*, 265–83.

61 **a research team at Loughborough University:** Lorin Taranis and Caroline Meyer, "Perfectionism and Compulsive Exercise Among Female Exercisers: High Personal Standards or Self-Criticism?," *Personality and Individual Differences* 49, no. 1 (2010): 3–7, https://doi.org/10.1016/j.paid.2010.02.024.

61 **Self-criticism is the core of humans' ability:** Bergner, *Pathological Self-Criticism*, 92.

61 **Eighteen-year-old Kareem Abdul-Jabbar:** Kareem Abdul-Jabbar and Raymond Obstfeld, *Becoming Kareem: Growing Up On and Off the Court* (New York: Little, Brown, 2017).

62 **Individually, Abdul-Jabbar:** Wikipedia, s.v. "Kareem Abdul-Jabbar," accessed March 24, 2024, https://en.wikipedia.org/w/index.php?title=Kareem_Abdul-Jabbar&oldid=1215256424.

62 **"Today, we are going to learn how":** Abdul-Jabbar, and Obstfeld *Becoming Kareem,* 184.

62 **"His pale pink feet":** Abdul-Jabbar and Obstfeld, *Becoming Kareem,*184.

63 **cracked the code by studying:** Roland Tharp and Ronald Gallimore, "Basketball's

John Wooden: What a Coach Can Teach a Teacher," *Psychology Today* 9, no. 8 (1976): 74–78; Ronald Gallimore and Roland Tharp, "What a Coach Can Teach a Teacher, 1975–2004: Reflections and Reanalysis of John Wooden's Teaching Practices," *Sport Psychologist* 18, no. 2 (2004): 119–37, https://doi.org/10.1123/tsp.18.2 .119; Ronald Gallimore, "Surprising Consequences of Researching John Wooden's Teaching Practices: The Backstory of the 1976 Study of the Legendary University of California, Los Angeles Basketball Coach," *International Sport Coaching Journal* 7, no. 2 (2020): 256–60, https://doi.org/10.1123/iscj.2020-0008; Ronald Gallimore, Wade Gilbert, and Swen Nater, "Reflective Practice and Ongoing Learning: A Coach's 10-Year Journey," *Reflective Practice* 15, no. 2 (2014): 268–88, https://doi.org/10.1080 /14623943.2013.868790.

63 **teacher praise and reproof were hot topics:** Roland G. Tharp and Ralph J. Wetzel, eds., *Behavior Modification in the Natural Environment* (San Diego: Academic Press, 1970).

63 **"Pass the ball to someone short!":** Gallimore and Tharp, "What a Coach Can Teach."

63 **"short, punctuated, and numerous":** "Wooden 1975 Study," UCLA, http://ronaldg .bol.ucla.edu/Rons_UCLA_Homepage/Wooden_1975_study.html.

63 **"It was the information that promoted change.":** Gallimore and Tharp, "What a Coach Can Teach."

63 **used instructional comments 36 percent of the time:** Ronald Gallimore and Roland Tharp, "Revisiting John Wooden's Teaching Practice and Philosophy: 'Everyone's a Teacher Who Has Someone Under Their Supervision,'" *Sport Psychologist*, no. 18 (2004): 119–37.

63 **Wooden bested them all:** Tharp and Gallimore, "Basketball's John Wooden."

65 **Eunice's day started out healthy:** Eunice, in discussion with the author, September 24, 2019.

67 **it diminishes us:** Bergner, *Pathological Self-Criticism.*

68 **Self-compassion, according to psychologist:** Kristin Neff, *Self-Compassion: The Proven Power of Being Kind to Yourself* (New York: William Morrow, 2015); "What Is Self-Compassion?," Self-Compassion, March 22, 2011, https://self-compassion.org /what-is-self-compassion.

68 **An avalanche of research:** Angus MacBeth and Andrew Gumley, "Exploring Compassion: A Meta-Analysis of the Association Between Self-Compassion and Psychopathology," *Clinical Psychology Review* 32, no. 6 (2012): 545–52, https://doi .org/10.1016/j.cpr.2012.06.003; Alexander C. Wilson et al., "Effectiveness of Self-Compassion Related Therapies: A Systematic Review and Meta-Analysis," *Mindfulness* 10, no. 6 (2019): 979–95, https://doi.org/10.1007/s12671-018-1037-6.

68 **giant analysis of seventy-nine different studies:** Ulli Zessin, Oliver Dickhäuser, and Sven Garbade, "The Relationship Between Self-Compassion and Well-Being: A Meta-Analysis," *Applied Psychology: Health and Well-Being* 7, no. 3 (2015): 340–64, https://doi.org/10.1111/aphw.12051.

68 **But those of us with perfectionism:** Allison Kelly et al., "Why Would I Want to Be More Self-Compassionate? A Qualitative Study of the Pros and Cons to Cultivating Self-Compassion in Individuals with Anorexia Nervosa," *British Journal of Clinical*

Psychology 60, no. 1 (2021): 99–115, https://doi.org/10.1111/bjc.12275; Marios Biskas, Fuschia M. Sirois, and Thomas L. Webb, "Using Social Cognition Models to Understand Why People, Such as Perfectionists, Struggle to Respond with Self-Compassion," *British Journal of Social Psychology* 61, no. 4 (2022): 1160–82, https://doi.org/10.1111/bjso .12531.

69 **self-compassion is a Vitamixed smoothie:** "What Is Self-Compassion?"

69 **can be *validation*, which is the recognition:** Alan E. Fruzzetti and Allison K. Ruork, "Validation Principles and Practices in Dialectical Behavior Therapy," in *The Oxford Handbook of Dialectical Behaviour Therapy*, ed. Michaela A. Swales (Oxford, England: Oxford University Press, 2018).

70 **A reader emailed me with her method:** Reader DS, email message to author, August 18, 2023.

70 **"behaviors are the things we can control":** Clarissa Ong, in discussion with the author, February 8, 2023.

70 **"I take good care of myself":** Reader CM, email message to author, August 18, 2023.

70 **"I am allowed to do things":** Reader SA, email message to author, August 18, 2023.

70 **"my overactive conscience poking":** Reader DH, email message to author, August 19, 2023.

70 **"I have realized that I really cannot":** Reader KC, email message to author, August 18, 2023.

70 **"Not imposing impossible standards":** CM, email to author.

70 **"Saying what I *can't* do":** Reader KC, email message to author, August 18, 2023.

71 **When Eunice and I reconnected:** Eunice, personal communication, September 24, 2019.

73 **But this gives us a metaphor:** "ACT for Depression and Anxiety Disorders," Psychwire, online course, https://psychwire.com/harris/act-depression.

74 **All cognitive defusion techniques:** "Cognitive Defusion (Deliteralization)," Association for Contextual Behavioral Science, https://contextualscience.org/cognitive _defusion_deliteralization.

74 **Other variations popularized:** "ACT for Depression and Anxiety Disorders"; Russ Harris, *The Happiness Trap: Stop Struggling, Start Living* (London: Robinson, 2012).

74 **Playing with the thoughts:** "ACT for Depression and Anxiety Disorders."

75 **The clean, sharp smell of sagebrush:** Jesse Crosby, in discussion with the author, February 7, 2023.

76 **"I think about that a lot":** Jesse Crosby, in discussion with the author, January 30, 2023.

77 **mind-bendingly complicated theory:** Steven C. Hayes et al., "Acceptance and Commitment Therapy and Contextual Behavioral Science: Examining the Progress of a Distinctive Model of Behavioral and Cognitive Therapy," *Behavior Therapy* 44, no. 2 (2013): 180–98, https://doi.org/10.1016/j.beth.2009.08.002; Roger Vilardaga et al., "Creating a Strategy for Progress: A Contextual Behavioral Science Approach," *Behavior Analyst* 32, no. 1 (2009): 105–33, https://doi.org/10.1007/bf03392178; S. C.

Hayes, D. Barnes-Holmes, and B. Roche, *Relational Frame Theory: A Post-Skinnerian Account of Human Language and Cognition* (New York: Plenum, 2001); Rebecca J. Linnett and Fraenze Kibowski, "A Multidimensional Approach to Perfectionism and Self-Compassion," *Self and Identity* 19, no. 7 (2020): 757–83, https://doi.org/10 .1080/15298868.2019.1669695; Clarissa W. Ong et al., "Is Perfectionism Always Unhealthy? Examining the Moderating Effects of Psychological Flexibility and Self-Compassion," *Journal of Clinical Psychology* 77, no. 11 (2021): 2576–91, https://doi.org /10.1002/jclp.23187; Deborah Lee, *The Compassionate Mind Approach to Recovering from Trauma Using Compassion-Focused Therapy* (London: Robinson, 2012).

Chapter 5: The Outer Critics

81 **"What's wrong with you?":** Lisa Brennan-Jobs, *Small Fry: A Memoir* (New York: Grove, 2018).

81 **"He screams at subordinates":** Malcolm Gladwell, "The Real Genius of Steve Jobs," *New Yorker*, November 6, 2011, https://www.newyorker.com/magazine/2011/11/14 /the-tweaker.

82 **Drs. Gordon Flett and Paul Hewitt:** P. L. Hewitt and G. L. Flett, "Perfectionism in the Self and Social Contexts: Conceptualization, Assessment, and Association with Psychopathology," *Journal of Personality and Social Psychology* 60, no. 3 (1991): 456–70, https://doi.org/10.1037/0022-3514.60.3.456.

83 **One of the first to describe:** Karen Horney, *Neurosis and Human Growth: The Struggle Towards Self-Realization* (New York: W. W. Norton, 1950).

83 **"gentle rebel of psychoanalysis":** Jack L. Rubins, *Karen Horney: Gentle Rebel of Psychoanalysis* (New York: Dial Press, 1978).

83 **"A person may primarily impose":** Horney, *Neurosis and Human Growth*.

83 **a questionnaire meant to measure:** P. L. Hewitt and G. L. Flett, *Multidimensional Perfectionism Scale (MPS): Technical Manual* (Toronto: Multi-Health Systems, 2004).

84 **"high self-regard but low regard":** Joachim Stoeber, "How Other-Oriented Perfectionism Differs from Self-Oriented and Socially Prescribed Perfectionism," *Journal of Psychopathology and Behavioral Assessment* 36, no. 2 (2014): 329–38, https://doi.org /10.1007/s10862-013-9397-7.

84 **Healthy narcissism:** Elsa Ronningstam, *NPD Basic: A Brief Overview of Identifying, Diagnosing and Treating Narcissistic Personality Disorder*, 4th ed. (Boston: Harvard Medical School, 2021).

84 **But there's a whole lot of variation:** "Level 1 Radically Open Dialectical Behavior Therapy Blended Learning Course," Radically Open, online course, https://www .radicallyopen.net/training/product/level-1-test.html; "Level 2 for RO DBT Practitioners in Radically Open Dialectical Behavior Therapy," Radically Open, online course, https://www.radicallyopen.net/training/product/radically-open-dialectical -behavior-therapy-blended-learning-course-level-2.html.

84 **Radically Open Dialectical Behavior Therapy:** Thomas R. Lynch, *Radically Open Dialectical Behavior Therapy: Theory and Practice for Treating Disorders of Overcontrol* (Oakland, CA: New Harbinger, 2017); Thomas R. Lynch, *The Skills Training Manual*

for Radically Open Dialectical Behavior Therapy: A Clinician's Guide for Treating Disorders of Overcontrol (Oakland, CA: New Harbinger, 2017); "Level 1 Radically Open Dialectical Behavior Therapy"; "Level 2 for RO DBT Practitioners."

85 **"sensitive and specific as a nerve"**: Brennan-Jobs, *Small Fry*.

85 **"Because he noticed the details"**: Brennan-Jobs, *Small Fry*.

86 **"You guys don't know"**: Walter Isaacson, *Steve Jobs* (New York: Simon & Schuster, 2021).

86 **Next up, empathy.**: Aysel Köksal Akyol and Güneş Sali, "A Study on the Perfectionist Personality Traits and Empathic Tendencies of Working and Non-Working Adolescents Across Different Variables," *Educational Sciences Theory & Practice* 13, no. 4 (2013): 2032–42, https://doi.org/10.12738/estp.2013.4.1861.

86 **"We're just cold people."**: Brennan-Jobs, *Small Fry*.

87 **hidden engine of the Outer Critic**: "Level 1 Radically Open Dialectical Behavior Therapy"; "Level 2 for RO DBT Practitioners."

89 **"The least helpful thing we can do"**: Harriet Lerner, *The Dance of Connection: How to Talk to Someone When You're Mad, Hurt, Scared, Frustrated, Insulted, Betrayed, or Desperate* (New York: William Morrow, 2002).

89 **As she was leaving**: Brennan-Jobs, *Small Fry*.

89 **his version of "honesty"**: Nellie Bowles, "In 'Small Fry,' Steve Jobs Comes Across as a Jerk. His Daughter Forgives Him. Should We?," *New York Times*, August 23, 2018, https://www.nytimes.com/2018/08/23/books/steve-jobs-lisa-brennan-jobs-small-fry.html.

90 **a technique called *self-enquiry***: Lynch, *Radically Open Dialectical Behavior Therapy*; Lynch, *Skills Training Manual*; "Level 1 Radically Open Dialectical Behavior Therapy"; "Level 2 for RO DBT Practitioners."

90 **"finding your edge"**: Lynch, *Radically Open Dialectical Behavior Therapy*; Lynch, *Skills Training Manual*; "Level 1 Radically Open Dialectical Behavior Therapy"; "Level 2 for RO DBT Practitioners."

90 **Dr. Lynch gives examples**: "Level 1 Radically Open Dialectical Behavior Therapy"; "Level 2 for RO DBT Practitioners."

91 **"That shit was in the trash can"**: Josh Eells, "Bruno Mars: The Private Anxiety of a Pop Perfectionist," *Rolling Stone*, November 2, 2016, https://www.rollingstone.com/music/music-features/bruno-mars-the-private-anxiety-of-a-pop-perfectionist-191397/.

92 **Welcome to the world of *socially prescribed perfectionism***: Hewitt and Flett, "Perfectionism in the Self and Social Contexts."

92 **Bruno Mars traces his intensity**: Eells, "Bruno Mars."

92 **come out of socially prescribed perfectionism**: Christine Liwag Dixon, "The Untold Truth of Bruno Mars," List, August 31, 2017, https://www.thelist.com/83646/untold-truth-bruno-mars/; "Bruno Mars Is Such a Perfectionist That 'Uptown Funk' Almost Didn't Happen," MTV, November 2, 2016. http://www.mtv.com/news/2950064/bruno-mars-24k-magic-perfectionist/.

92 **It's more of a cultural force**: Thomas Curran, *The Perfection Trap: Embracing the Power of Good Enough* (New York: Scribner, 2023).

93 **"Perfectionism is the defining psychology":** Curran, *The Perfection Trap*.

93 **"interpersonally motivated":** Aislin R. Mushquash and Simon B. Sherry, "Understanding the Socially Prescribed Perfectionist's Cycle of Self-Defeat: A 7-Day, 14-Occasion Daily Diary Study," *Journal of Research in Personality* 46, no. 6 (2012): 700–709, https://doi.org/10.1016/j.jrp.2012.08.006.

93 *perfectionistic discrepancy:* Kenneth G. Rice et al., "Addressing Concerns about How Perfectionistic Discrepancy Should Be Measured with the Revised Almost Perfect Scale," *Assessment* 26, no. 3 (2019): 432–44, https://doi.org/10.1177/1073191117702241.

93 *perfectionistic self-presentation:* Paul L. Hewitt et al., "The Interpersonal Expression of Perfection: Perfectionistic Self-Presentation and Psychological Distress," *Journal of Personality and Social Psychology* 84, no. 6 (2003): 1303–25, https://doi.org/10.1037/0022-3514.84.6.1303.

93 **fast track to predictable results:** Hewitt et al., "The Interpersonal Expression"; Mushquash and Sherry, "Understanding the Socially Prescribed Perfectionist's Cycle."

95 *whether we deserve it or not:* Theresa E. Robertson et al., "The True Trigger of Shame: Social Devaluation Is Sufficient, Wrongdoing Is Unnecessary," *Evolution and Human Behavior* 39, no. 5 (2018): 566–73, https://doi.org/10.1016/j.evolhumbehav.2018.05.010.

97 **It's a behavioral strategy:** Emma Reed Turrell, *Please Yourself: How to Stop People-Pleasing and Transform the Way You Live* (London: Fourth Estate, 2021).

97 **"I'm down with anything":** Nicole You Jeung Kim et al., "You Must Have a Preference: The Impact of No-Preference Communication on Joint Decision Making," *Journal of Marketing Research* 60, no. 1 (2023): 52–71, https://doi.org/10.1177/00222437221107593.

98 **Brain scans back this up:** Juan F. Domínguez, Sreyneth A. Taing, and Pascal Molenberghs, "Why Do Some Find It Hard to Disagree? An fMRI Study," *Frontiers in Human Neuroscience* 9 (2016), https://doi.org/10.3389/fnhum.2015.00718.

98 **"saying, 'Me first'":** Turrell, *Please Yourself*.

99 **"When they tell you that 'you've changed'":** Turrell, *Please Yourself*.

99 **"Conditional acceptance is no acceptance":** Turrell, *Please Yourself*.

ADDITIONAL SOURCES: Joachim Stoeber et al., "Perfectionism, Social Disconnection, and Interpersonal Hostility: Not All Perfectionists Don't Play Nicely with Others," *Personality and Individual Differences* 119 (2017): 112–17, https://doi.org/10.1016/j.paid.2017.07.008.

Daniel Sznycer et al., "Cross-Cultural Invariances in the Architecture of Shame," *Proceedings of the National Academy of Sciences of the United States of America* 115, no. 39 (2018): 9702–7, https://doi.org/10.1073/pnas.1805016115.

Chapter 6: From Labels to Values

104 **our labels start to determine our actions:** Clarissa Ong and Michael Twohig, *The Anxious Perfectionist: Acceptance and Commitment Therapy Skills to Deal with Anxiety, Stress, and Worry Driven by Perfectionism* (Oakland, CA: New Harbinger, 2022).

105 **"It's recognizing the chatter about ourselves":** Michael Twohig, in discussion with the author, February 2, 2023.

105 **acceptance and commitment therapy:** S. C. Hayes, K. Strosahl, and K. G. Wilson, *Acceptance and Commitment Therapy: An Experiential Approach to Behavior Change* (New York: Guilford Press, 1999).

107 **A true value:** Ong and Twohig, *The Anxious Perfectionist.*

109 **Dr. Ong gives an example:** Clarissa Ong, in discussion with the author, February 8, 2023.

109 **Dr. Twohig tells the story:** Twohig, discussion with the author.

110 **Dr. Ong gives the example:** Ong, discussion with the author.

110 **"I often say to my students":** Twohig, discussion with the author.

111 **A whopping 97 percent of respondents:** *Success Index* (n.p.: Populace/Gallup, 2019), https://populace.org/research.

111 **Dr. Twohig talks about values and rules:** Twohig, discussion with the author.

112 **"There's all this stuff that comes with 'smart'":** Ong, discussion with the author.

Chapter 7: Our Forgotten Baskets

113 **Tucked neatly in the rolling mountains:** "BCC to Host COVID-19 Vaccine Clinics," Berkshire Community College, https://www.berkshirecc.edu/news-events/2021/vaccine.php; "WATCH: Yo-Yo Ma Performs at Vaccine Clinic after Receiving Second COVID-19 Shot," WCVB, March 14, 2021, https://www.wcvb.com/article/watch-yo-yo-ma-performs-at-vaccine-clinic-after-receiving-second-covid-19-shot/35831169; Jennifer Jett, "Yo-Yo Ma Gives a Surprise Cello Concert at a Massachusetts Vaccination Site," *New York Times*, March 14, 2021, https://www.nytimes.com/2021/03/14/world/yo-yo-ma-berkshire-community-college.html; David Marchese, "Yo-Yo Ma and the Meaning of Life," *New York Times*, November 23, 2020, https://www.nytimes.com/interactive/2020/11/23/magazine/yo-yo-ma-interview.html.

114 **"I'm always happy to respond":** "Yo-Yo Ma Tells Story behind His Cello Performance at Vaccination Center," YouTube video, 2:11, posted by TODAY, March 16, 2021, https://www.youtube.com/watch?v=8t9-SvRv2zg.

114 **His first: Dvořák's "Going Home.":** Yo-Yo Ma (@YoYo_Ma), "In these days of anxiety, I wanted to find a way to continue to share some of the music that gives me comfort. The first of my #SongsOfComfort: Dvořák—'Going Home' stay safe," Twitter post, March 13, 2020, 5:08 p.m., https://twitter.com/YoYo_Ma/status/1238572657278431234.

114 **played pop-up concerts:** Amanda Burke, "Musicians Yo-Yo Ma, Emanuel Ax Surprise Essential Workers with Pop-up Performances," *Berkshire Eagle*, September 2, 2020, https://www.berkshireeagle.com/archives/musicians-yo-yo-ma-emanuel-ax-surprise-essential-workers-with-pop-up-performances/article_8ea51bbf-463d-54d9-ab45-8490068bfa2c.html.

114 **"At one point I had the audacity":** "Yo-Yo Ma Teachers Music and Connection," MasterClass, online course, https://www.masterclass.com/classes/yo-yo-ma-teaches-music-and-connection.

115 **"over-value performance and under-value the self.":** D. E. Hamachek, "Psychody-namics of Normal and Neurotic Perfectionism," *Psychology* 15 (1978): 27–33.

115 **This is *overevaluation*:** Roz Shafran, Zafra Cooper, and Christopher G. Fairburn, "Clinical Perfectionism: A Cognitive-Behavioural Analysis," *Behaviour Research and Therapy* 40, no. 7 (2002): 773–91, https://doi.org/10.1016/s0005-7967(01)00059-6.

115 **working toward goals boosts happiness:** Ed Diener et al., "Subjective Well-Being: Three Decades of Progress," *Psychological Bulletin* 125, no. 2 (1999): 276–302, https://doi .org/10.1037/0033-2909.125.2.276; James T. Austin and Jeffrey B. Vancouver, "Goal Constructs in Psychology: Structure, Process, and Content," *Psychological Bulletin* 120, no. 3 (1996): 338–75, https://doi.org/10.1037/0033-2909.120.3.338.

116 **"agency over communion":** A. E. Abele and B. Wojciszke, "Agency and Commu-nion from the Perspective Of Self Versus Others," *Journal of Personality and Social Psychology* 93, no. 5 (2007): 751–63, doi: 10.1037/0022–3514.93.5.751; A. E. Abele and B. Wojciszke, "Communal and Agentic Content in Social Cognition: A Dual Perspective Model," *Advances in Experimental Social Psychology*, 50 (2014): 195–255, https://doi.org/10.1016/B978-0-12-800284-1.00004-7.

116 **"'You know, I could actually just":** "Yo-Yo Ma Teachers Music and Connection."

117 **Paradoxically, we emphasize agency:** Joachim Stoeber et al., "Perfectionism and Interpersonal Problems Revisited," *Personality and Individual Differences* 169 (2021): 110106, https://doi.org/10.1016/j.paid.2020.110106; Joachim Stoeber et al., "Perfec-tionism, Social Disconnection, and Interpersonal Hostility: Not All Perfectionists Don't Play Nicely with Others," *Personality and Individual Differences* 119 (2017): 112–17, https://doi.org/10.1016/j.paid.2017.07.008.

117 **"gravitational pull to feel left out":** Thomas J. DeLong, *Flying Without a Net: Turn Fear of Change into Fuel for Success* (Boston: Harvard Business Review Press, 2011).

120 **Jon Bon Jovi looks out:** "Warren Buffett & Jon Bon Jovi: A Ukulele Duet for Char-ity," YouTube video, 2:40, posted by Forbes Digital Assets, June 28, 2012, https:// www.youtube.com/watch?v=nCm5–2UN2Ms.

120 **playing Sinatra's "My Way" on CNN:** "Piers Morgan-Warren Buffett Plays Ukulele for Piers-22/10/2013," YouTube video, 1:37, posted by "smtm: Entertainment," No-vember 13, 2013, https://www.youtube.com/watch?v=lxJw4QEglbA.

120 **"Red River Valley":** "Warren Buffett & The Quebe Sisters 'Red River Valley,'" YouTube video, 5:33, posted by the Quebe Sisters, January 28, 2008, https://www .youtube.com/watch?v=A0eEuDAtu2Q.

121 **coaxing Bill Gates into a duet:** "Philanthropists in Golf Carts Eating Dilly Bars," YouTube video, 3:49, posted by Bill Gates, July 8, 2016, https://www.youtube.com /watch?v=-WnoaY0X7bg.

122 **"I am neither drawn to, nor inspired by":** Harriet Lerner, *The Dance of Connection: How to Talk to Someone When You're Mad, Hurt, Scared, Frustrated, Insulted, Betrayed, or Desperate* (New York: William Morrow, 2002).

122 **type 1 fun, also called *hedonic happiness*:** R. M. Ryan and E. L. Deci, "On Hap-piness and Human Potentials: A Review of Research on Hedonic and Eudaimonic

Well-Being," *Annual Review of Psychology* 52, no. 1 (2001): 141–66, https://doi.org/10.1146/annurev.psych.52.1.141.

122 **type 2 fun, also called *eudaimonic happiness*:** Ryan and Deci, "On Happiness and Human Potentials."

123 **officially called *contingent self-worth*:** Patricia Marten DiBartolo et al., "Shedding Light on the Relationship Between Personal Standards and Psychopathology: The Case for Contingent Self-Worth," *Journal of Rational-Emotive and Cognitive-Behavior Therapy* 22, no. 4 (2004): 237–50, https://doi.org/10.1023/b:jore.0000047310.94044.ac.

124 **"a fucking human being":** Stephen J. Burn, ed., *Conversations with David Foster Wallace* (Jackson: University Press of Mississippi, 2012).

ADDITIONAL SOURCES: Jennifer Crocker, "Contingencies of Self-Worth: Implications for Self-Regulation and Psychological Vulnerability," *Self and Identity* 1, no. 2 (2002): 143–49, https://doi.org/10.1080/152988602317319320.

Jennifer Crocker, Amara T. Brook, Yu Niiya, and Mark Villacorta, "The Pursuit of Self-Esteem: Contingencies of Self-Worth and Self-Regulation," *Journal of Personality* 74, no. 6 (2006): 1749–71, https://doi.org/10.1111/j.1467-6494.2006.00427.x.

Kristin D. Neff and Roos Vonk. "Self-Compassion Versus Global Self-Esteem: Two Different Ways of Relating to Oneself," *Journal of Personality* 77, no. 1 (2009): 23–50, https://doi.org/10.1111/j.1467-6494.2008.00537.x.

Kenneth G. Rice, Clarissa M. E. Richardson, and Merideth E. Ray, "Perfectionism in Academic Settings," in *Perfectionism, Health, and Well-Being*, eds. Fuschia M. Sirois and Danielle Sirianni Molnar (Cham, Switzerland: Springer International: 2016), 245–64.

Edward D. Sturman, Gordon L. Flett, Paul L. Hewitt, and Susan G. Rudolph, "Dimensions of Perfectionism and Self-Worth Contingencies in Depression," *Journal of Rational-Emotive and Cognitive-Behavior Therapy* 27, no. 4 (2009): 213–31, https://doi.org/10.1007/s10942-007-0079-9.

Chapter 8: Rewriting the Inner Rulebook

138 **out-of-date laws:** Stephanie Morrow, "Top Craziest Laws Still on the Books," LegalZoom, October 7, 2009, https://www.legalzoom.com/articles/top-craziest-laws-still-on-the-books.

138 **definition of clinical perfectionism:** Roz Shafran, Zafra Cooper, and Christopher G. Fairburn, "Clinical Perfectionism: A Cognitive-Behavioural Analysis," *Behaviour Research and Therapy* 40, no. 7 (2002): 773–91, https://doi.org/10.1016/s0005-7967(01)00059-6.

138 **"maintained by the biased evaluation":** Shafran, Cooper, and Fairburn, "Clinical Perfectionism."

139 **"Success" includes how hard did I try:** Roz Shafran, in discussion with the author, December 13, 2021.

140 **"it's about giving back control":** Shafran, in discussion with the author.

141 **Dr. Albert Ellis dubbed "musturbation":** Albert Ellis and R. A. Harper, *A Guide to Rational Living* (Hoboken, NJ: Prentice Hall, 1961).

143 **"The shoulds . . . lack the moral seriousness":** Karen Horney, *Neurosis and Human Growth: The Struggle Towards Self-Realization* (New York: W. W. Norton, 1950).

146 **This is called a *behavioral experiment*:** Shafran, discussion with the author; Roz Shafran, Sarah J. Egan, and Tracey D. Wade, *Overcoming Perfectionism, 2nd Edition: A Self-Help Guide Using Scientifically Supported Cognitive Behavioural Techniques* (London: Robinson, 2018).

Chapter 9: Why We Turn Fun into a Chore

150 ***demand sensitivity*, which is a heightened sensitivity:** A. E. Mallinger, "Demand-Sensitive Obsessionals," *Journal of the American Academy of Psychoanalysis* 10, no. 3 (1982): 407–26, https://doi.org/10.1521/jaap.1.1982.10.3.407; Allan Mallinger and Jeannette De Wyze, *Too Perfect: When Being in Control Gets out of Control* (New York: Random House, 1992).

151 **the same magic word:** Mallinger, "Demand-Sensitive Obsessionals."

151 **"tyranny of the shoulds":** Karen Horney, *Neurosis and Human Growth: The Struggle Towards Self-Realization* (New York: W. W. Norton, 1950).

151 **"the volitional into the obligatory":** Mallinger, "Demand-Sensitive Obsessionals."

152 **"feel easily influenced by the force fields":** Allan Mallinger, in discussion with the author, July 30, 2020.

152 **"chaos associated with autonomy":** Mallinger, discussion with the author.

153 ***demand resistance*:** Mallinger, "Demand-Sensitive Obsessionals"; Mallinger and De Wyze, *Too Perfect*.

154 **"It feels so organic to the person":** Mallinger, discussion with the author.

155 **"I oppose; therefore, I am":** Mallinger, "Demand-Sensitive Obsessionals."

155 **"You have to assume if someone is stubbornly oppositional":** Mallinger, discussion with the author.

155 **one of the most difficult things to change:** Mallinger, discussion with the author.

158 **"Run toward what you're interested in":** Michael Twohig, in discussion with the author, February 2, 2023.

158 **"the quality of the experience will shift":** Clarissa Ong, in discussion with the author, February 8, 2023.

158 **"the decision to comply or not":** Mallinger and De Wyze, *Too Perfect*.

158 **"Don't let the ownership of your life":** Mallinger and De Wyze, *Too Perfect*.

ADDITIONAL SOURCE: Allan Mallinger, "The Myth of Perfection: Perfectionism in the Obsessive Personality," *American Journal of Psychotherapy* 63, no. 2 (2009): 103–31, https://doi.org/10.1176/appi.psychotherapy.2009.63.2.103.

Chapter 10: From "Failure" to the Human Condition

164 **our expectations are often subjective:** Roz Shafran, Zafra Cooper, and Christopher G. Fairburn, "Clinical Perfectionism: A Cognitive-Behavioural Analysis," *Behaviour Research and Therapy* 40, no. 7 (2002): 773–91, https://doi.org/10.1016/s0005-7967(01)00059-6.

165 **"constantly on the alert ":** Marc H. Hollender, "Perfectionism," *Comprehensive Psychiatry* 6, no. 2 (1965): 94–103, https://doi.org/10.1016/s0010-440x(65)80016-5.

165 **high moral certitude:** Thomas R. Lynch, Roelie J. Hempel, and Christine Dunkley, "Radically Open-Dialectical Behavior Therapy for Disorders of Over-Control: Signaling Matters," *American Journal of Psychotherapy* 69, no 2 (2015): 141–62, https://doi.org/10.1176/appi.psychotherapy.2015.69.2.141.

166 **look back and see a string of failures:** Martin Smith, in discussion with the author, February 10, 2020.

166 **"I'm calling with the Department":** Sara Hopkins (@sayhopkins), TikTok video, May 5, 2020, https://www.tiktok.com/@sayhopkins/video/6823207652412099846?lang=en.

167 **fodder for the cringe attack:** Melissa Dahl, "How to Stop Reliving Embarrassing Memories," Cut, February 6, 2018, https://www.thecut.com/article/how-to-stop-reliving-embarrassing-memories.html.

167 **alone and doing something mindless:** Ferris Jabr, "Mind-Pops: Psychologists Begin to Study an Unusual Form of Proustian Memory," *Scientific American*, May 23, 2012. https://www.scientificamerican.com/article/mind-pops/.

167 **"I did ecstasy and made out with two guys":** Melissa Dahl, *Cringeworthy: A Theory of Awkwardness* (New York: Portfolio, 2018).

168 **Many of the following examples:** Thomas R. Lynch, *The Skills Training Manual for Radically Open Dialectical Behavior Therapy: A Clinician's Guide for Treating Disorders of Overcontrol* (Oakland, CA: New Harbinger, 2017).

169 **just like we can grieve:** Lynch, *Skills Training Manual*; "Level 1 Radically Open Dialectical Behavior Therapy Blended Learning Course," Radically Open, online course, https://www.radicallyopen.net/training/product/level-1-test.html; "Level 2 for RO DBT Practitioners in Radically Open Dialectical Behavior Therapy," Radically Open, online course, https://www.radicallyopen.net/training/product/radically-open-dialectical-behavior-therapy-blended-learning-course-level-2.html.

169 **when we try to avoid "feel":** T. D. Borkovec, O. M. Alcaine, and E. Behar, "Avoidance Theory of Worry and Generalized Anxiety Disorder," in *Generalized Anxiety Disorder: Advances in Research and Practice*, ed. R. G. Heimberg, C. L. Turk, and D. S. Mennin (New York: Guilford Press, 2004), 77–108.

170 **He calls it physicalizing:** "ACT for Depression and Anxiety Disorders," Psychwire, online course, https://psychwire.com/harris/act-depression.

172 **Enter self-forgiveness:** Antonio Pierro et al., "'Letting Myself Go Forward Past Wrongs': How Regulatory Modes Affect Self-Forgiveness," *PLOS ONE* 13, no. 3 (2018): e0193357, https://doi.org/10.1371/journal.pone.0193357; Julie H. Hall and

Frank D. Fincham, "Self-Forgiveness: The Stepchild of Forgiveness Research," *Journal of Social and Clinical Psychology* 24, no. 5 (2005): 621–37, https://doi.org/10.1521/jscp .2005.24.5.621; Marilyn A. Cornish and Nathaniel G. Wade, "A Therapeutic Model of Self-forgiveness with Intervention Strategies for Counselors," *Journal of Counseling and Development* 93, no. 1 (2015): 96–104, https://doi.org/10.1002/j.1556-6676.2015 .00185.x; Lydia Woodyatt et al., eds. *Handbook of the Psychology of Self-Forgiveness*, 1st ed. (Basel, Switzerland: Springer International, 2017).

FOOTNOTE: "Guilt is one of the cements": Jane E. Brody, "Guilt: Or Why It's Good to Feel Bad," *New York Times*, November 29, 1983, https://www.nytimes.com /1983/11/29/science/guilt-or-why-it-s-good-to-feel-bad.html.

173 **are linked to empathy, honesty, and altruism:** C. W. Leach, "Understanding Shame and Guilt," in *Handbook of the Psychology of Self-Forgiveness*, ed. L. Woodyat et al. (Cham, Switzerland: Springer Nature, 2017), 17–28, https://doi.org/10.1007/978-3 -319-60573-9_2.

173 **Guilt and shame occur:** Annette Kämmerer, "The Scientific Underpinnings and Impacts of Shame," *Scientific American*, August 9, 2019, https://www.scientificamerican .com/article/the-scientific-underpinnings-and-impacts-of-shame/; Helen Block Lewis, *Shame and Guilt in Neurosis* (Madison, WI: International Universities Press, 1974); June Tangney and Ronda Dearing, "Shame and Guilt," in *Encyclopedia of Crime and Punishment*, ed. David Levinson (Thousand Oaks, CA: SAGE, 2002).

174 **Emotion researchers continue to quibble:** Maria Miceli and Cristiano Castelfranchi, "Reconsidering the Differences Between Shame and Guilt," *Europe's Journal of Psychology* 14, no. 3 (2018): 710–33, https://doi.org/10.5964/ejop.v14i3.1564; June Price Tangney et al., "Are Shame, Guilt, and Embarrassment Distinct Emotions?," *Journal of Personality and Social Psychology* 70, no. 6 (1996): 1256–69, https://doi.org /10.1037/0022-3514.70.6.1256.

175 **It's not about finding someone else:** Michael Wenzel, Lydia Woodyatt, and Kyli Hedrick, "No Genuine Self-Forgiveness Without Accepting Responsibility: Value Reaffirmation as a Key to Maintaining Positive Self-regard," *European Journal of Social Psychology* 42, no. 5 (2012): 617–27, https://doi.org/10.1002/ejsp.1873.

175 **do the opposite of concealment:** "Opposite Action—Marsha," Vimeo video, 8:32, posted by NowMattersNow.org, July 22, 2014, https://vimeo.com/101373270; Marsha M. Linehan, *DBT (R) Skills Training Manual*, 2nd ed. (New York: Guilford Publications, 2014).

ADDITIONAL SOURCE: M. Landers, D. Sznycer, and P. Durkee, "Are Self-Conscious Emotions About the Self? Testing Competing Theories of Shame and Guilt Across Two Disparate Cultures," *Emotion*, advance online publication, https://doi.org /10.1037/emo0001321.

Chapter 11: From Exam to Experiment

176 **It was time:** Tricia Park, in discussion with the author, March 1, 2022; Is It Recess Yet?, March 14, 2016, https://www.isitrecessyet.com.

177 **"You know, Tricia":** Is It Recess Yet?

177 **perfectionism as a form of overcompensation:** Alfred Adler, *Study of Organ Inferi-*

ority and Its Psychical Compensation, trans. Smith Ely Jelliffe (New York: Nervous and Mental Disease Publishing, 1917).

178 **"That was the arithmetic"**: Park, discussion with the author.

178 **"to demand of oneself"**: Marc H. Hollender, "Perfectionism," *Comprehensive Psychiatry* 6, no. 2 (1965): 94–103, https://doi.org/10.1016/s0010-440x(65)80016-5.

180 **Sometimes the expectation of overcompensation**: Paul Massari, "The Costs of 'Twice as Good,'" Harvard Kenneth C. Griffin Graduate School of Arts and Sciences, February 15, 2023, https://gsas.harvard.edu/news/costs-twice-good; Garry S. Mitchell and Cara E. Furman, "Striver·*ish*: Young Strivers and the Formation of Ethical Narratives," *Studies in Philosophy and Education* 40, no. 6 (2021): 665–70, https://doi.org/10.1007/s11217-021-09788-3.

180 **higher standards of behavior**: Winston C. Thompson, Abigail J. Beneke, and Garry S. Mitchell, "Legitimate Concerns: On Complications of Identity in School Punishment," *Theory and Research in Education* 18, no. 1 (2020): 78–97, https://doi.org/10.1177/1477878520903400; Chela White, "Twice as Good to Get Half as Much? Research Confirms That Your Mama Was Right All Along," LinkedIn, October 7, 2015, https://www.linkedin.com/pulse/twice-good-get-half-much-research-confirms-your-mama-all-chela/.

180 **Overperformance feels required**: Lee Edward Colston II, "The Problem with Being 'Twice as Good,'" Medium, August 29, 2018, https://medium.com/@Mr.Write/the-problem-with-being-twice-as-good-1de095dcacee.

180 **Andrew Tobias's classic memoir**: Andrew Tobias, *Best Little Boy in the World: The 25th Anniversary Edition of the Classic Memoir* (New York: Random House, 1993); Adam D. Chandler, "The Best Little Boy in the World—That's Me," *New York Times*, Opinion, May 7, 2013, https://www.nytimes.com/2013/05/07/opinion/the-best-little-boy-in-the-world-thats-me.html.

180 **"Another important line of defense"**: Tobias, *Best Little Boy*.

180 **underpinned Tobias's memoir with data**: John E. Pachankis and Mark L. Hatzenbuehler, "The Social Development of Contingent Self-Worth in Sexual Minority Young Men: An Empirical Investigation of the 'Best Little Boy in the World' Hypothesis," *Basic and Applied Social Psychology* 35, no. 2 (2013): 176–90, https://doi.org/10.1080/01973533.2013.764304.

180 **conceptually replicated the study**: Benjamin T. Blankenship and Abigail J. Stewart, "The Best Little *Kid* in the World: Internalized Sexual Stigma and Extrinsic Contingencies of Self-worth, Work Values, and Life Aspirations Among Men *and* Women." *European Journal of Social Psychology* 52, no. 2 (2022): 361–76, https://doi.org/10.1002/ejsp.2800.

181 **"That thick sense of cohort"**: Massari, "The Costs of 'Twice as Good.'"

183 **the *felt sense***: Eugene T. Gendlin, *Focusing* (New York: Bantam, 1981); "Part One: What Is Felt Sense—CUNY COMPosition & Rhetoric Community," CUNY, https://compcomm.commons.gc.cuny.edu/feltsense/part-one-what-is-felt-sense/.

184 **"the body's sense of a particular situation"**: Gendlin, *Focusing*.

184 **let's say you're trying to write**: "Part One: What Is Felt Sense."

185 *psychological flexibility*: Esta A. Berg, "A Simple Objective Technique for Measuring Flexibility in Thinking," *Journal of General Psychology* 39, no. 1 (1948): 15–22, https://doi.org/10.1080/00221309.1948.9918159; Todd B. Kashdan and Jonathan Rottenberg, "Psychological Flexibility as a Fundamental Aspect of Health," *Clinical Psychology Review* 30, no. 7 (2010): 865–78, https://doi.org/10.1016/j.cpr.2010.03.001; Kathlyn M. Cherry et al., "Defining and Measuring 'Psychological Flexibility': A Narrative Scoping Review of Diverse Flexibility and Rigidity Constructs and Perspectives," *Clinical Psychology Review* 84 (March 2021): 101973, https://doi.org/10.1016/j.cpr.2021.101973.

188 **As Tricia matured, she realized:** Park, discussion with the author; Is It Recess Yet?

188 **"It was unequivocally awful.":** Park, discussion with the author.

188 **"He started by banging on a bowl":** Park, discussion with the author.

189 **she test-drove an interest:** Park, discussion with the author; Is It Recess Yet?

190 **our physical and social neural pain:** Naomi I. Eisenberger and Matthew D. Lieberman, "Why Rejection Hurts: A Common Neural Alarm System for Physical and Social Pain," *Trends in Cognitive Sciences* 8, no. 7 (2004): 294–300, https://doi.org/10.1016/j.tics.2004.05.010.

190 **Simple reminders of our deepest values:** Geoffrey L. Cohen and David K. Sherman, "The Psychology of Change: Self-Affirmation and Social Psychological Intervention," *Annual Review of Psychology* 65, no. 1 (2014): 333–71, https://doi.org/10.1146/annurev-psych-010213-115137; David K. Sherman et al., "Deflecting the Trajectory and Changing the Narrative: How Self-Affirmation Affects Academic Performance and Motivation Under Identity Threat," *Journal of Personality and Social Psychology* 104, no. 4 (2013): 591–618, https://doi.org/10.1037/a0031495; Emily K. Lindsay and J. David Creswell, "Helping the Self Help Others: Self-Affirmation Increases Self-Compassion and Pro-Social Behaviors," *Frontiers in Psychology* 5 (2014), https://doi.org/10.3389/fpsyg.2014.00421.

191 **"The goal is not to appraise":** Cohen and Sherman, "The Psychology of Change."

192 **Today, Tricia tries to let herself:** Park, discussion with the author.

192 **She launched a blog and a podcast:** Is It Recess Yet?; Tricia Park, "The 'Is It Recess Yet?' Podcast!," Is It Recess Yet?, December 30, 2018, https://www.isitrecessyet.com/the-is-it-recess-yet-podcast.

192 **Tricia also revisited improvisation:** Park, discussion with the author.

192 **"I think about the character, the art":** Park, discussion with the author.

192 **The other day, Tricia told me:** Park, discussion with the author.

ADDITIONAL SOURCE: Janet Metcalfe, "Learning from Errors," *Annual Review of Psychology* 68, no. 1 (2017): 465–89, https://doi.org/10.1146/annurev-psych-010416-044022.

Chapter 12: It's Not About Time Management

195 *Tomorrow at 9:00 a.m.*: Dianne M. Tice, Ellen Bratslavsky, and Roy F. Baumeister, "Emotional Distress Regulation Takes Precedence over Impulse Control: If You Feel Bad, Do It!," *Journal of Personality and Social Psychology* 80, no. 1 (2001): 53–67, https://doi.org/10.1037/0022-3514.80.1.53.

198 **"common self-regulation problem":** "Do It Now: Overcoming Procrastination with Fuschia Sirois," Great Courses, online course, 2021.

198 **20 percent of adults:** Jesse Harriott and Joseph R. Ferrari, "Prevalence of Procrastination Among Samples of Adults," *Psychological Reports* 78, no. 2 (1996): 611–16, https://doi.org/10.2466/pr0.1996.78.2.611.

198 **50 percent of college students:** Victor Day, David Mensink, and Michael O'Sullivan, "Patterns of Academic Procrastination," *Journal of College Reading and Learning* 30, no. 2 (2000): 120–34, https://doi.org/10.1080/10790195.2000.10850090.

198 **getting a colonoscopy or a mammogram:** Fuschia M. Sirois, Michelle L. Melia-Gordon, and Timothy A. Pychyl, "'I'll Look After My Health, Later': An Investigation of Procrastination and Health," *Personality and Individual Differences* 35, no. 5 (2003): 1167–84, https://doi.org/10.1016/s0191-8869(02)00326-4; Eve-Marie C. Blouin-Hudon, Fuschia M. Sirois, and Timothy A. Pychyl, "Temporal Views of Procrastination, Health, and Well-Being," in *Procrastination, Health, and Well-Being*, ed. Fuschia M. Sirois, and Timothy A. Pychyl (Amsterdam: Elsevier, 2016), 213–32.

198 **lifelong trait:** Daniel E. Gustavson et al., "Genetic Relations Among Procrastination, Impulsivity, and Goal-Management Ability: Implications for the Evolutionary Origin of Procrastination," *Psychological Science* 25, no. 6 (2014): 1178–88, https://doi.org/10.1177/0956797614526260; Henri C. Schouwenburg and Clarry H. Lay, "Trait Procrastination and the Big-Five Factors of Personality," *Personality and Individual Differences* 18, no. 4 (1995): 481–90, https://doi.org/10.1016/0191-8869(94)00176-s.

198 **it's in our very genes:** Richard D. Arvey et al., "The Determinants of Leadership Role Occupancy: Genetic and Personality Factors," *Leadership Quarterly*, 17, no. 1 (2006): 1–20, https://doi.org/10.1016/j.leaqua.2005.10.009.

198 **46 percent heritability:** Gustavson et al., "Genetic Relations Among Procrastination."

198 **self-regulation deteriorates under emotional distress:** Dianne M. Tice and Ellen Bratslavsky, "Giving In to Feel Good: The Place of Emotion Regulation in the Context of General Self-Control," *Psychological Inquiry* 11, no. 3 (2000): 149–59, https://doi.org/10.1207/s15327965pli1103_03.

199 **procrastination steps in as a coping mechanism:** Piers Steel, "The Nature of Procrastination: A Meta-Analytic and Theoretical Review of Quintessential Self-Regulatory Failure," *Psychological Bulletin* 133, no. 1 (2007): 65–94, https://doi.org/10.1037/0033-2909.133.1.65.

199 **in fMRI studies, procrastination is linked:** Marek Wypych et al., "Attenuated Brain Activity During Error Processing and Punishment Anticipation in Procrastination-a Monetary Go/No-Go fMRI Study," *Scientific Reports* 9, no. 1 (2019): 11492, https://doi.org/10.1038/s41598-019-48008-4.

199 **whatever initial emotions we were trying:** R. L. Fee and J. P. Tangney, "Procrastination: A Means of Avoiding Shame or Guilt?," *Journal of Social Behavior & Personality* 15, no. 5 (2000): 167–84.

199 **Our negative-emotion seesaw:** Tim Urban, "Inside the Mind of a Master Procrastinator," TED video, 13:54, filmed February 2016, https://www.ted.com/talks/tim_urban_inside_the_mind_of_a_master_procrastinator?language=en.

201 **failure to launch:** Dan Kiley, *The Peter Pan Syndrome: Men Who Have Never Grown Up* (New York: Dodd, Mead, 1983); Melek Kalkan et al., "Peter Pan Syndrome 'Men Who Don't Grow': Developing a Scale," *Men and Masculinities* 24, no. 2 (2021): 245–57, https://doi.org/10.1177/1097184x19874854.

201 **procrastination-related self-criticism:** Murray Stainton, Clarry Lay, and Gordon Flett, "Trait Procrastinators and Behavior/Trait-Specific Cognitions Stainton," *Journal of Social Behavior and Personality* 15, no. 5 (2000): 297–312.

202 **The work of Dr. Patricia DiBartolo:** Patricia Marten DiBartolo et al., "The Relationship of Perfectionism to Judgmental Bias and Psychopathology," *Cognitive Therapy and Research* 31, no. 5 (2007): 573–87, https://doi.org/10.1007/s10608-006-9112-z.

203 **We procrastinators, research shows:** Fuschia M. Sirois and Natalia Tosti, "Lost in the Moment? An Investigation of Procrastination, Mindfulness, and Well-Being," *Journal of Rational-Emotive and Cognitive-Behavior Therapy* 30, no. 4 (2012): 237–48, https://doi.org/10.1007/s10942-012-0151-y.

203 *overidentification with affective states:* Johannes A. Karl and Ronald Fischer, "The Relationship Between Negative Affect, State Mindfulness, and the Role of Personality," *Mindfulness* 13, no. 11 (2022): 2729–37, https://doi.org/10.1007/s12671-022-01989-2.

204 **the intensity of emotion drops:** Philippe Verduyn and Saskia Lavrijsen, "Which Emotions Last Longest and Why: The Role of Event Importance and Rumination," *Motivation and Emotion* 39, no. 1 (2015): 119–27, https://doi.org/10.1007/s11031-014-9445-y; Philippe Verduyn et al., "Predicting the Duration of Emotional Experience: Two Experience Sampling Studies," *Emotion* 9, no. 1 (2009): 83–91, https://doi.org/10.1037/a0014610; Karen Brans and Philippe Verduyn, "Intensity and Duration of Negative Emotions: Comparing the Role of Appraisals and Regulation Strategies," *PLOS ONE* 9, no. 3 (2014): e92410, https://doi.org/10.1371/journal.pone.0092410; Nico H. Frijda, Batja Mesquita, Joep Sonnemans, and Stephanie van Goozen, "The Duration of Affective Phenomena or Emotions, Sentiments and Passions," in *International Review of Emotion and Motivation*, ed. K. Strongman (New York: Wiley, 1991), 187–225.

204 **breaking tasks down into small steps:** Sirois, *Do It Now*; Alan R. Frank, "Breaking Down Learning Tasks: A Sequence Approach," *Teaching Exceptional Children* 6, no. 1 (1973): 16–19, https://doi.org/10.1177/004005997300600104.

204 **a study for individuals with depression:** Steven A. Safren et al., "A Randomized Controlled Trial of Cognitive Behavioral Therapy for Adherence and Depression (CBT-AD) in Patients with Uncontrolled Type 2 Diabetes," *Diabetes Care* 37, no. 3 (2014): 625–33, https://doi.org/10.2337/dc13-0816.

204 **"Never in my wildest imagination":** Harriet Goldhor Lerner, *Fear & Other Uninvited Guests* (New York: HarperCollins, 2004).

205 **forgave themselves for procrastinating:** Michael J. A. Wohl, Timothy A. Pychyl, and Shannon H. Bennett, "I Forgive Myself, Now I Can Study: How Self-Forgiveness for Procrastinating Can Reduce Future Procrastination," *Personality and Individual Differences* 48, no. 7 (2010): 803–8, https://doi.org/10.1016/j.paid.2010.01.029.

205 **can be changed through self-compassion:** Fuschia M. Sirois, "Procrastination and

Stress: Exploring the Role of Self-Compassion," *Self and Identity* 13, no. 2 (2014): 128–45, https://doi.org/10.1080/15298868.2013.763404.

207 **more disconnected than average:** Fuschia Sirois and Timothy Pychyl, "Procrastination and the Priority of Short-Term Mood Regulation: Consequences for Future Self," *Social and Personality Psychology Compass* 7, no. 2 (2013): 115–27, https://doi.org/10.1111/spc3.12011; Fuschia M. Sirois, "Out of Sight, Out of Time? A Meta-Analytic Investigation of Procrastination and Time Perspective: Procrastination and Time Perspective," *European Journal of Personality* 28, no. 5 (2014): 511–20, https://doi.org/10.1002/per.1947.

207 **Neuroscience research backs her up:** Hal Ersner-Hershfield, G. Elliott Wimmer, and Brian Knutson, "Saving for the Future Self: Neural Measures of Future Self-Continuity Predict Temporal Discounting," *Social Cognitive and Affective Neuroscience* 4, no. 1 (2009): 85–92, https://doi.org/10.1093/scan/nsn042; Johanna Peetz and Anne E. Wilson, "The Temporally Extended Self: The Relation of Past and Future Selves to Current Identity, Motivation, and Goal Pursuit," *Social and Personality Psychology Compass* 2, no. 6 (2008): 2090–106, https://doi.org/10.1111/j.1751-9004.2008.00150.x.

207 **"mental imagery intervention":** Eve-Marie C. Blouin-Hudon and Timothy A. Pychyl, "A Mental Imagery Intervention to Increase Future Self-Continuity and Reduce Procrastination," *Psychologie Appliquee [Applied Psychology]* 66, no. 2 (2017): 326–52, https://doi.org/10.1111/apps.12088.

208 **can make us feel more empathetic:** Hal Hershfield, *Your Future Self: How to Make Tomorrow Better Today* (New York: Little, Brown Spark, 2023); Hal E. Hershfield, "Future Self-Continuity: How Conceptions of the Future Self Transform Intertemporal Choice," *Annals of the New York Academy of Sciences* 1235, no. 1 (2011): 30–43, https://doi.org/10.1111/j.1749-6632.2011.06201.x.

ADDITIONAL SOURCES: Monica Ramirez Basco, *The Procrastinator's Guide to Getting Things Done* (New York: Guilford Publications, 2010).

Marie My Lien Rebetez, Lucien Rochat, and Martial Van der Linden, "Cognitive, Emotional, and Motivational Factors Related to Procrastination: A Cluster Analytic Approach," *Personality and Individual Differences* 76 (2015): 1–6, https://doi.org/10.1016/j.paid.2014.11.044.

Chapter 13: Hardwired but Not Haywire

214 **we humans constantly compare ourselves:** Leon Festinger, "A Theory of Social Comparison Processes," *Human Relations* 7, no. 2 (1954): 117–40, https://doi.org/10.1177/001872675400700202.

214 **it begins as early as preschool:** Marjorie Rhodes and Daniel Brickman, "Preschoolers' Responses to Social Comparisons Involving Relative Failure," *Psychological Science* 19, no. 10 (2008): 968–72, https://doi.org/10.1111/j.1467-9280.2008.02184.x.

214 **can even occur unconsciously:** Stanislas Dehaene et al., "Imaging Unconscious Semantic Priming," *Nature* 395, no. 6702 (1998): 597–600, https://doi.org/10.1038/26967; Thomas Mussweiler, Katja Rüter, and Kai Epstude, "The Man Who Wasn't

There: Subliminal Social Comparison Standards Influence Self-Evaluation," *Journal of Experimental Social Psychology* 40, no. 5 (2004): 689–96, https://doi.org/10.1016/j.jesp.2004.01.004.

214 **negative and directed toward others:** Richard H. Smith, "Assimilative and Contrastive Emotional Reactions to Upward and Downward Social Comparisons," in *Handbook of Social Comparison*, ed. Jerry Suls and Ladd Wheeler (Boston: Springer, 2000), 173–200.

214 **feel a little bit superior:** Laura M. Bogart, Eric G. Benotsch, and Jelena D. Pavlovic Pavlovic, "Feeling Superior but Threatened: The Relation of Narcissism to Social Comparison," *Basic and Applied Social Psychology* 26, no. 1 (2004): 35–44, https://doi.org/10.1207/s15324834basp2601_4.

215 **"That's the thing about being a borderline anorexic":** Liz Jones, "Fatten Me up! What Happened When Former Anorexic Liz Jones Had to Eat Normally for Three Weeks," *Daily Mail*, June 8, 2009, https://www.dailymail.co.uk/femail/article-1191429/Fatten-What-happened-anorexic-Liz-Jones-eat-normally-weeks.html.

215 **separated from potential community:** Emma Nicholls and Arthur A. Stukas, "Narcissism and the Self-Evaluation Maintenance Model: Effects of Social Comparison Threats on Relationship Closeness," *Journal of Social Psychology* 151, no. 2 (2011): 201–12, https://doi.org/10.1080/00224540903510852.

215 **and simple enjoyment:** Dian A. de Vries et al., "Social Comparison as the Thief of Joy: Emotional Consequences of Viewing Strangers' Instagram Posts," *Media Psychology* 21, no. 2 (2018): 222–45, https://doi.org/10.1080/15213269.2016.1267647.

215 **we feel intimidated or dejected:** Smith, "Assimilative and Contrastive Emotional Reactions."

215 **if we think they're unqualified:** Hyunji Kim et al., "Social Comparison Processes in the Experience of Personal Relative Deprivation," *Journal of Applied Social Psychology* 48, no. 9 (2018): 519–32, https://doi.org/10.1111/jasp.12531.

216 **social comparison was automatic and inevitable:** Festinger, "A Theory of Social Comparison Processes."

216 **a host of neural evidence has emerged:** Gayannée Kedia, Thomas Mussweiler, and David E. J. Linden, "Brain Mechanisms of Social Comparison and Their Influence on the Reward System," *Neuroreport* 25, no. 16 (2014): 1255–65, https://doi.org/10.1097/wnr.0000000000000255; K. Fliessbach et al., "Social Comparison Affects Reward-Related Brain Activity in the Human Ventral Striatum," *Science* 318, no. 5854 (2007): 1305–8, https://doi.org/10.1126/science.1145876.

216 **scanned participants' brains while they earned:** Fliessbach et al., "Social Comparison Affects Reward-Related Brain Activity."

216 **why billionaires try to one-up:** Tobias Greitemeyer and Christina Sagioglou, "The Experience of Deprivation: Does Relative More Than Absolute Status Predict Hostility?," *British Journal of Social Psychology* 58, no. 3 (2019): 515–33, https://doi.org/10.1111/bjso.12288.

217 **we compare ourselves to people:** Festinger, "A Theory of Social Comparison Processes."

217 **social media is designed with surgical precision:** Claire Sanford, "Facebook Whistleblower Frances Haugen Testifies on Children & Social Media Use: Full Senate Hearing Transcript," *Rev* blog, October 6, 2021, http://www.rev.com/blog /transcripts/facebook-whistleblower-frances-haugen-testifies-on-children-social -media-use-full-senate-hearing-transcript.

217 **when our basic human needs are not satisfied:** Andrew K. Przybylski et al., "Motivational, Emotional, and Behavioral Correlates of Fear of Missing Out," *Computers in Human Behavior* 29, no. 4 (2013): 1841–48, https://doi.org/10.1016/j.chb .2013.02.014.

217 **passive social media use:** Philippe Verduyn et al., "Social Comparison on Social Networking Sites," *Current Opinion in Psychology* 36 (2020): 32–37, https://doi.org/10 .1016/j.copsyc.2020.04.002.

218 **comparison declines as we age:** Mitchell J. Callan, Hyunji Kim, and William J. Matthews, "Age Differences in Social Comparison Tendency and Personal Relative Deprivation," *Personality and Individual Differences* 87 (2015): 196–99, https://doi.org /10.1016/j.paid.2015.08.003.

218 **Social comparison has survived evolutionarily:** Thomas Mussweiler and Kai Epstude, "Relatively Fast! Efficiency Advantages of Comparative Thinking," *Journal of Experimental Psychology: General* 138, no. 1 (2009): 1–21, https://doi.org/10.1037 /a0014374.

220 **"self-organizing life aim":** Patrick E. McKnight and Todd B. Kashdan, "Purpose in Life as a System That Creates and Sustains Health and Well-Being: An Integrative, Testable Theory," *Review of General Psychology* 13, no. 3 (2009): 242–51, https://doi .org/10.1037/a0017152.

220 **asked study participants to post a selfie:** Anthony L. Burrow and Nicolette Rainone, "How Many Likes Did I Get?: Purpose Moderates Links Between Positive Social Media Feedback and Self-Esteem," *Journal of Experimental Social Psychology* 69 (2017): 232–36, https://doi.org/10.1016/j.jesp.2016.09.005.

221 **do the opposite of what our negative emotions:** "Opposite Action—Marsha," Vimeo video, 8:32, posted by NowMattersNow.org, July 22, 2014, https://vimeo.com /101373270.

FOOTNOTE: **Both are complex negative social emotions:** W. Gerrod Parrott and Richard H. Smith, "Distinguishing the Experiences of Envy and Jealousy," *Journal of Personality and Social Psychology* 64, no. 6 (1993): 906–20, https://doi.org/10.1037/0022-3514 .64.6.906.

221 **Envy stems from perceived scarcity:** Richard H. Smith and Sung Hee Kim, "Comprehending Envy," *Psychological Bulletin* 133, no. 1 (2007): 46–64, https://doi.org/10 .1037/0033-2909.133.1.46.

221 **So doing the opposite of shame:** "Opposite Action—Marsha."

ADDITIONAL SOURCE: Matthew Baldwin and Thomas Mussweiler, "The Culture of Social Comparison," *Proceedings of the National Academy of Sciences of the United States of America* 115, no. 39 (2018): E9067–74, https://doi.org/10.1073/pnas .1721555115.

Chapter 14: Rolling Back Emotional Perfectionism

226 **getting along with the group is essential:** Charles Darwin, *The Expression of the Emotions in Man and Animals* (Chicago: University of Chicago Press, 1965); R. Plutchik, "A General Psychoevolutionary Theory of Emotion," in *Emotion: Theory, Research, and Experience*, ed. R. Plutchik and H. Kellerman (San Diego: Academic Press, 1980).

226 **"Feelings are the most alive part":** Karen Horney, *Neurosis and Human Growth: The Struggle Towards Self-Realization* (New York: W. W. Norton, 1950).

226 **a phenomenon fittingly called *emotional perfectionism*:** Olga Mecking, "The Flip Side of Toxic Positivity: Emotional Perfectionism," *Washington Post*, June 9, 2022, https://www.washingtonpost.com/wellness/2022/06/09/what-is-emotional-perfectionism-toxic-positivity/; Annie Hickox, "Emotional Perfectionism," Dr. Annie Hickox's website, https://dranniehickox.co.uk/resources-blog-neuropsychology/10-mindfulness.

227 **we think others do the same:** Thomas Lynch and Erica Smith Lynch, in discussion with the author, May 10, 2023.

227 **PBS sent none other than Fred Rogers:** "May 1, 1969: Fred Rogers Testifies before the Senate Subcommittee on Communications," YouTube video, 6:50, posted by "danieldeibler," February 8, 2015, https://www.youtube.com/watch?v=fKy7ljRr0AA.

227 **how we feel inside, our *emotional experience*:** Magda B. Arnold, *Emotion and Personality* (New York: Columbia University Press, 1960); Nico H. Frijda, *The Emotions* (Cambridge, England: Cambridge University Press, 1986); Carroll Izard, *Human Emotions* (New York: Plenum, 1977).

227 **plus our attempts at managing them:** James J. Gross, "The Emerging Field of Emotion Regulation: An Integrative Review," *Review of General Psychology* 2, no. 3 (1998): 271–99, https://doi.org/10.1037/1089-2680.2.3.271; J. J. Gross and R. A. Thompson, "Emotion Regulation: Conceptual Foundations," in *Handbook of Emotion Regulation*, ed. J. J. Gross (New York: Guilford Press, 2007), 3–24.

227 **our *emotional expression* (and its opposing counterpart):** James J. Gross and Robert W. Levenson, "Emotional Suppression: Physiology, Self-Report, and Expressive Behavior," *Journal of Personality and Social Psychology* 64, no. 6 (1993): 970–86, https://doi.org/10.1037/0022-3514.64.6.970; Emily A. Butler et al., "The Social Consequences of Expressive Suppression," *Emotion* 3, no. 1 (2003): 48–67, https://doi.org/10.1037/1528-3542.3.1.48; Christine R. Harris, "Cardiovascular Responses of Embarrassment and Effects of Emotional Suppression in a Social Setting," *Journal of Personality and Social Psychology* 81, 5 (2001): 886–97, https://doi.org/10.1037/0022-3514.81.5.886.

228 **There are oodles of ways:** Gross, "The Emerging Field of Emotion Regulation"; Gal Sheppes, Gaurav Suri, and James J. Gross, "Emotion Regulation and Psychopathology," *Annual Review of Clinical Psychology* 11, no. 1 (2015): 379–405, https://doi.org/10.1146/annurev-clinpsy-032814-112739; Thomas L. Webb, Eleanor Miles, and Paschal Sheeran, "Dealing with Feeling: A Meta-Analysis of the Effectiveness of Strategies Derived from the Process Model of Emotion Regulation," *Psychological Bulletin* 138, no. 4 (2012): 775–808, https://doi.org/10.1037/a0027600.

228 **worry or ruminate:** T. D. Borkovec, "The Nature, Functions, and Origins of Worry," in *Worrying: Perspectives on Theory, Assessment and Treatment*, ed. G. C. L. Davey

and F. Tallis (Hoboken, NJ: John Wiley, 1994), 5–33; T. D. Borkovec, O. Alcaine, and E. Behar, "Avoidance Theory of Worry and Generalized Anxiety Disorder," in *Generalized Anxiety Disorder: Advances in Research and Practice*, ed. R. G. Heimberg, C. L. Turk, and D. S. Mennin (New York: Guilford Press, 2004), 77–108; Amelia Aldao and Susan Nolen-Hoeksema, "Specificity of Cognitive Emotion Regulation Strategies: A Transdiagnostic Examination," *Behaviour Research and Therapy* 48, no. 10 (2010): 974–83, https://doi.org/10.1016/j.brat.2010.06.002; Susan Nolen-Hoeksema, Blair E. Wisco, and Sonja Lyubomirsky, "Rethinking Rumination," *Perspectives on Psychological Science* 3, no. 5 (2008): 400–24, https://doi.org/10.1111/j .1745-6924.2008.00088.x; Edward R. Watkins, "Constructive and Unconstructive Repetitive Thought," *Psychological Bulletin* 134, no. 2 (2008): 163–206.

229 **40 to 75 percent of psychological disorders:** James J. Gross and Hooria Jazaieri, "Emotion, Emotion Regulation, and Psychopathology: An Affective Science Perspective," *Clinical Psychological Science* 2, no. 4 (2014): 387–401, https://doi.org/10 .1177/2167702614536164; Hooria Jazaieri, Heather L. Urry, and James J. Gross, "Affective Disturbance and Psychopathology: An Emotion Regulation Perspective," *Journal of Experimental Psychopathology* 4, no. 5 (2013): 584–99, https://doi.org/10 .5127/jep.030312.

229 **Often, we grow up in a household:** Anne G. Halberstadt, V. William Crisp, and Kali L. Eaton, "Family Expressiveness: A Retrospective and New Directions for Research," in *The Social Context of Nonverbal Behavior*, ed. P. Philippot, R. S. Feldman, and E. J. Coats (Cambridge, England: Cambridge University Press, 1999); Sara F. Waters et al., "Keep It to Yourself? Parent Emotion Suppression Influences Physiological Linkage and Interaction Behavior," *Journal of Family Psychology* 34, no. 7 (2020): 784–93, https://doi.org/10.1037/fam0000664; Nancy Eisenberg, Amanda Cumberland, and Tracy L. Spinrad, "Parental Socialization of Emotion," *Psychological Inquiry* 9, no. 4 (1998): 241–73, https://doi.org/10.1207/s15327965pli0904_1.

230 **This rule was articulated by our old friend:** Horney, *Neurosis and Human Growth*.

231 **"Never give in except to convictions":** "Never Give In, Never, Never, Never, 1941," America's National Churchill Museum, https://www.nationalchurchillmuseum.org /never-give-in-never-never-never.html.

231 **very different from failing:** Clarissa Ong and Michael Twohig, *The Anxious Perfectionist: Acceptance and Commitment Therapy Skills to Deal with Anxiety, Stress, and Worry Driven by Perfectionism* (Oakland, CA: New Harbinger, 2022).

231 **a difference between *valid* and *justified* emotion:** "The Role of Emotion Regulation in DBT (Part 1)," Behavioral Tech Institute, April 8, 2019, https://behavioraltech .org/role-of-emotion-regulation-dbt-part-1.

232 **a little overregulated:** Thomas R. Lynch, *The Skills Training Manual for Radically Open Dialectical Behavior Therapy: A Clinician's Guide for Treating Disorders of Overcontrol* (Oakland, CA: New Harbinger, 2017).

232 **as Dr. Lynch calls it, *distress overtolerance*:** "Level 1 Radically Open Dialectical Behavior Therapy Blended Learning Course," Radically Open, online course, https:// www.radicallyopen.net/training/product/level-1-test.html; "Level 2 for RO DBT Practitioners in Radically Open Dialectical Behavior Therapy," Radically Open, online

course, https://www.radicallyopen.net/training/product/radically-open-dialectical
-behavior-therapy-blended-learning-course-level-2.html.

233 **can slide into medical problems or depression:** Benjamin P. Chapman et al., "Emotion Suppression and Mortality Risk over a 12-Year Follow-Up," *Journal of Psychosomatic Research* 75, no. 4 (2013): 381–85, https://doi.org/10.1016/j.jpsychores.2013.07
.014; L. Campbell-Sills et al., "Acceptability and Suppression of Negative Emotion
in Anxiety and Mood Disorders," *Emotion* 6, no. 4 (2006): 587–95, https://doi.org
/10.1037/1528-3542.6.4.587; Martin M. Smith et al., "Perfectionism and the Five-
Factor Model of Personality: A Meta-Analytic Review," *Personality and Social Psychology Review* 23, no. 4 (2019): 367–90, https://doi.org/10.1177/1088868318814973.

233 **Emotional suppression has even been linked:** Kathleen D. Vohs et al., "Ego De-
pletion Is Not Just Fatigue: Evidence from a Total Sleep Deprivation Experiment,"
Social Psychological and Personality Science 2, no. 2 (2011): 166–73, https://doi.org/10
.1177/1948550610386123.

233 **I Am Fine extends the duration:** Debora Cutuli, "Cognitive Reappraisal and Expressive Suppression Strategies Role in the Emotion Regulation: An Overview on
Their Modulatory Effects and Neural Correlates," *Frontiers in Systems Neuroscience* 8
(2014): 175, https://doi.org/10.3389/fnsys.2014.00175.

233 **crosses the line into martyrdom:** Lynch, *Skills Training Manual.*

233 **even if that emotion is negative:** Emily A. Butler et al., "The Social Consequences
of Expressive Suppression," *Emotion* 3, no. 1 (2003): 48–67, https://doi.org/10.1037
/1528-3542.3.1.48.

233 **without lambasting ourselves, falling apart:** "Level 1 Radically Open Dialectical
Behavior Therapy"; "Level 2 for RO DBT Practitioners."

234 **we might have gotten pushback:** Lynch, *Skills Training Manual.*

234 **it's totally okay to be wired:** Katharina Bernecker, Daniela Becker, and Aiste Guobyte,
"If the Party Is Good, You Can Stay Longer—Effects of Trait Hedonic Capacity on
Hedonic Quantity and Performance," *Motivation and Emotion* 47, no. 5 (2023): 711–
25, https://doi.org/10.1007/s11031-023-10021-6; James Goodnight, "Reward Sensitivity," in *The SAGE Encyclopedia of Lifespan Human Development*, vol. 5, 1854–1855
(Thousand Oaks, CA: SAGE, 2018); Luke Wayne Henderson, Tess Knight, and
Ben Richardson, "An Exploration of the Well-Being Benefits of Hedonic and Eudaimonic Behaviour," *Journal of Positive Psychology* 8, no. 4 (2013): 322–36, https://
doi.org/10.1080/17439760.2013.803596.

234 **Not all fun is created equal:** I. C. McManus and Adrian Furnham, "'Fun, Fun,
Fun': Types of Fun, Attitudes to Fun, and Their Relation to Personality and Bi-
ographical Factors," *Psychology* 1, no. 3 (2010): 159–68, https://doi.org/10.4236
/psych.2010.13021; Veronika Huta and Richard M. Ryan, "Pursuing Pleasure or
Virtue: The Differential and Overlapping Well-Being Benefits of Hedonic and Eudaimonic Motives," *Journal of Happiness Studies* 11, no. 6 (2010): 735–62, https://
doi.org/10.1007/s10902-009-9171-4; Veronika Huta, and Alan S. Waterman, "Eu-
daimonia and Its Distinction from Hedonia: Developing a Classification and Ter-
minology for Understanding Conceptual and Operational Definitions," *Journal of*

Happiness Studies 15, no. 6 (2014): 1425–56, https://doi.org/10.1007/s10902-013 -9485-0.

234 **self-consciousness is a social phenomenon:** Lynch and Lynch, discussion with the author.

235 **"He's in a situation":** Lynch and Lynch, discussion with the author.

235 **"critical scrutiny":** Lynch and Lynch, discussion with the author.

235 **Opting out separates us:** Lynch and Lynch, discussion with the author.

235 *participate without planning*: Lynch, *Skills Training Manual*; "Level 1 Radically Open Dialectical Behavior Therapy"; "Level 2 for RO DBT Practitioners."

236 **Not as efficiently as in a skills class:** Lynch and Lynch, discussion with the author.

236 **"Beneath my laid-back college-kid demeanor":** Michelle Obama, *Becoming* (New York: Crown, 2021).

237 **There is dispassionate awareness:** Lynch, *Skills Training Manual*; "Level 1 Radically Open Dialectical Behavior Therapy"; "Level 2 for RO DBT Practitioners."

238 **bring up the houselights:** "ACT for Depression and Anxiety Disorders," Psychwire, online course, https://psychwire.com/harris/act-depression.

238 **what they call "hedonic success":** Katharina Bernecker and Daniela Becker, "Beyond Self-Control: Mechanisms of Hedonic Goal Pursuit and Its Relevance for Well-Being," *Personality & Social Psychology Bulletin* 47, no. 4 (2021): 627–42, https:// doi.org/10.1177/0146167220941998.

238 **"more difficult to enjoy an after-work drink":** Bernecker and Becker, "Beyond Self-Control."

238 **why we can't enjoy the ice cream:** Daniela Becker, Nils B. Jostmann, Wilhelm Hofmann, and Rob W. Holland, "Spoiling the Pleasure of Success: Emotional Reactions to the Experience of Self-Control Conflict in the Eating Domain," *Emotion* 19, no. 8 (2019): 1377–95, https://doi.org/10.1037/emo0000526.

238 **"Those thoughts about conflicting long-term goals":** "Hedonism Leads to Happiness," University of Zurich, July 27, 2020, https://www.news.uzh.ch/en/articles /2020/Hedonism.

239 **a sign of healthy self-regulation:** Bernecker and Becker, "Beyond Self-Control"; Malte Friese and Wilhelm Hofmann, "State Mindfulness, Self-Regulation, and Emotional Experience in Everyday Life," *Motivation Science* 2, no. 1 (2016): 1–14, https://doi.org/10.1037/mot0000027.

Chapter 15: Rolling Back Perfectionistic Self-Presentation

242 **two fundamental dimensions—competence and warmth:** Susan T. Fiske, Amy J. C. Cuddy, and Peter Glick, "Universal Dimensions of Social Cognition: Warmth and Competence," *Trends in Cognitive Sciences* 11, no. 2 (2007): 77–83, https://doi .org/10.1016/j.tics.2006.11.005; Charles M. Judd, Laurie James-Hawkins, Vincent Yzerbyt, and Yoshihisa Kashima, "Fundamental Dimensions of Social Judgment: Understanding the Relations between Judgments of Competence and Warmth," *Journal*

of Personality and Social Psychology 89, no. 6 (2005): 899–913, https://doi.org/10.1037
/0022-3514.89.6.899.

FOOTNOTE: The exact names of the dimensions: Andrea E. Abele and Bogdan
Wojciszke, "Agency and Communion from the Perspective of Self versus Others," *Journal of Personality and Social Psychology* 93, no. 5 (2007): 751–63, https://doi.org/10.1037
/0022-3514.93.5.751;

Andrea E. Abele and Bogdan Wojciszke, "Communal and Agentic Content in Social
Cognition," in *Advances in Experimental Social Psychology*, ed. Bertram Gawronski (Amsterdam: Elsevier, 2014), 195–255.

FOOTNOTE: intellectual and social: Seymour Rosenberg, Carnot Nelson, and
P. S. Vivekananthan, "A Multidimensional Approach to the Structure of Personality
Impressions," *Journal of Personality and Social Psychology* 9, no. 4 (1968): 283–94, https://
doi.org/10.1037/h0026086.

FOOTNOTE: respecting and liking: Fiske, Cuddy, and Glick, "Universal Dimensions."

242 *Competence* is being smart: Fiske, Cuddy, and Glick, "Universal Dimensions"; Abele
and Wojciszke, "Agency and Communion."

242 "Although both dimensions are fundamental": Fiske, Cuddy, and Glick, "Universal
Dimensions."

242 warmth and competence in individuals: Charles M. Judd et al., "Fundamental
Dimensions of Social Judgment: Understanding the Relations between Judgments
of Competence and Warmth," *Journal of Personality and Social Psychology* 89, no. 6
(2005): 899–913, https://doi.org/10.1037/0022-3514.89.6.899.

243 "If we don't show much": "Level 1 Radically Open Dialectical Behavior Therapy Blended Learning Course," Radically Open, online course, https://www
.radicallyopen.net/training/product/level-1-test.html; "Level 2 for RO DBT Practitioners in Radically Open Dialectical Behavior Therapy," Radically Open, online
course, https://www.radicallyopen.net/training/product/radically-open-dialectical
-behavior-therapy-blended-learning-course-level-2.html.

243 emotions evolved as a form of communication: Charles Darwin, *The Expression of
the Emotions in Man and Animals* (Chicago: University of Chicago Press, 1965); Ross
Buck, "Social and Emotional Functions in Facial Expression and Communication: The Readout Hypothesis," *Biological Psychology* 38, no. 2–3 (1994): 95–115, doi:
10.1016/0301-0511(94)90032-9; R. Thomas Boone and Ross Buck, "Emotional
Expressivity and Trustworthiness: The Role of Nonverbal Behavior in the Evolution of Cooperation," *Journal of Nonverbal Behavior* 27, no. 3 (2003): 163–82, doi:
10.1023/a:1025341931128; Eckart Altenmüller, Sabine Schmidt, and Elke Zimmermann, eds., *Evolution of Emotional Communication: From Sounds in Nonhuman Mammals to Speech and Music in Man*, Series in Affective Science (Oxford, England: Oxford
Academic, 2013), online edition; Eva Jablonka, Simona Ginsburg, and Daniel Dor,
"The Co-Evolution of Language and Emotions," *Philosophical Transactions of the Royal
Society of London. Series B, Biological Sciences* 367, no. 1599 (2012): 2152–59, https://doi
.org/10.1098/rstb.2012.0117.

243 emotional state is *emotional expression*: APA Dictionary of Psychology, s.v. "Emotional Expression," https://dictionary.apa.org/emotional-expression; APA Dictio-

nary of Psychology, s.v. "Suppression," https://dictionary.apa.org/suppression; James J. Gross and Robert W. Levenson, "Emotional Suppression: Physiology, Self-Report, and Expressive Behavior," *Journal of Personality and Social Psychology* 64, no. 6 (1993): 970–86, https://doi.org/10.1037/0022-3514.64.6.970.

244 *Perfectionistic self-presentation* **is when:** Paul L. Hewitt et al., "The Interpersonal Expression of Perfection: Perfectionistic Self-Presentation and Psychological Distress," *Journal of Personality and Social Psychology* 84, no. 6 (2003): 1303–25, https://doi.org/10.1037/0022-3514.84.6.1303.

244 *overly agreeable face***:** "Level 1 Radically Open Dialectical Behavior Therapy"; "Level 2 for RO DBT Practitioners"; Thomas Lynch and Erica Smith Lynch, in discussion with the author, May 10, 2023.

244 *overly disagreeable face***:** "Level 1 Radically Open Dialectical Behavior Therapy"; "Level 2 for RO DBT Practitioners"; Lynch and Lynch, discussion with the author.

FOOTNOTE: But Erica Smith Lynch explained to me: Lynch and Lynch, discussion with the author.

245 **Our faces and bodies send:** "Level 1 Radically Open Dialectical Behavior Therapy"; "Level 2 for RO DBT Practitioners."

245 **"When we're in self-protection mode":** Mariana G. Franco, *Platonic: How the Science of Attachment Can Help You Make—and Keep—Friends* (New York: Putnam, 2022).

245 **makes us anxious and uncomfortable:** Emily A. Butler et al., "The Social Consequences of Expressive Suppression," *Emotion* 3, no. 1 (2003): 48–67, https://doi.org/10.1037/1528-3542.3.1.48.

245 **It literally increases our blood pressure:** Butler et al., "The Social Consequences"; Gross and Levenson, "Emotional Suppression"; Nicole A. Roberts, Robert W. Levenson, and James J. Gross, "Cardiovascular Costs of Emotion Suppression Cross Ethnic Lines," *International Journal of Psychophysiology* 70, no. 1 (2008): 82–87, https://doi.org/10.1016/j.ijpsycho.2008.06.003.

245 **stressful to interact with someone we can't read:** Butler et al., "The Social Consequences."

245 **but it raises our chance of heart disease:** Benjamin P. Chapman et al., "Emotion Suppression and Mortality Risk over a 12-Year Follow-Up," *Journal of Psychosomatic Research* 75, no. 4 (2013): 381–85, https://doi.org/10.1016/j.jpsychores.2013.07.014.

245 **It also undermines our memory:** Jane M. Richards and James J. Gross, "Emotion Regulation and Memory: The Cognitive Costs of Keeping One's Cool," *Journal of Personality and Social Psychology* 79, no. 3 (2000): 410–24, https://doi.org/10.1037/0022-3514.79.3.410; Boris Egloff et al., "Spontaneous Emotion Regulation during Evaluated Speaking Tasks: Associations with Negative Affect, Anxiety Expression, Memory, and Physiological Responding," *Emotion* 6, no. 3 (2006): 356–66, https://doi.org/10.1037/1528-3542.6.3.356.

245 **habitual suppressors report lower satisfaction:** James J. Gross and Oliver P. John, "Individual Differences in Two Emotion Regulation Processes: Implications for Affect, Relationships, and Well-Being," *Journal of Personality and Social Psychology* 85, no. 2 (2003): 348–62, https://doi.org/10.1037/0022-3514.85.2.348; Iris B. Mauss et al.,

"Don't Hide Your Happiness! Positive Emotion Dissociation, Social Connectedness, and Psychological Functioning," *Journal of Personality and Social Psychology* 100, no. 4 (2011): 738–48, https://doi.org/10.1037/a0022410; Tammy English and Oliver P. John, "Understanding the Social Effects of Emotion Regulation: The Mediating Role of Authenticity for Individual Differences in Suppression," *Emotion* 13, no. 2 (2013): 314–29, https://doi.org/10.1037/a0029847; Michael H. Kernis and B. Matthew Goldman, "A Multicomponent Conceptualization of Authenticity: Theory and Research," in *Advances in Experimental Social Psychology*, vol. 38, ed. Mark P. Zanna (Amsterdam: Elsevier, 2006), 283–357.

246 **tracked almost three hundred first-year students:** Sanjay Srivastava et al., "The Social Costs of Emotional Suppression: A Prospective Study of the Transition to College," *Journal of Personality and Social Psychology* 96, no. 4 (2009): 883–97, https://doi.org/10.1037/a0014755.

246 **others can still think we're pretty cool:** Lynch and Lynch, discussion with the author.

248 **We use nonverbal signals:** John D. Eastwood, Daniel Smilek, and Philip M. Merikle, "Differential Attentional Guidance by Unattended Faces Expressing Positive and Negative Emotion," *Perception & Psychophysics* 63, no. 6 (2001): 1004–13, https://doi.org/10.3758/bf03194519; Arne Öhman, Anders Flykt, and Francisco Esteves, "Emotion Drives Attention: Detecting the Snake in the Grass," *Journal of Experimental Psychology: General* 130, no. 3 (2001): 466–78, https://doi.org/10.1037/0096-3445.130.3.466; Jukka M. Leppännen and Jari K. Hietanen, "Positive Facial Expressions Are Recognized Faster than Negative Facial Expressions, but Why?," *Psychological Research* 69, no. 1–2 (2004): 22–29, https://doi.org/10.1007/s00426-003-0157-2; Judith A. Hall, Erik J. Coats, and Lavonia Smith LeBeau, "Nonverbal Behavior and the Vertical Dimension of Social Relations: A Meta-Analysis," *Psychological Bulletin* 131, no. 6 (2005): 898–924, https://doi.org/10.1037/0033-2909.131.6.898; Alexander Todorov et al., "Understanding Evaluation of Faces on Social Dimensions," *Trends in Cognitive Sciences* 12, no. 12 (2008): 455–60, https://doi.org/10.1016/j.tics.2008.10.001.

249 **Overall, the point is flexibility:** George A. Bonanno et al., "The Importance of Being Flexible: The Ability to Both Enhance and Suppress Emotional Expression Predicts Long-Term Adjustment," *Psychological Science* 15, no. 7 (2004): 482–87, https://doi.org/10.1111/j.0956-7976.2004.00705.x.

249 **Dr. Lynch teaches a technique:** "Level 1 Radically Open Dialectical Behavior Therapy"; "Level 2 for RO DBT Practitioners"; Thomas R. Lynch, *The Skills Training Manual for Radically Open Dialectical Behavior Therapy: A Clinician's Guide for Treating Disorders of Overcontrol* (Oakland, CA: New Harbinger, 2017).

250 **"It has the added advantage":** Lynch and Lynch, discussion with the author.

250 **assures us that it's not fake:** Lynch and Lynch, discussion with the author.

251 **"What's really cool about the eyebrows":** Lynch and Lynch, discussion with the author.

251 **disclosure should be *sustained*:** Arthur Aron et al., "The Experimental Generation of Interpersonal Closeness: A Procedure and Some Preliminary Findings," *Personality & Social Psychology Bulletin* 23, no. 4 (1997): 363–77, https://doi.org/10.1177/0146167297234003.

252 **well over half of conversation:** Henry T. Moore, "Further Data Concerning Sex Differences," *Journal of Abnormal Psychology and Social Psychology* 17, no. 2 (1922): 210–14, https://doi.org/10.1037/h0064645.

252 **an indigenous Zinacantan:** John B. Haviland, *Gossip, Reputation and Knowledge in Zinacantan* (Chicago: University of Chicago Press, 1977).

252 **or a man in Liverpool in the 1990s:** R. I. M. Dunbar, Anna Marriott, and N. D. C. Duncan, "Human Conversational Behavior," *Human Nature* 8, no. 3 (1997): 231–46, https://doi.org/10.1007/bf02912493.

252 *not* **talking about yourself:** Michael Kardas, Amit Kumar, and Nicholas Epley, "Overly Shallow?: Miscalibrated Expectations Create a Barrier to Deeper Conversation," *Journal of Personality and Social Psychology* 122, no. 3 (2022): 367–98, https://doi.org/10.1037/pspa0000281; Nicole You Jeung Kim et al., "You Must Have a Preference: The Impact of No-Preference Communication on Joint Decision Making," *Journal of Marketing Research* 60, no. 1 (2023): 52–71, https://doi.org/10.1177/00222437221107593.

253 **"digressions and confessions":** Adam Mastroianni, "Good Conversations Have Lots of Doorknobs," Experimental History, February 23, 2022. https://www.experimental-history.com/p/good-conversations-have-lots-of-doorknobs.

255 **"felt excluded during a subsequent":** Gerald Cooney, Daniel T. Gilbert, and Timothy D. Wilson, "The Unforeseen Costs of Extraordinary Experience," *Psychological Science* 25, no. 12 (2014): 2259–65.

255 **"can make the people who have them":** Cooney, Gilbert, and Wilson, "The Unforeseen Costs."

255 **There are different levels of sharing:** Levels inspired by Lynch, *Skills Training Manual.*

259 **These embarrassment signals are vital:** Lynch, *Skills Training Manual*; "Level 1 Radically Open Dialectical Behavior Therapy"; "Level 2 for RO DBT Practitioners."

259 **withholding information, even about shady stuff:** L. K. John, K. Barasz, and M. I. Norton, "Hiding Personal Information Reveals the Worst," *Proceedings of the National Academy of Sciences of the United States of America* 113, no. 4 (2016): 954–59, https://doi.org/10.1073/pnas.1516868113.

260 **We feel close to people we trust:** Fiske, Cuddy, and Glick, "Universal Dimensions."

260 **Dr. Thomas Lynch calls this skill:** Lynch, *Skills Training Manual*; "Level 1 Radically Open Dialectical Behavior Therapy"; "Level 2 for RO DBT Practitioners."

ADDITIONAL SOURCES: Thomas R. Lynch, Shannon A. Lazarus, and Jennifer S. Cheavens, "Mindfulness Interventions for Undercontrolled and Overcontrolled Disorders: From Self-Control to Self-Regulation," in *Handbook of Mindfulness: Theory, Research, and Practice*, eds. Kirk W. Brown, J. David Creswell, and Richard M. Ryan, (New York: Guilford Press, 2015), 329–47.

Kristin D. Scheider, Roelie J. Hempel, and Thomas R. Lynch, "That 'Poker Face' Just Might Lose You the Game! The Impact of Expressive Suppression and Mimicry on Sensitivity to Facial Expressions of Emotion," *Emotion* 13, no. 5 (2013): 852–66, https://doi.org/10.1037/a0032847.

Epilogue

262 **"say the unsayable"**: Tom Junod, "My Friend Mister Rogers," *Atlantic*, November 7, 2019, https://www.theatlantic.com/magazine/archive/2019/12/what-would-mister-rogers-do/600772/.

262 **resulted in a threatened boycott**: Junod, "My Friend Mister Rogers."

262 **"the nicest man in the world"**: Junod, "My Friend Mister Rogers."

262 **Junod was secretly wondering**: Junod, "My Friend Mister Rogers."

262 **"Well, Tom, I'm in my bathrobe"**: Tom Junod, "Can You Say . . . 'Hero'?," *Esquire*, November 1, 1998, http://classic.esquire.com/article/1998/11/1/can-you-say-hero.

263 **"sure enough, there was Mister Rogers"**: Junod, "Can You Say . . . 'Hero'?"

263 **"There was an energy to him"**: Junod, "Can You Say . . . 'Hero'?"

263 **"This was not a dragged-out process"**: "'He Wanted Me to See That I Was a Good Person': How a Writer's Friendship with Mr. Rogers Inspired a Movie," CBC News, updated August 21, 2020, https://www.cbc.ca/radio/day6/impeachment-fallout-in-ukraine-starmetro-shuts-down-new-pokemon-neil-gaiman-remembering-mr-rogers-more-1.5367148/he-wanted-me-to-see-that-i-was-a-good-person-how-a-writer-s-friendship-with-mr-rogers-inspired-a-movie-1.5367152.

263 **"I've been trying to figure out"**: "'He Wanted Me to See That I Was a Good Person.'"

263 **to compensate for some perceived inner shortcoming**: Maxwell King, *The Good Neighbor: The Life and Work of Fred Rogers* (New York: Abrams, 2018).

263 **"Look at us—I've just met you"**: Junod, "Can You Say . . . 'Hero'?"

263 **"He gave so much to me"**: Junod, "My Friend Mister Rogers."

264 **reflected on the elusive energy**: King, *The Good Neighbor*.

264 **"'Fred, were you talking to me?'"**: Kai Lindholm, "StoryCorps 462: In the Neighborhood," StoryCorps, https://storycorps.org/podcast/storycorps-462-in-the-neighborhood/.

264 **AFTER ALL THESE YEARS**: King, *The Good Neighbor*.

264 **"every imaginable childhood disease"**: Anne Fritz, "The Sad Story Behind Mr. Rogers' Hallmark Empathy," *Reader's Digest*, February 21, 2021, https://www.rd.com/article/mr-rogers/.

264 **"Hey, fat Freddy!"**: Fritz, "The Sad Story."

264 **"mystified" by teenagers**: King, *The Good Neighbor*.

265 **growing marijuana in the basement**: King, *The Good Neighbor*.

265 **"yelled and screamed at each other for an hour"**: John Rogers. Interview by Jessica Wiederhorn, The Narrative Trust: Fred Rogers Oral History Collection, Fred Rogers Center for Early Learning and Children's Media at St. Vincent College, April 24, 2008.

265 **painful battle with stomach cancer**: King, *The Good Neighbor*.

265 **"A perfectionistic thought"**: Michael Twohig, in discussion with the author, February 2, 2023.

265 **The root,** *telos***:** Wikipedia, s.v. "Christian Perfection," accessed November 12, 2023, http://en.wikipedia.org/w/index.php?title=Christian_perfection&oldid=1184836014; Online Etymology Dictionary, s.v. "Perfection," accessed November 19, 2023, https://www.etymonline.com/word/perfection.

ADDITIONAL SOURCE: George Wirth. Interview by Jessica Wiederhorn. The Narrative Trust. April 24, 2008. Fred Rogers Oral History Collection. Fred Rogers Center for Early Learning and Children's Media, St. Vincent College, Latrobe, PA.

ABOUT THE AUTHOR

Matthew Guillory

ELLEN HENDRIKSEN is a clinical psychologist at Boston University's Center for Anxiety and Related Disorders. She is the author of *How to Be Yourself: Quiet Your Inner Critic and Rise Above Social Anxiety*. Her work has been featured in *The New York Times*, *The Washington Post*, BBC News, *New York*, *The Guardian*, *Harvard Business Review*, *Scientific American*, and *Psychology Today*, among others. She lives in the Boston area with her family.